THE END OF
THE GERMAN
MONARCHY

THE END OF
THE GERMAN
MONARCHY

THE DECLINE AND FALL OF
THE HOHENZOLLERNS

JOHN VAN DER KISTE

FONTHILL

Fonthill Media Language Policy

Fonthill Media publishes in the international English language market. One language edition is published worldwide. As there are minor differences in spelling and presentation, especially with regard to American English and British English, a policy is necessary to define which form of English to use. The Fonthill Policy is to use the form of English native to the author. John Van der Kiste was born and educated in England; therefore British English has been adopted in this publication.

Fonthill Media Limited
Fonthill Media LLC
www.fonthillmedia.com
office@fonthillmedia.com

First published in the United Kingdom and the United States of America 2017

British Library Cataloguing in Publication Data:
A catalogue record for this book is available from the British Library

Copyright © John Van der Kiste 2017

ISBN 978-1-78155-636-8

Typeset in 10.5pt on 13pt Sabon
Printed and bound in England

CONTENTS

Introduction

The date 18 January 1901 marked the bicentenary of the elevation of the Hohenzollerns to Kings of Prussia, and the Prussian sovereign William II, also German Emperor, intended to celebrate in style. The anniversary had been slightly overshadowed by the death of the octogenarian Charles Alexander, Grand Duke of Saxe-Weimar, the younger and only surviving brother of William's paternal grandmother, the late Empress Augusta. Court mourning was accordingly declared, but then cut short on 17 January in preparation for the grand day, which was marked by a *Festspiel* or celebratory play at the Berlin Opera House.

Among guests at the festivities was the Emperor's uncle, Arthur, Duke of Connaught, the younger surviving son of Queen Victoria of England. On 19 January, the Duke was warned that his mother, who had been in poor health for some time, was seriously ill and that he should return to England at once. Despite their differences in the past, the Emperor had always admired and respected Queen Victoria, whom he called his 'unparalleled grandmama'. He told his court that, anniversary or no anniversary in Berlin, his place was at her side across the North Sea. All the remaining celebrations were cancelled, while he and the Duke accordingly travelled from Berlin to Osborne House on the Isle of Wight, where they were in time to take their place with the other sorrowing relations around her deathbed and be with her as she breathed her last three days later.

The King of Prussia had welcomed the second Hohenzollern centenary, even if the celebrations had been abruptly curtailed, and in 1913, he would mark the twenty-fifth anniversary of his accession. Yet this would be his last milestone before he and his empire stumbled into war, and four years beyond that lay defeat, abdication, over twenty years of exile, and the end of the German monarchy. Yet throughout the troubled years of the

Weimar republic and the Third Reich, the possibility of a restoration could never be disregarded.

My particular thanks for help and advice during my writing and research are due to Marlene Eilers-Koenig, Kori Roff Lawrence, Sue Woolmans, Chris Warwick, to Alan Sutton, Jay Slater, and Josh Greenland at Fonthill Media, and, as ever, to my wife Kim, for her support throughout.

1

'By Iron and Blood'

On 18 January 1871, William I, King of Prussia, was proclaimed German Emperor at the Salle des Glaces, Versailles. It was 170 years to the day since his three-times-great-grandfather Frederick I, Elector of Brandenburg and Duke of Prussia, had crowned himself King in Prussia in Königsberg, establishing his status as a monarch whose royal territory lay outside the boundaries of the Holy Roman Empire, with the full agreement of Leopold I, Holy Roman Emperor. Frederick was King in, rather than of, Prussia as part of Prussia's lands were under the suzerainty of the crown of the Kingdom of Poland. In 1772, the Duchy of Prussia was elevated to a kingdom, and Frederick's grandson, Frederick II ('Frederick the Great'), assumed the title King of Prussia, a title borne by his successors.

At the Congress of Vienna in 1815, convened after the defeat of Napoleon Bonaparte at the Battle of Waterloo, Prussia absorbed various additional territories, including the Rhineland and Westphalia, which resulted in the doubling of Prussia's population. Another consequence of the Congress was the creation of the German Confederation, or *Deutscher Bund*, an association of thirty-nine German states in Central Europe, with the aim of coordinating the economies of separate German-speaking lands and replacing the former Holy Roman Empire. Prussia was one of these, and rivalry between Austria and the ambitious Prussia would ultimately lead to its collapse.

The first half of the nineteenth century saw a prolonged struggle throughout Germany between liberals, who wanted a united, federal state under a democratic constitution, and conservatives and nationalists, intent on maintaining Germany as a patchwork of independent, monarchical states, with Prussia and Austria competing for ultimate mastery. One school of thought that aimed for unity in this period was the *Burschenschaft*, or student movement, led by students who wanted to see the territories unite as one nation under a progressive, liberal political system. Due to Prussia's size and economic importance, smaller states began to join its free trade area in the 1820s. Prussia thus benefited from the creation in 1834 of the German Customs Union, or *Zollverein*, which by then included most of the other states apart from Austria.

In 1848, during the year of revolutions, King Frederick William IV agreed under pressure to convene a National Assembly and grant a constitution. Much to the disappointment of German liberals and nationalists, when the Frankfurt Parliament offered him the crown of a united Germany, he refused on the grounds that he could not accept it from a revolutionary assembly without the full approval of Germany's other monarchs. The Parliament was dissolved in 1849, and the King issued Prussia's first constitution on his own authority the following year. This conservative document provided for a two-house parliament. The lower house, or *Landtag*, elected by all taxpayers, was divided into three classes, whose votes were weighted according to the amount they paid, with the vote denied to women and those who were not subject to taxes. This enabled just over one-third of the voters to choose 85 per cent of the legislature, all but assuring dominance by the more well-to-do male population. The upper house, later renamed the *Herrenhaus*, or 'House of Lords', was appointed by the King, who retained full executive authority, with ministers responsible only to him. The grip of the landowning classes, or *Junkers*, remained dominant, especially in the eastern provinces.

The liberals had always sought a more democratic Prussia, and they had high hopes on the prince who was second in line to the throne after his uncle and father, the present heir. Aged seventeen in the revolutionary year, Prince Frederick William had little in common with his military minded, arch-conservative father Prince William, whose interests hardly extended beyond the army. William's artistically inclined wife, Augusta, had been born a princess of Saxe-Weimar, one of the most liberal of German states, and despite his respect for the military, their only son had taken more after her in personality and outlook. In 1855, he became engaged to the fourteen-year-old Victoria, Princess Royal of England, the eldest child of Queen Victoria and Prince Albert. The former Prince Albert of Saxe-Coburg Gotha and his uncle Leopold, King of the Belgians, had been among those who also hoped for a united liberal Germany under Prussian leadership. With Frederick William as King and his supportive English wife by his side a generation ahead, it all seemed possible. Their wedding on 25 January 1858 was meant to herald a new dawn.

The couple's first child, William, born one year and two days after the wedding, had a troubled entry into the world. Princess Frederick William had been very unwell during her pregnancy, but her physician, Dr August

Wegner, saw no grounds for concern. The services of Eduard Martin, a professor of gynaecology and obstetrics at the University of Berlin, were secured for her accouchement. There was some professional jealousy between both men, and Wegner, more courtier than physician, hesitated to jeopardise the sensibilities of his royal patient by conducting the necessary examination, even at the risk of allowing nature to take its course by letting mother and child die. Mortality in childbirth being not uncommon, his professional reputation would probably not have suffered had this been the outcome. Once her labour pains began and various doctors, a midwife, and a lady of the bedchamber arrived, Wegner examined her and realised all was not well, and only then was Martin urgently summoned by messenger. At around the same time, he was handed a note from the anxious Prince Frederick William written the previous evening (and inadvertently put in the post instead of being handed to another messenger for immediate delivery), asking him to come at once. A horrified Martin arrived to find Wegner and his colleagues in a corner of the room while the distraught prince held his semi-conscious wife in his arms. He immediately administered chloroform and delivered the baby boy, then devoted his attention to saving the mother, extremely weak after her ordeal.

When the midwife realised that the baby had not yet uttered a sound, she feared he might be stillborn. She and Martin proceeded to slap him gently until he began to cry. A subsequent examination showed that his left arm was hanging limply from its socket. His mother was bitterly distressed by the injury, and during his early years, she was desperately worried that he would never grow up to be normal. On her child's first birthday, she wrote to her father: '[It] cuts me to the heart when I see all the other children with the use of all their limbs, and that mine is denied that. The idea of his remaining a cripple haunts me'.[1] Moreover, a 'reduced blood flow to the brain during delivery' would leave the baby with the possibility of various mental problems.[2] For a child destined to be one of the most dominant sovereigns of Europe, the consequences could be disastrous. Prince Albert, created Prince Consort in June 1857, had come to know and respect Frederick William's father who, as Prince of Prussia, heir to a childless brother, had, despite his bluff military exterior, given a somewhat deceptive appearance of being amenable to liberal ideas. In October 1857, William was appointed acting regent for the ailing King Frederick William IV, an alcoholic increasingly enfeebled by several strokes. On his death in January 1861, King William revealed himself as anything but a liberal, and he had no patience with the Prince Consort's well-meaning, if ill-advised letters of advice from England. The new heir and his wife, now Crown Prince and Princess Frederick William, were mildly discouraged but not completely disheartened, for they had assumed the Prince Consort would be there to offer them guidance for many years yet. However, later that year, he became seriously ill and he died on 14 December at the early age of forty-two.

Shortly after his accession, King William had demanded a programme of army reform and was furious when the *Landtag* refused to approve an increase in military spending that he was determined to push through. In September 1862, he considered abdicating in favour of the Crown Prince, while probably well aware that his diffident heir would be far too astonished and lacking in confidence to accept a crown under such circumstances—and also too devoted a son to contemplate replacing his father on the throne. He told him with tears in his eyes that he had already drawn up a letter to his people announcing his intention to step down from the throne: 'God and my conscience do not allow me to do anything else'.[3] It was little more than a hollow threat. By then, his Minister for War, Albrecht von Roon, had advised him to send for the recently appointed Prussian Ambassador to Paris, Otto von Bismarck, a 'hard man' prepared to pass any reforms without parliamentary approval. The King accepted his advice and made Bismarck his Minister-President and Foreign Minister.

A few days later, when appearing before the *Landtag* Budget Committee, Bismarck stressed how important he believed it was for them to have adequate defences. He finished his speech with the statement that Prussia's position in Germany would not be determined by its liberalism but by its power. Since the treaties of Vienna, he said, their frontiers had been 'ill-designed for a healthy body politic'. It was not through speeches and majority decisions that the great questions of the day would be decided—'that was the great mistake of 1848 and 1849—but by iron and blood [*Eisen und Blut*]'.

In June 1863, he issued a decree empowering the suppression of newspapers and periodicals in Prussia 'for persisting in an attitude endangering the commonweal', making it an offence to undermine 'respect and loyalty towards the King', and expose 'to hatred or contempt state institutions'.[4] The Prussian constitution guaranteed freedom of the press, and the Crown Prince—who had a few days earlier written to the King, asking him not to infringe the constitution, in return for him honouring an undertaking not to oppose His Majesty's views openly— said he considered the cabinet proceedings illegal and contrary to state and dynastic interests. He received no reply. The King endorsed the decree and dissolved the *Landtag*, and the liberals protested that it was an unconstitutional measure as there was no 'unusual emergency' to justify such an action, while the Berlin city council voted to send a delegation to the King expressing its disquiet at the government's arbitrary action. While the Crown Prince stopped short of siding with the liberals by openly criticising the measure, he said it went against 'the true spirit of the constitution'. He admitted that the opposition press posed a threat to the government, but suggested that the decrees should be rescinded as they would only incite the opposition to further protest. He had just begun a tour of military inspection in East Prussia, and later that week, he was present at a parade by the Danzig garrison and a reception at the town hall in his honour. After being welcomed by the *Oberbürgermeister* (Mayor), he made a speech saying that he regretted the conflict between government and constitution; he had not known of the measures in advance and took no part in the deliberations leading to their announcement.

When the contents of this address were reported to him, the King wrote to his son, ordering him to retract his words in the press or else he would 'recall him and take his place in the Army and the Council from him'.[5] Bismarck knew that to make a martyr of the Crown Prince would only strengthen liberal resistance against the government, and he advised him to 'deal gently with the young man Absalom'. It would be best to warn him that any repetition of the Danzig speech would not be tolerated.

Within the next seven years, Bismarck's Prussia fought three European wars and was victorious in each. The first was against Denmark over a dispute concerning ownership of the duchies of Schleswig and Holstein in the spring of 1864, while two years later, the long-simmering rivalry between Austria and Prussia was resolved in the Seven Weeks' War of 1866. Austria and her allies among the southern German states, including Bavaria, Hanover, and Württemberg, which had sided with her, were beaten in a swift but decisive campaign, leading to the creation of the North German Confederation under Prussian leadership in 1867. After the Second French Empire under Napoleon III was vanquished in the Franco–Prussian War in 1870, Prussia's ascendancy under the rule of Bismarck was complete and King William I was elevated to imperial status.

At Bismarck's suggestion, he was now 'by the grace of God German Emperor and King of Prussia'. According to Crown Prince Frederick William, the stubborn monarch was 'miserably unhappy at seeing the title of King taking second place' and having to say farewell to the old Prussia.[6] Both men were in a bad temper at the ceremony in the Salle des Glaces, Versailles, but it was the Minister-President whose decision prevailed. The new Emperor entered the room, filled with a crowd of princes, officers, and deputations from army regiments, mounted the dais decorated with brightly coloured regimental banners, and addressed the throng brokenly before handing over to Bismarck, who read out the imperial proclamation in an expressionless voice. Next, the Emperor's son-in-law Frederick, Grand Duke of Baden, requested three cheers for His Majesty the Emperor, who stood glowering beside him and then stumped out of the room without even glancing at the politician who had made it possible.

The Crown Prince had been a keen advocate of a German Empire, although he regretted it should have come about as a result of conquest in war. Despite having commanded Prussian forces in all three wars, he hated war and everything it stood for. He was also annoyed by the bad atmosphere caused by the ungracious demeanour of his father and Bismarck at the declaration, as well as having been defeated in his hopes of helping the Reichstag to present German unity as a popular cause. He wrote to the Crown Princess the following year, and as an advocate of an united Germany under Prussian leadership, the Prince Consort would have been impressed by such changes and the end result, but he 'would not have approved of the methods whereby unification was achieved any more than [the Crown Prince and Princess]'.[7] The heir to the throne and his wife knew well how dismayed Queen Victoria's late husband would have been at German unity having been forged on the field of battle.

Aged seventy-three at the time, the Emperor expected his reign to be short. Nobody could have foreseen that he would reach his ninetieth birthday. The Crown Prince and Princess naturally expected to be Emperor and Empress within a few years. In England, Queen Victoria was thought to be a little jealous that her son-in-law and eldest daughter would soon have an imperial title, and suspected that the notion had gone to the future Emperor's head. In 1874, she told her private secretary Sir Henry Ponsonby that the heir was 'rather weak & to a certain extent obstinate not conceited but absurdly proud, as all his family are, thinking no family higher or greater than the Hohenzollerns'.[8]

Prussia's place within Imperial Germany was defined by the constitution of 16 April 1871, the result being not so much a political contract or definition of rights in the traditional sense, but more a treaty among the sovereign territories that formed the Empire.[9] The latter had a federal constitution, a slightly amended version of the one observed by the North German Confederation. The imperial crown was a hereditary office of the House of Hohenzollern, with the Minister-President of Prussia also holding the position of Imperial Chancellor, except during two brief periods one from January to November 1873 and one from 1892 to 1894. The Empire itself had no right to collect taxes directly from its subjects, the only incomes totally under federal control being the customs duties, common excise duties, and the revenue from postal and telegraph services. The other sovereign principalities (*Fürstenbund*) of the Empire all had their own hereditary princes, sovereigns, or dukes. Each continued to operate their own parliamentary legislatures and constitutions, and they retained responsibility for their affairs, governments, and elections for their own assemblies. Prussia was the largest state in Germany, comprising about three-fifths of the empire and two-thirds of the population. The Imperial

German Army was in practice an enlarged Prussian Army, although the other three kingdoms, Bavaria, Saxony, and Württemberg, retained their own armies as well as their kings. Like the other German hereditary rulers, they all owed allegiance to the German Emperor. He was responsible for appointing the imperial government or Reich, with his Minister-President and Chancellor, now elevated to the style of Prince, as head of government. Also vested in the monarch and his ministerial officials was the right to conduct his country's foreign policy, to decide upon the deployment of his armed forces in war and peace, and the power to nominate and dismiss his Chancellor. The Crown was involved in major areas of executive decision-making, and in his capacity as King of Prussia, he was empowered to select the members of the Ministry of State and the Civil Service. Every bill had to be approved by the King, the upper chamber (*Herrenhaus*), and the lower chamber (*Landtag*), and the right to institute or initiate legislation rested with the monarch, although he was prepared to delegate such duties to his Chancellor.

The imperial parliament comprised two bodies, the Reichstag and the Bundesrat. The Reichstag, which met in Berlin, elected by all German men above the age of twenty-five, had no leader, and its responsibilities were to vote on legislation and the imperial budget. The Chancellor, who had direct authority on behalf of the Emperor on foreign policy matters, addressed it on a frequent basis. Although elections were held regularly, the government was empowered to dissolve it and order fresh elections whenever it wished. The Bundesrat was a council of representatives from the states, which gave a voice to state governments within the Empire, and as the largest state, Prussia had the greatest representation. While Bismarck needed the cooperation of both bodies in passing legislation and obtaining consent for the federal budget, he was not directly responsible to them, and he was accountable only to the Emperor. Whereas in the British parliamentary system, hostile votes at Westminster could result in general elections and changes of government; in Imperial Germany, a hostile parliament might obstruct the government but do no more than delay legislation with which it disagreed.

Bismarck's relations with Emperor William were generally good. Though the monarch would sometimes complain about his Chancellor's methods and policies, he knew he was too valuable a servant to lose. Empress Augusta, who loved neither her husband nor his politics, detested Bismarck, an antipathy he repaid with interest. With the Crown Prince and Princess, his relationship was more complex. They had looked on with apprehension at his appointment to high office in 1862—politically, he stood for much of what they actively opposed. While they disagreed with his politics and his methods, at length they could not but accept that he had made Prussia strong, and that they could ill-afford to do without him. They admired him for having brought about the unification of Germany, though they resented the way it was done. He likewise had a love-hate relationship with them, professing to hold them in contempt while at times unable to conceal his admiration for both. The Crown Princess had her reservations about the new imperial era, which her husband had greeted so enthusiastically. Shortly before the proclamation of the Empire in January 1871, she had expressed to him her fears that their political judgement, interest in social progress, and in the progressive development of their own country had diminished as a result of the war against France: 'I fear that an era of reaction will ensue—I can already see its dark shadows hovering over us!'[10]

Throughout Germany, Britain, and the rest of Europe, Crown Prince Frederick William had acquired a reputation as a forward-thinking personality at odds with the ingrained conservatism of his father and uncles as well as most of the German military elite. His views on contemporary issues such as anti-Semitism, socialism, and religious toleration, and his interest in the fine arts, all marked him out as a liberal. Nonetheless, there were doubts as to whether he would remain thus once he ascended the throne. Some suggested that during his reign he would show himself to be a true autocrat, while others suspected that his liberal convictions were only skin deep, and that once he succeeded his father, he would be able to exert little, if any influence on the course of political events. Much as he loathed the butchery of war and the waste of life that he had witnessed on the battlefield, he was still a product of the dynasty of 'soldier kings', with its love of all things military. To the end of his days, he retained a particular interest in the passage of any bills through the Reichstag dealing with the army and with the minutiae of detail such as soldiers' and officers' uniforms and procedures for drill on the parade ground.

During the first few years of empire, regarded by some as Prussia's 'liberal era', the Crown Prince and Princess had grounds for optimism. The National Liberals comprised the majority party in the Reichstag, while the Prussian cabinet included three liberal ministers, and they pursued a policy of free trade that inaugurated several years of economic prosperity. Despite some setbacks for the liberals during the crisis that had brought Bismarck to power in 1862, they had subsequently made gains in the ten years or so afterwards, with the constitution intact and unification achieved. With an elderly Emperor and a Chancellor in possibly uncertain health—although his complaints about illness were more those of the *prima donna* or the lifelong hypochondriac than of a genuine invalid—liberals hoped for the day when politicians of their stamp would hold the highest offices of state. While recent advances promised further progressive reforms, they were divided as to the benefits of an increase in parliamentary power. The

Crown Prince and some of his leading liberal allies saw the foundation of the empire as the fulfilment of the liberal programme, and they began to question the desirability of transferring English governmental institutions to Germany. Other National Liberals and Progressives hoped the future course of democratic reform would see the arrival of a government responsible to parliament that would control the budget of the military, in which the monarchy found its strongest support.

The Crown Prince's endorsement of Bismarck's policies during the early 1870s made it likely that, should the Emperor suddenly die, the Chancellor would be retained in office during the next reign. A heavy smoker throughout his adult life, the Crown Prince was prone to colds, sore throats, loss of voice, and respiratory complaints during the winter. In November 1872, he left Berlin to convalesce for a few weeks at Karlsruhe and Wiesbaden. At around this time, a right-wing newspaper, *Rheinische Kurier*, reported that the Crown Prince had privately warned his wife that his father was old, their eldest son was still a minor, and that if the worst came to the worst, she might be called upon to act as Regent for a time. Should this happen, she made a promise to her husband: '[I will] do nothing without Prince Bismarck, whose counsels have raised our House to undreamed-of power and greatness'.[11]

Much as the Crown Princess distrusted the Chancellor, she knew he would be indispensable during her husband's reign. She fully supported his foreign policy, particularly with regard to maintaining the status quo in the Mediterranean, an area of importance to British trading interests, while protecting Germany against any further attack from France through the *Dreikaiserbund* between the empires of Germany, Austria-Hungary, and Russia. While she considered him 'a misfortune for Germany and for the development of liberties, [their] trade &c. and certainly a danger for the Crown', she felt he was 'entirely for England, and [had] a sincere wish to be well with England, and that England's power should on all occasions rise superior to Russia's'.[12]

The Crown Princess's endorsement of some of Bismarck's policies, and her husband's agreement with many of his aims for government policy in the imperial era, did not prevent him from instigating many unpleasant stories about husband and wife. It still suited him to portray the heir—a reluctant warrior but a war hero nonetheless, an intelligent and enlightened potential ruler awaiting his inheritance, with a self-deprecating demeanour and lack of confidence in himself—as a weakling dominated by his more forceful wife, *die Engländerin* (the Englishwoman), who surely had the interests of her native country above all else at heart. Bismarck's spite towards anybody who ever opposed him robbed the Crown Prince of his rightful reputation as a military commander. Baron Hugo von Reischach, who served under all three Emperors, thought him a superior general to his cousin Prince Frederick Charles, and despite a profound humanitarian dislike of war, bloodshed, and the arrogant militarism of contemporary Prussia, just as dedicated to the army as his father.

Although the Crown Prince might have disappointed some of the more progressive liberals and radicals—occasionally even his own wife—by his caution and respect for the power of the crown, he was nevertheless widely admired as a kindly, humane man with pronounced artistic interests, a good leader on the battlefield, and a devoted husband. In some ways, he was well ahead of his time. With his respect for a free press, he surprised many of the authorities in class-conscious Berlin by receiving reporters and editors at the palace, and by making an effort to seek them out and speak to them at official functions. Openly favouring the advancement of women, he was among those who supported a petition sent to the Reichstag in 1872, advocating that they should be allowed to pursue careers in such professions as the postal, telegraphic, and railway services—at that time, bastions of male bureaucracy.

In 1878, on two separate occasions within the space of a few weeks, attempts were made on the Emperor's life in Berlin. During the first one, shots fired at him missed, but on the next one, he was severely wounded. While he was convalescing, the Crown Prince was appointed Regent, but it was a token gesture as all power remained in the hands of the Chancellor. The robust octogenarian monarch was fully restored to health within six months, although to those around him, it seemed afterwards that he had lost some of his mental alertness. Two years later, Lady Emily Russell, wife of the British Ambassador to Berlin, commented to Queen Victoria:

> ['The initiated' knew that since then the Emperor had allowed Bismarck] to have his own way in everything: and the great Chancellor revels in the absolute power he has acquired and does as he pleases. He lives in the country and governs the German Empire without even taking the trouble to consult the Emperor about his plans, who only learns what is being done from the documents top which his signature is necessary, and which His Majesty signs without question or hesitation. Never has a subject been granted so much irresponsible power from his Sovereign, and never has a Minister inspired a nation with more abject individual, as well as general, terror before.[13]

A few weeks after this, the Crown Prince was shocked to discover that the Emperor was signing all documents the Chancellor sent him, without reading them first. When he tried to point out the dangers of such blind trust, the Emperor retorted, 'Prince Bismarck knows what he is doing.'[14]

2

'Endless Mischief and Endless Harm'

In the elections of 1881, the Progressives won an impressive victory in the Reichstag at the expense of the National Liberals and Free Conservatives. The Crown Princess wrote to her mother how pleased she was, hoping it would show Bismarck how the Germans felt:

> [They are] not all delighted with his government, though I do not think he cares a bit! I wonder why he does not say straight out 'As long as I live both the constitution and the crown are suspended'; because that is the exact state of the matter.[1]

Bismarck, who admittedly resented, if not actively feared her political influence, particularly on her husband, readily dismissed him as 'delusional, lazy, stupid, haughty, and keen on flattery', while his son, Herbert, who served as foreign secretary later in the decade, said the heir to the throne was characterised by 'measureless personal pride and the most complete lack of judgment'.[2]

Meanwhile, the Chancellor attempted to mould their eldest son and heir, the younger William, in the conservative traditions of the Hohenzollern family. The prince worshipped his grandfather and Bismarck as the men who, between them, had created the German Empire, realising that his parents' liberal aspirations had had nothing to do with it. In character, he took more after his mother than his father, saying it was the English blood that ran through their veins. Both were headstrong personalities, often impatient of opposition, unlike the more self-effacing Crown Prince. Relations between the son and his parents gradually deteriorated after his wedding in February 1881 to the mild, yet fiercely Anglophobe Princess Augusta Victoria of Schleswig-Holstein. Ironically, it was a match the Crown Prince and Princess had ardently championed despite hostility from some sections of Berlin society on the grounds that she was not of sufficient royal blood for a future German Empress. Within a couple of years, William was paying only occasional visits to his parents, and when he did, their differences in opinion and character meant that they rarely passed without ill-tempered argument.

As a young mother, the Crown Princess had not been allowed to nurse her three eldest children herself, her sons, William and Henry, and daughter, Charlotte. This had invariably created some distance between them and their mother. By the time the five younger ones were born— her sons, Sigismund and Waldemar, and daughters, Victoria, Sophie, and Margaret—she was granted more say in their upbringing, and she and her husband always enjoyed a better relationship with them. However, Sigismund died of meningitis at twenty-one months in 1866 and Waldemar of diphtheria at eleven years in 1879. The loss of the latter completely broke his parents; the Crown Princess came close to a complete nervous breakdown, and her husband's moods of depression and weariness increased. All this contributed to their unsatisfactory relationship with William, who had been fond of his youngest brother, but his undemonstrative manner seemed to them to show a want of feeling. It added to their irritation with his political views and arrogance, until, at times, it seemed like the son was barely on speaking terms with them.

Meanwhile, Bismarck was treating the young prince as though he was first in line to the throne already. In 1886, he arranged for him to enter the Foreign Office at Berlin and gain some experience in international affairs. The Crown Prince, who had never been shown any such privilege, protested in a letter to Bismarck that the appointment was a dangerous one in view of his son's 'tendency towards overbearingness and self-conceit'.[3] He thought it more important for his son to learn more about the domestic affairs of his own country first before concerning himself with foreign policy, all the more given a tendency for over-hasty and highly impetuous judgment. Bismarck pointed out that the plan had been endorsed by the Emperor, who told Herbert Bismarck that his grandson was extraordinarily mature, unlike the Crown Prince with his 'regrettable political views', and who was to be regarded as of no account. Even so, the Chancellor allowed himself occasional misgivings about the ambition and character of his young protégé. To his wife, Johanna, he stated: '[There is] a little bit of Frederick the Great in him, but he also possesses the aptitude to become a despot like him—it is a real blessing that we have a parliamentary regime'.[4]

By the mid-1880s, Crown Prince Frederick William seemed increasingly resigned to the possibility that he would never reign or rule, and that the succession would skip a generation. Having recovered from the attempts on his life in 1878, Emperor William looked increasingly indestructible until weakened by a series of minor strokes a few years later. In January 1882, the Crown Prince's adjutant noted that his mood was very worrying: 'he likes to indulge in dark thoughts and pessimistic notions'.[5] On his fiftieth birthday, he noted despondently in his diary that he felt he was ageing and that if he did not have his wife and children as his all, he 'would long since have wished to be out of this world'.[6] He was dismayed by years of being treated as a virtual political pariah by the official world in Germany, and by the differences with his eldest son, increasingly estranged from his parents. The Crown Princess wrote to Queen Victoria: '[The young prince] fancies his opinion quite infallible—and that his conduct is always perfect—and cannot stand the smallest rebuke—though he criticises and abuses his elders and his relations, as though he knew far better than they did'.[7] Some of the army officers in the prince's circle declared that the Crown Prince ought to renounce his rights of succession to the throne and the court should be purged of English influences.[8]

Full of admiration for his grandson, Emperor William was increasingly dismissive of his 'dangerous' son and heir, whom he accused of being a supporter of parties hostile to the state; he told Empress Augusta—who had become increasingly distant from the son with whom she had once had so much in common—that if he was not the Crown Prince, 'he would be worth getting rid of'. He treated his grandson William as heir instead, endorsing Bismarck's policy of sending him as representative of the Hohenzollerns on important visits abroad, such as the coming-of-age celebrations for the Tsarevich Nicholas at St Petersburg in May 1886. The Crown Princess shared her husband's irritation that 'such things [were] always arranged between the Emperor and William without consulting or informing [them]', which they found a source of 'endless mischief and endless harm'.[9] Early the next year, the Crown Prince told the governor of Alsace-Lorraine that although he was an Emperor-in-waiting, he was frustrated at hearing nothing about home or foreign policy from official sources, learning everything through the newspapers, 'and that with the Emperor being ninety years old'.[10] Others commented increasingly on his apparent lack of energy and a 'paralysing pessimism'.

During the last three years of Emperor William's reign, the family were divided by a matter in which foreign affairs and a family issue were inextricably combined. Prince Alexander of Battenberg, a particular favourite of his uncle, Tsar Alexander II, had been chosen as ruling Prince of Bulgaria in 1879 after the Congress of Berlin, summoned to agree on generally acceptable peace terms following Russia's victory in war against Turkey. He was one of the sons of Prince Alexander of Hesse, all of whom were disadvantaged in being of insufficiently royal birth. In 1851, their father had morganatically married Countess Julie von Hauke, a former lady-in-waiting to the late Empress Marie of Russia, and they were banished from the Russian court. With the assassination of Alexander II in St Petersburg in 1881, Prince Alexander lost his most powerful protector. He was never on good terms with his successor, Tsar Alexander III, who resented his determination to govern without Russian interference. The situation became complicated when he went visiting the courts of Europe, partly in search of a suitable consort. While at Berlin, he became attached to Princess Victoria of Prussia, the second and eldest unmarried daughter of the Crown Prince and Princess, and plans were made for them to become betrothed. Two factors made him *persona non grata* as far as the German Emperor, Empress, and Bismarck were concerned: firstly, his morganatic birth, and secondly his apparent setting himself up as an independently minded opponent of Russia, something which would conflict sharply with the general direction of German foreign policy.

Crown Prince Frederick William liked Alexander, but he was reluctant to let his daughter marry a Battenberg prince. He stopped short of forbidding the engagement, but knew it could never be with his parents, Bismarck, and also his by now semi-estranged eldest son, William, so strongly opposed to it. The Crown Princess fully supported the idea and championed Alexander so passionately as a son-in-law that gossips at court even started to insinuate that she was in love with 'Sandro' herself. Queen Victoria of England not only admired the prince, but also saw benefits to England with Bulgaria becoming part of an anti-Russian faction in the Balkans. Her own family links with the Battenberg family were about to be strengthened for, in April 1884, one of Alexander's brothers, Louis, married the Queen's eldest Hessian granddaughter, Princess Victoria, and another, Henry, married her youngest daughter, Princess Beatrice, fifteen months later. She was annoyed when the Crown Prince wrote of Henry 'as not being of *Geblut* [stock], a little like animals'.[11] However, Alexander eventually exhausted the Tsar's patience, and in August 1886, he was taken prisoner in a Russian coup and forced to abdicate. He himself had long seen the impracticality of a marriage that would cause such fierce controversy and political resentment. After leaving Bulgaria and retiring into private life, he fell in love with and married Joanna Loisinger, an opera singer.

Once he became Emperor, Crown Prince Frederick William would have been in a position to give his consent to the marriage had the young couple still wished it, but the former Prince of Bulgaria evidently did not. The increasingly enfeebled Emperor William was in his late eighties and could not be expected to live much longer. Yet there were ominous signs that the reign of the second German Emperor would not be a long one—

and might not even happen at all. During the winter of 1886, he seemed unable to shake off a winter cold, sore throat, and general hoarseness. When the trouble persisted for several months, his physician suspected it might be something more serious. On 6 March, Professor Karl Gerhardt, a throat specialist, examined the Crown Prince's throat and discovered a small growth on the left vocal cord that he tried to remove surgically—at first with little success. It came at an inconvenient time, for two weeks later, various European royalties, including the Prince of Wales and Crown Prince Rudolf of Austria, gathered at Berlin to celebrate Emperor William's ninetieth birthday. It was alleged that, during the festivities, the elderly and now possibly senile Emperor quipped that he would not die, since the Crown Prince was still alive.[12] Notwithstanding his own personal feelings about the parent who seemed well-nigh immortal, it was an occasion for family and national solidarity. As befitted his position as heir, the Crown Prince made a speech of congratulation to the assembled company. It was noticed that his normally resonant voice sounded unusually rough.

After a month, following several sessions of painful treatment, the lesion was removed and the Crown Prince went to recuperate at the spa resort of Bad Ems. No one could be certain that the growth would not return after a few weeks. At first, he made a good recovery and his voice briefly returned to normal, but by May, the old symptoms had returned. When he went back to Berlin for another examination, Gerhardt found that the growth on his vocal cord was there again—and larger than before. Consultation with more specialists took place and they decided to seek advice from an eminent British laryngologist, Dr Morell Mackenzie. At the request of the German doctors and of Bismarck himself, he was summoned from London in May and arrived in Berlin to take charge of the case.

Within a few days of Mackenzie's starting to treat the Crown Prince, arguments began between him and the German doctors, who insisted that an immediate operation on the throat was vital. He insisted that if they did operate, the Crown Prince would almost certainly die. The Crown Princess had an unexpected ally in Bismarck, who for years had disparaged the Crown Prince, but was now appalled by the possibility that the immature and headstrong Prince William might succeed his grandfather and ascend the throne long before he was ready to do so. The Chancellor agreed with her that such a course of action without due consideration and the likelihood of death as a result was too terrible to contemplate. They would rather take a chance on the natural order of things in that the elderly Emperor would predecease his son, even if it meant that the latter was a dying man by then.

In Britain, the celebration of Queen Victoria's Jubilee to mark her fifty years on the throne in June 1887 was being planned. The Crown Prince and Princess had been invited and were determined to attend. Once his illness became common knowledge throughout Berlin, Prince William assumed that he and his wife would be at the festivities as his father would not be well enough to go. He therefore asked his grandfather, Emperor William, to appoint him as the Hohenzollerns' official representative in London that summer, a request the Emperor granted without bothering to consult his son. Deeply upset at being passed over in this unthinking manner, the Crown Prince wrote to Queen Victoria confirming his intention to be there and requesting that she consider him as the official representative of the family. Happy to oblige, the Queen reprimanded her grandson for his presumption, a scolding he took with very bad grace. Such plans fitted in perfectly with the planned medical treatment, for Mackenzie had recommended that if the Crown Prince came to England, he could attend as a private patient in his surgery. Several warning voices were raised against this plan, particularly from those who feared the Emperor did not have long to live, and that there would be difficulties if he died while his son and heir was abroad, had a relapse, and was too ill to return to Berlin. Although the Crown Princess was increasingly worried by her husband's condition, and 'struggling between hopes and fears', she maintained that 'one cannot be kept a prisoner here, or be prevented from following a useful course by the fear of what might happen'.[13]

As the Crown Prince was heir to the throne, the Emperor's permission for such questions as to whether any operations could take place or whether his son could go abroad in order to receive medical treatment was always required. Whenever he was consulted, he always responded in a curiously detached manner, as if to suggest that he no longer really cared about his son. On being urged by Bismarck to receive the doctors before deciding whether to permit a life-threatening operation on the heir to go ahead, he complained it would be inconvenient as the Crown Prince was due to inspect troops in Potsdam. Even Bismarck was astonished by such a heartless response. The Emperor reluctantly conceded, but only as long as the doctors arrived early so that it would not interfere with or delay the inspection. Later, when asked to grant permission for the Crown Prince to travel to London, the Emperor assented, remarking casually that this would perhaps be his son's final wish.

Among those in the procession for the service of thanksgiving at Westminster Abbey on 21 June, no one looked more magnificent than Crown Prince Frederick William in his gleaming white cuirassier uniform, towering above those riding next to him. Very few present outside the family were aware that he could barely speak above a whisper.

The Crown Prince and Princess stayed in Britain for several weeks, dividing their time between Osborne, on the Isle of Wight, and the rest at Braemar, near Balmoral, the Queen's Highland residence. The newly knighted Sir Morell Mackenzie advised them to avoid the bitter cold of Berlin over the winter, so after leaving Scotland in September, they went first to Toblach in the Austrian Tyrol then to Venice and Baveno. The patient and his family still hoped that the illness was not cancer, and by the end of the month, the Crown Prince was writing from Venice to his old tutor Professor Karl Schellbach that his convalescence was 'in full swing', but that he should stay in the milder southern climate rather than return home. Mackenzie, he said, was convinced that the real trouble had been overcome and that it was only necessary for him to strengthen his health by avoiding speaking and catching cold, 'so that [he] may be able to return to [his] duties at home by the beginning of the winter'.[14] Meanwhile, in Berlin, the Emperor showed no interest in the medical reports and instead grumbled about how much his son's protracted stay abroad was costing the exchequer.

At the beginning of November, the Crown Prince and Princess moved to San Remo, close to the French border on the Italian coast, but he failed to improve. He lost colour and appetite and found the heat irritating. For some time, it had been rumoured that he was suffering from cancer of the larynx. After a further examination, Mackenzie had to admit this was almost certainly the case.

By now, Prince William was not just showing contempt for his parents' liberal leanings in favour of the conservative politics of his grandfather and Prince Bismarck, but also beginning to behave as if he was Emperor-in-waiting. Endlessly fawned upon and flattered by the reactionary elements at court and the military establishment, he became more arrogant and dismissive of his parents' ways than ever. Any sympathy he felt for his seriously ill father and desperately worried mother was concealed all too well. He seemed to regard his father as a noble, but helpless victim, at the mercy of a steely wife who seemed to be looking after her own interests as well as those of her British homeland. Some said she meant to keep her husband alive just long enough to become Emperor, and once he was dead, she would be left with her chamberlain Count Götz von Seckendorff, whom gossips insinuated was now the object of her affections. Another of their chamberlains, Count Hugo von Radolinski, spoke to an angry Prince William in July 1887, just after the jubilee celebrations, and was convinced as a result that he now hated his mother. Shortly after his parents arrived at San Remo, he warned the German Foreign Office not to send any confidential information to the Crown Prince because he was sure the Crown Princess was opening and screening his correspondence and would certainly pass on everything of political interest to their counterparts in London.

Over Christmas and the new year, the Crown Prince rallied a little and, despite the German doctors' comments, Mackenzie appeared less convinced that his patient was suffering from cancer after all. In January 1888, he noted that the symptoms seemed to be a more severe form of chronic laryngitis, but there was nothing malignant about the disease. A few days later, his condition worsened again. After one particularly bad night when he was in danger of suffocation and speedy death, an immediate tracheotomy was decided upon and performed by Dr Friedrich Bramann. By this stage, it was clear that he only had a few weeks left. Since late the previous year, he had been in constant pain, unable to speak at all except in a hoarse whisper and reduced to writing everything he wanted to say on a pad of paper that he always kept within reach.

The ninety-year-old Emperor had been unwell since catching a severe cold during a naval inspection the previous summer. Nevertheless, it was decided that the Crown Prince should stay at San Remo and not return to Berlin until the spring, by which time the weather would have improved. However, on 9 March, while taking his regular morning walk in the garden at San Remo, he was handed a telegram addressed to His Majesty the Emperor. It told him that Emperor William had just passed away, within two weeks of what would have been his ninety-first birthday.

Announcing that he would reign as Emperor Frederick III, he and the Empress returned to Berlin that week, but he was obviously dying. Matters were made worse by the tactless behaviour of Crown Prince William, surrounded by those who already had an eye on their own advancement during the forthcoming reign. Despite his political differences with the new Emperor, Bismarck still believed it was in no one's interests for the young new Crown Prince to ascend the throne while he was still so immature and headstrong. Knowing he had to prepare himself for the inevitable, he asked the German doctors how much longer he had to put up with the uncertainty of a dying Emperor. They assured him that His Majesty would not survive the summer.

Although becoming ever weaker, he managed to attend the wedding of his second son, Prince Henry, to his cousin Princess Irene, the third daughter of Louis, Grand Duke of Hesse and the Rhine, on 24 May. He leaned on a stick for support the whole time he was present, and every step he took caused him great agony. The doctors' prognosis was proved correct. On the morning of 15 June, members of the family were warned that the end was near and they gathered in the sickroom as he passed away, aged fifty-six.

During the previous twenty-four hours, while his father lay dying, the then Crown Prince William had filled the grounds and corridors of Friedrichskron—the former *Neues Palais* at Potsdam, which Frederick had renamed after himself, where he was born and where he had returned to end his days—with troops in readiness for a virtual state of siege. The building was effectively sealed off from the outside world by armed guards and orders were issued that neither doctors nor members of the imperial family could leave without a signed permit, while all outgoing letters, telegrams, and parcels were to be checked. The new Emperor William II had to be dissuaded from issuing an order for the immediate arrest of Dr Mackenzie. He had been prepared for the secret removal of some, if not all of his parents' private correspondence, knowing that it would not show him in a favourable light, but though his soldiers ransacked every desk they could lay their hands on, they found nothing. Knowing better than to trust their son, during the previous year, the Crown Prince and Princess had ensured that everything was or would soon be in safe storage at Windsor.

The funeral of Emperor William I in March had been held a week after his death, so as to give those from foreign courts who wanted to attend adequate time for preparation. In contrast, the obsequies for his son were rushed through and he was buried three days later, on 18 June, at the Friedenskirche, Potsdam. No invitations were sent out to other European sovereigns or princes, but as his death had been anticipated for several weeks, some had made their plans and were ready to leave for Berlin at once. They included the Prince and Princess of Wales and their elder son, Albert Victor; Ernest, Duke of Saxe-Coburg Gotha; and Grand Duke Vladimir of Russia, brother of Tsar Alexander III. While waiting for the coffin to arrive at the start of the ceremony, the clergymen and military officers stood around laughing and chattering with each other. Chancellor Bismarck was not there, and had sent his son Herbert to represent him. To discourage members of the public who wanted to pay their last respects to 'our Fritz', whose reign they had hoped would have been the start of a new era in German history, the Emperor had the route of the procession cordoned off by soldiers so that nobody could see anything. The Dowager Empress could not face attending the official obsequies, and she and her three younger daughters held a small private service of their own instead that same day.

Just as hard to bear as the loss of her beloved husband was the realisation that all their political hopes and efforts had come to nothing. 'We had a mission, we felt it and we knew it, we were Papa's and your children!' she wrote that same day to her mother, 'We were faithful to what we believed and we knew to be right. We loved Germany—we wished to see her strong and great, not only with the sword, but in all that was righteous, in culture, in progress and in liberty.'[15]

'Full Steam Ahead'

Almost from the start of his reign, Emperor William II made it clear that he intended to rule as well as reign over his empire. Despite their occasional disagreements, his grandfather had always trusted Bismarck completely in allowing him mastery of domestic and foreign matters without interference. Crown Prince Frederick William had let it be known that he disagreed with the Chancellor's conservatism and sometimes repressive legislation, though since the Franco-Prussian War, they had generally been in broad agreement with his handling of affairs outside their borders. When Queen Victoria had paid a brief visit to her daughter and dying son-in-law in April 1888, and told Bismarck she was anxious about the then Crown Prince William's inexperience and lack of travel, he reassured her that though the young Emperor-in-waiting knew nothing at all about civil affairs: 'should he be thrown into the water, he would be able to swim'.[1] William was intelligent, a quick thinker, had a very good memory, and could be charming when he chose; however, his views were all too often distorted by prejudice, and he could be tactless, lacked concentration, and was easily distracted. A few months after he ascended the throne, Bismarck remarked that the young Emperor was 'like a balloon, if one did not hold him fast on a string, he would go no one knows whither'.[2]

Like his father and grandfather before him, he was devoted to all things military, with an almost obsessive passion for ceremonial and uniforms. One of his first acts after ascending the throne was to issue a proclamation to the Prussian Army, speaking in glowing terms of its 'stout, unbreakable allegiance to the Commander-in-Chief'. He declared that the army and he 'were born for one another and will stick together forever, be it, by God's will, through peace or war'.[3]

In view of his love of pageantry, some of those around him were surprised that he chose to dispense with a coronation. Bismarck confirmed that such a ceremony was not constitutionally required, as his grandfather had 'laid special emphasis in his coronation on the principle of monarchy by divine right', and had done all that was necessary for his successors by crowning himself King 'by the grace of God' in Königsberg Castle at the start of his reign in October 1861.[4, 5]

Instead, he inaugurated his reign ten days after his accession, on 25 June, with a ceremonial opening of his first Reichstag in the White Hall of the Old Palace. After a service in the chapel of the imperial palace, all members of the parliament (apart from the eleven Social Democrats, who refused to take part) assembled in the hall, where they were joined by the sovereign German princes, the Empress and the new six-year-old Crown Prince William, and various other members of the family, plus representatives of the government and military, and court officials. In his speech from the throne, after a brief reference to his grief at the loss of his grandfather and father, he declared that he was 'resolved to follow the same path by which [his] late, revered grandfather won the trust of his allies, the love of the German people and the goodwill of other nations'.[6] He also mentioned his personal friendship with Tsar Alexander III of Russia, in addition to the German alliance with Austria-Hungary and Italy. While he later came to recognise that he had become the successor to his grandfather—'in other words that, to a certain extent, [he] skipped one generation'—his mother was annoyed and upset that no reference was made to Anglo-German relations, fearing that it augured badly for the peace of Europe in the years ahead.[7]

The Emperor showed no great wish to keep on the right side of his British relations. Within hours of his accession, he received a telegram from Queen Victoria: 'help and do all you can for your poor dear mother and try to follow in your best noblest and kindest of father's footsteps'.[8] He soon made it clear that he intended to stamp his own personality on his reign, and that he thought his father's brief reign had been an interlude best forgotten. His cousin, Princess Louis of Battenberg, was more ready than most to make allowances for his shortcomings, blaming them on the environment in which he had been schooled. She wrote to the Queen that she pitied him greatly as he was so young for his position, and more than anything, he needed a wise and honest friend to guide him: 'When I think how warm hearted & nice he was as a boy, how greatly he changed during the last years, I cannot but think it is a great measure the fault of his surroundings'.[9] The Queen was less sanguine, thinking it 'too dreadful for [them] all to think of Willy & Bismarck & Dona [Empress Augusta Victoria]' now at the head of Germany—'two so unfit & one so wicked'.[10]

Under the imperial constitution, the Emperor was answerable to no one, with very few encroachments on his powers. Such limitations as there were on his sovereign authority were a reflection of the necessity for imperial decrees to carry the signature of the Chancellor as well as his own, and an obligation to respect the rights of the other German monarchs and princes. These merely curtailed to a negligible extent, if at all, his use of the powers normally assigned to a head of state, together with the right to summon and dissolve the Reichstag and Bundesrat, to propose legislation, and to appoint and dismiss ministers from the Chancellor downwards.

When the Emperor had alluded to his friendship with Tsar Alexander III, he was deceiving himself. Though the latter was never a friend of Britain and neither liked nor respected Queen Victoria, he was unimpressed by the Queen's eldest grandson. The Queen had assumed or rather expected that he would observe an appropriate period of mourning for his father, and in view of their close family ties, ensure that his first visit abroad would be to Britain. The Emperor had other ideas, and in July 1888, he paid the first of his visits abroad to St Petersburg. He informed his grandmother grandly of this:

> [A meeting with the Tsar would] be of good effect for the peace of Europe, and for the rest and quiet of my Allies. I would have gone later if possible, but State interest goes before personal feelings, and the fate which sometimes hangs over nations does not wait until the etiquette of Court mournings has been fulfilled.[11]

Herbert Bismarck accompanied him, and between them, they tried to stir up the Tsar against what he called the 'English leanings' of his mother and late father. It did nothing to endear the elder sovereign to the younger, and he commented coldly on this washing of dirty linen in public of the differences between Bismarck and Emperor Frederick and Germany's attitude towards England. Nevertheless, the young Emperor and his foreign minister mistakenly believed that the visit had been a great success.

His second visit abroad was to have repercussions that would poison family relations for some time to come. In August 1888, Emperor Francis Joseph of Austria had invited the Prince of Wales to attend army manoeuvres that autumn. The Prince knew that the German Emperor had planned to pay an official visit to Vienna at the same time, and wrote him two friendly letters expressing pleasure at the likelihood of their meeting on that occasion, neither of which were acknowledged. The Prince went to Vienna as planned on 10 September, and only after plans were being made for his itinerary was he told that Emperor William had informed Emperor Francis Joseph that no other royal guest should be allowed 'to dim the glory of his own stay in Vienna'. As he had wished to avoid provoking ill-natured gossip by staying away from the capital while his nephew was present, he was thoroughly offended. Within a day, it was common knowledge throughout Vienna that the German Emperor had threatened to cancel his visit unless the Prince of Wales was asked to leave at once. He complied with this request, going to stay in Hungary and Romania, only returning to Vienna after his nephew was back in Berlin.

Yet he and Queen Victoria were furious at the Emperor's high-handed attitude, especially as she had always treated her grandson with understanding and courtesy. In a letter to her Prime Minister, Lord Salisbury, she said that political relations between both governments should not be affected if possible by personal quarrels, but she feared that 'with such a hot-headed, conceited, and wrong-headed young man, devoid of all feeling, this may at ANY moment become impossible'.[12] The Emperor insisted there had been a misunderstanding, and only after several months and numerous letters was 'the Vienna affair' laid to rest. It left the Prince of Wales with a sense of grievance, which he would never completely forget.

If both Bismarcks, father and son, had taken it for granted that they would remain in power until they wished to return the seals of office at a time of their own choosing, they would soon find themselves mistaken. They had imagined that after the unwelcome, but brief interval of the reign of Emperor Frederick, his son would be content to follow in his grandfather's footsteps and leave the matters of government in the hands of his chief minister, while indulging in the more outward imperial manifestations of dressing up in uniforms, making formal speeches, and inspecting his troops. Now aged seventy-three, and after more than twenty-five years in his post, the Chancellor was spending more time on his estates at Friedrichsruh and Varzin than in the government offices in Berlin, while leaving Herbert to keep an eye on the young ruler. Neither realised that the Emperor was increasingly prepared to listen more to others with whom the Bismarcks had little in common, such as Baron Friedrich von Holstein, a secretary in the foreign ministry, the diplomat Philipp von Eulenburg, and the senior naval officer, later naval secretary, Alfred von Tirpitz. None of these men had much sympathy with Bismarck's methods.

Differences between the young master and his ageing servant would soon become apparent. German industrial development was growing, and while the Emperor had little idea of what living conditions were like in the poorer quarters of Berlin, he had visited mines and factories during his adolescence as part of the educational regime that his childhood tutor Georg Hinzpeter had devised for him. He therefore had more sympathy than Bismarck when it came to a question of restricting the number of daily or weekly hours worked by individuals. A countryman and landowner himself, Bismarck knew he had to accept some responsibility for industrial workers, as he did for the peasants on his estate. With this in mind, he proposed insurance schemes and old age pensions, well in advance of state welfare programmes in other industrial nations. Nevertheless, he did not believe in limiting hours of work on humanitarian grounds, believing that people were entitled to work longer if they wanted to earn more, and he did not support legislation intended to restrain the rights of employers to determine the length of the working day. In 1888, German industrial workers averaged a sixty-three-hour week, compared with fifty-two hours for those in Britain.

Bismarck thought better than to intervene in the spring of 1889 when miners in the Ruhr coalfields went on strike. He thought hunger would soon force the men to accept the mine owners' conditions. To his annoyance, they found an unexpected ally in their Emperor. Defying convention, on 14 May, he strode unannounced into the ministerial chamber of the Reichstag and ordered his ministers to settle the dispute at once. By the end of the week, the strikers had won their demands and called off their action. Bismarck declared angrily afterwards that it would soon be necessary to protect the monarch from his 'excessive zeal'.

Early in 1890, the Emperor informed the Crown Council that he would mark his thirty-first birthday on 27 January with two proclamations: one promising new laws to protect working men and women and limit their hours of labour; the other summoning an international conference at Berlin, where delegates would discuss how to improve conditions of work throughout Europe. Bismarck was unimpressed. When elections were held in February, the Roman Catholic Centre party emerged as the largest single group, with more than a quarter of all seats in the chamber. The Bismarckian Conservatives lost heavily, and to retain power, he was prepared to reach a compromise with the centre party, having talks with its leader, Ludwig Windthorst, for the purpose. As he left the chancellery after their discussion, Windthorst said he felt he had come from the political deathbed of a great man.[13]

The Emperor told Bismarck he had no right to negotiate with party leaders without his consent, reminding him that his responsibilities were to him as Emperor and not to the Reichstag. When Bismarck insisted that he must be free to consult the party leaders, the Emperor insisted he could not if he himself forbade it. Bismarck retorted that the power of his sovereign ceased at the door of his wife's drawing room, and in support of his case, he invoked a statute of King Frederick William IV from 1852, which declared that all ministerial communications to the King of Prussia had to pass through the Minister-President. The Emperor insisted that this was out of date and a fresh decree would have to be drawn up; if his Chancellor was spending so much of the year on his country estates, the sovereign could hardly be expected to rule without discussing matters with his ministers. Aware that they were approaching a point of no return, Bismarck pretended to fumble with some papers he had brought with him, making no real effort to conceal them. As the Emperor asked to see them, snatching them from his hands, he caught sight of a comment from Tsar Alexander III, calling him (William), '*C'est un garcon mal élevé et de mauvaise foi*'—'an ill-mannered boy of bad faith'.[14] Without a further word, the furious Emperor walked back to his carriage.

Afterwards, he sent messengers three times to the Chancellor requesting cancellation of the 1852 statute or instead his resignation, although he received no reply. Next, he sent a note passed openly through departmental offices, angry at not being kept informed of Russian troop movements. Bismarck protested at the Emperor interfering in foreign policy and talking of war with Russia. On 18 March, he sent a letter laying down his burden of office. It was so abusive that the Emperor suppressed its publication.

Despite the misery he had caused her over many years, the Empress Frederick magnanimously told Queen Victoria that she could not approve of the way in which Bismarck had resigned, as it looked like 'a dangerous experiment'.[15] He had been forced into leaving office for the wrong reasons, she believed, and despite his advancing years, his genius and prestige could still have been useful for Germany and for the cause of peace. To Queen Victoria, the Emperor wrote that he and his Chancellor took leave of each other tearfully 'after a warm embrace', and that he had 'resolved to part from him, in order to keep him alive' after the doctor had assured him that if Bismarck remained in office for a few more weeks, he would have died of apoplexy.[16] The Emperor received a supportive message from Emperor Francis Joseph, saying that Bismarck 'had the misfortune to be unable to find his exit from the stage, and to remain too long'. According to William, Tsar Alexander III told him Bismarck's disobedience had brought about his fall, and in his position, he would have done the same.[17] In view of the Tsar's opinion of his younger fellow-sovereign, this was probably less than accurate.

The Emperor declared that 'the position of officer of the watch on the ship of state' had fallen to him, and the course remained the same—'full steam ahead'.[18] In London, *Punch* magazine also adopted a naval metaphor with Sir John Tenniel's cartoon, 'Dropping the pilot', showing an angry Bismarck stumping off the ship while the Emperor watched nonchalantly. The ship of state would soon enter stormy waters.

When Princess Augusta Victoria married Prince William in 1881, she vowed to be a good wife and make the imperial succession secure for her husband. She was as good as her word. The birth of their eldest son William in May 1882 was soon followed by five more boys. Eitel

Frederick was born in July 1883, Adalbert exactly a year later, Augustus William in January 1887, Oscar in July 1888, and Joachim in December 1890. The first five were very robust infants, which was more than could be said of the sixth: Joachim was born prematurely, only a few weeks after a bitter family argument. The third of the Emperor's sisters, Sophie, had married Constantine, Crown Prince of Greece, in October 1889. As wife of the next king, the next year she decided to enter the Greek Orthodox Church. The Emperor tried to forbid her to do so without his consent on the grounds that he was head of the family, and he threatened to ban her from Germany for life if she disobeyed him. Thinking she would not dare to argue or even disagree with her heavily pregnant sister-in-law, he asked the Empress to try and dissuade her from such a step. Always the most pious and God-fearing of women, she haughtily told Sophie that if she persisted in her intentions, she would be forbidden from visiting the country of her birth again and would end up in hell. Sophie told her calmly that it was nothing to do with her. At this, the Empress became very excited and when she went into labour three weeks prematurely, the furious Emperor told the family that if the baby did not live, it would be Sophie's fault and she would have killed it. The boy survived, but as an infant, he was sickly and suffered from epileptic fits. In the end, the Crown Princess of Greece's ban was reduced to three years, but when she quietly accompanied her husband on a family visit to Germany just over a year later, her brother made no effort to stop her. Even so, the whole business created a rift between the siblings which would never be fully healed.

In September 1892, the Empress gave birth to the last of her seven children, a daughter named Victoria Louise. As the succession was safe, the Emperor was pleased to have a little girl at last. She could often get her way with him where her brothers failed, and Crown Prince William would later say that she was the only one 'who succeeded in her childhood in winning a warm corner in his heart'. He treated his sons like small recruits to be barked at and kept under strict discipline. With some generosity, the eldest recalled in middle age that their father was always very friendly and, 'in his way, loving towards [them]', but had little time to devote to them. He could barely recall a time when the proud father would join in '[their] childish games with unconstrained mirth or happy abandon'. It was as if 'he was unable to divest himself of the dignity and superiority of the mature adult man as to enable him to be properly young with [his sons]'.[19] When they came into his study, where they were not normally welcome, they had to hold their hands behind their backs so they would not knock anything off the tables.

Once old enough, they had to accompany him on early morning horse rides. Fearing it would put too much of a strain on them, especially the delicate Joachim, the Empress begged him to let her come with him instead. Although she was exhausted when they returned to the stables afterwards, she usually took them for a gentler ride afterwards so their father could never complain that they were poor horsemen from lack of practice. Their mother was always their protector, the one who 'radiated a love which ... warmed and comforted [them]', and she was the one to show them sympathy and understanding when needed.[20]

The princes and their sister regularly joined their cousins each summer on visits to their grandmother at Friedrichshof, but they were warned to be on their best behaviour. The Empress Frederick, they were told, was 'sickly', perhaps as an excuse for her being so strict with them, for they soon discovered she was much more so with them than with her other grandchildren. It was as if the Empress's difficult relations with her eldest son and daughter-in-law meant that she regarded them less indulgently than their cousins. The Crown Prince and Princess of Greece's family were evidently allowed to make as much noise as they liked without fear of a scolding.

Joachim was 'a continual source of anxiety' to their mother. When playing with his siblings, he was much less sturdy than them and could not run as fast. Once, when he fell over, he cried out in English, 'I'm dying, I'm dying'. At this, his sister snapped that if he really was going to die, then when he reached heaven would he please find out for her the name of Frederick the Great's horse. She was much closer to Oscar, who she noted always had a great influence over the younger ones, and she obeyed him more than their governesses and teachers. He assumed the mantle of their protector, and invariably felt it his duty to guard the smaller ones. He was the one to whom they would generally go for advice; he was to them 'an upright, straightforward character, modest and devoted to duty, and remained so all his life'.[21]

Ethel Howard was appointed English governess to the princes in 1895, and until retirement through ill-health three years later, she was largely responsible for their welfare. Twenty years later, she published a memoir in which she recalled her individual impressions of each during their adolescent years. She found the Crown Prince 'terribly overbearing and tyrannical with his brothers, though with [her] he always behaved well'. Very clever, he also showed considerable tact when discussing relations between England and Germany: '[He is] very affectionate, and is essentially a gentleman at heart'. Eitel Friedrich, always known in the family as Fritz, was 'such a gentle, long-suffering, sweet lad, but quite cracked on soldiering', seemed to know everything possible about the German, French, and other armies, their colours and regiments, 'a nice boy, and far gentler than his eldest brother'. Adalbert, who was in appearance his father's double, was 'all heart and naughtiness', by turns very rough and affectionate, often up to mischief, 'with no feeling for others.' On first acquaintance, Augustus Wilhelm was 'a silly little person. A dear little thing, [with] very little in him'. As she got to know him better, she was impressed by his gifts: '[He was] the teller of fairy tales and legends, and the reciter of poems … talented beyond the ordinary, and if he does not eventually produce some great literary or artistic work I shall be much surprised'. Oscar, she thought, had the most character and had a very deep nature. He was 'one who would take a long time to like you, and if he once did so he would not forget you'. Joachim and their sister were 'funny little things, rather wild and unmanageable'. She had little to do with either of them, and what she saw of Joachim she did not like: '[A] weak, frightened little cry-baby [who] certainly gave little promise of developing much character'.[22]

William was King of Prussia and German Emperor, but he was also the head of the house of Hohenzollern, and never did he let the rest of his family forget it. Having always had a difficult relationship with his mother, once he came to the throne, he treated her with scant consideration. Perhaps the hardest cross she had to bear was the way in which he made it evident that his father's reign was a brief aberration and best forgotten, with his memory unworthy of any respect. 'William allows his Father and me to be insulted and attacked, and sanctions it!' she wrote bitterly to Queen Victoria four months after his death.[23]

While William was devoted to his wife, not until much later in his reign did he consult her about affairs of state. In the early years, he was content to give the impression that her opinions counted for nothing. Sometimes he found her constant affection almost stifling, and she fussed after him so much that he found it necessary for his peace of mind to escape from time to time. Whenever they were apart, no matter how briefly, she wrote him sentimental letters saying how much she missed him. Courtiers at Berlin thought she 'bored and agitated' her husband. About two years after coming to the throne, he decided to spend a few days at Wilhelmshaven after completing one of his regular Scandinavian cruises, instead of coming straight back to Berlin to be with her again before leaving for a visit to England—again without her. She wrote to him that it made her cry to think that if only he had come back she could have been with him for almost three days, and that it was very hard 'when one loves one's little husband so much'. Just before another visit to England, one of the royal ladies-in-waiting, Marie Adeane (later Marie Mallet), noted in her diary that everybody around her dreaded his arrival. 'The more I hear of him the more I dislike him, he must be such a despot and so terribly vain,' she wrote: 'However, poor man, he has a most insipid and boring wife whom he does not care for and from whom he escapes by prancing to the four corners of the world'.[24]

With his eldest sister Charlotte and only surviving brother Henry, his relations were good at the start of his reign but later deteriorated. As young adults, both had generally sided with him in his opposition to their parents, much to the distress of their mother in particular. However, they soon tired of his high-handed behaviour, and the good-natured Henry, who served in the Imperial Navy, became ever less ready to indulge in the general hero-worship of his brother after his wedding in May 1888 to Princess Irene, a strong-minded woman who disliked the Hohenzollern obsession with all things military.

His three younger sisters, whom he disdainfully nicknamed 'the English colony', had always been devoted to their parents. With them, the Emperor had little in common. His relations improved a little with Victoria, the eldest of the three, after plans for her to marry Prince Alexander of Battenberg had been dashed with his marriage to an Austrian opera singer, Joanna Loisinger, and Victoria's subsequent, none-too-happy marriage to Prince Adolf of Schaumburg-Lippe. After she entered the Greek Orthodox Church, Sophie was always treated with coldness by her brother. The youngest sister, Margaret, a quiet, amenable woman, married Prince Frederick Charles, later Landgrave of Hesse. While she had always been loyal to her mother and for some years there was little love lost between her and her brother, she took care never to cause offence and seemed to get on better with him than the rest of the family, especially in later life.

Bismarck's successor as Chancellor and Minister-President, General Leo von Caprivi, was a former Chief of the Imperial Navy. Aged fifty-nine and more straightforward and less devious than his predecessor, he was something of an innocent in government circles. He had been chosen partly as he appeared an amenable character, likely to do the bidding of his imperial master without question. Moreover, Bismarck had recommended him as 'a strong man' likely to deal ruthlessly with the socialists should Germany be threatened by radicals or revolutionaries. In fact, he soon demonstrated a will of his own, told the *Landtag* in his first speech that he was ready to steer 'a new course', and would give ministers more freedom in their individual departments. He was conciliatory with potential opponents of his government, making concessions to the radical members, knowing that if he had their support, they would reciprocate in approving for new measures that he intended to pass.

At home, he presided over modest reforms in taxation, local government, and labour relations. In foreign policy, he strengthened the Triple Alliance by seeking trade treaties linking the German economy with those of Italy and Austria-Hungary. However, he had little knowledge of the empire's relations with foreign powers. Bismarck had retained a virtual monopoly on the details of relevant information. The cornerstone of his diplomacy had been the isolation of France. In order to help control Russian and Austrian expansion in the Balkans, he had signed a defensive alliance with Austria that provided for Germany to come to the dual monarchy's aid in the event of Russian attack. The Reinsurance Treaty, signed by Bismarck in 1887 and due to expire in June 1890, provided for mutual assistance if Austria-Hungary should attack Russia or should France attack Germany. The Emperor alleged that he knew nothing of it until the spring of 1890, when he was informed rather belatedly of its existence by Bismarck. Nikolai Giers, the Russian foreign minister, had seen through Bismarck's strategy and warned that if Germany did not renew the alliance, the Tsar would have to consider one with the French republic. Caprivi was likewise unaware of these matters and of assurances the Emperor had given Count Paul Shuvalov, Russian ambassador in Germany, that Bismarck's resignation would mean no changes in German policy and that the Emperor would personally give his word that the agreement would be renewed. Holstein recommended letting it lapse on the grounds that it undermined that Austro-German alliance, and the Emperor took his advice. It was a mistake he would regret.

There was one major issue on which Emperor and Chancellor did not agree. The Emperor had decided that German needed a large fleet, and took it for granted that Caprivi, as a former head of the navy, would consent. Caprivi begged to differ on the grounds that good Anglo-German relations were vital for the peace of Europe and it would be endangered if they built more battleships.

Where Anglo-German relations were concerned, His Majesty blew hot and cold. Though he sometimes railed to his entourage about Queen Victoria and his irritation with her, he never ceased to respect her as a ruler and a woman. The same could not be said about her eldest son, the Prince of Wales, whom he never lost an opportunity to tease or provoke, while the Empress thoroughly disliked England and the 'immoral English', only accompanying her husband on state visits there under duress. When the Prince was called as a witness in a court case after participating in a game of baccarat, in which one of the players had been involved in cheating on a major scale, the Emperor sent the Queen a high-handed message protesting against the impropriety of anyone holding the honorary rank of a colonel of Prussian Hussars becoming implicated in a gambling dispute with men young enough to be his children.

Soon afterwards, the Emperor became interested in yachting. Purchasing a vessel, the *Thistle*, which he renamed the *Meteor*, he paid annual visits to Cowes each summer to compete with the Prince of Wales and his yacht the *Britannia*. The Prince soon lost patience with his nephew's yachting obsession, making endless trouble about handicaps and rulings and his implication that the committee unduly favoured the Prince at the expense of others, especially himself. He nicknamed the Prince of Wales 'the old peacock', while the latter complained about the self-appointed 'Boss of Cowes', and a few years later, he sold his yacht as the Emperor had completely spoiled his sporting activities.

Caprivi served as Chancellor for four and a half years, during which he repeatedly threatened to resign, as had Bismarck had on many occasions under the previous two Emperors' reigns. Increasingly alarmed by the advance of German socialism, and in particular the assassination in June 1894 of Sadi Carnot, President of the French Republic, the Emperor believed that the lives of himself and his family were at risk, and he appealed for further repressive legislation against 'subversive elements'. Caprivi told him the Reichstag was ill-inclined to pass any more anti-socialist laws. The Minister-President Count Botho Eulenburg, who had been appointed in 1892 when Caprivi resigned the post after the Emperor opposed one of his reform bills (though he remained Chancellor), tried to persuade the Emperor to sanction a *coup d'état* similar to that with which Bismarck had come to power in 1862, reducing the powers of the Reichstag. Caprivi persuaded him against it, but by then, he was weary of trying to control his wayward ruler. He and Eulenburg realised they could not work together any more, and in October, both resigned.

Despite saying he would appoint a younger man for his next Chancellor, the Emperor chose Prince Chlodwig zu Hohenlohe-Schillingsfürst, Governor of Alsace-Lorraine. At seventy-five years of age, he was two years older than Bismarck had been at his resignation, and as a distant kinsman of the houses of Saxe-Coburg and Schleswig-Holstein, he was jocularly called 'Uncle Clovis' by the Emperor. Major-General Swaine, a British military *attaché* in Berlin, was cynical about the replacement of two chancellors with a mere stopgap of a successor—a man who admitted he was too old, too ill, and had a poor memory, thus allowing the ruler to 'pull the strings without opposition' and trust him to continue carrying out the policies of his successor.

In November 1894, Tsar Alexander III died. Emperor William had gradually realised he would never enjoy friendly relations with the man whom he referred to in private as 'the barbarian'. His diffident eldest son and heir, now Tsar Nicholas II, engaged to the Emperor's cousin Princess Alix of Hesse, saw a new opportunity for Russo-German relations. Although Nicholas was careful to maintain friendly relations with William, he soon learned better than to accept his policy initiatives at face value. As for the Emperor, he considered Tsar Nicholas weak, unreliable, and 'only fit to live in a country house and grow turnips'.[25] At the same time, he rarely missed an opportunity to try and wean him from the Russian alliance with France, which for him might be one of the great European powers; however, because of its history over the last two centuries, it was or should have been anathema to all right-thinking sovereigns:

> The Blood of their Majesties is still on that country! Look at it, has it since then ever been happy or quiet again? Has it not staggered from bloodshed to bloodshed? And in its great moments did it not go from war to war? till it soused all Europe and Russia in streams of blood? till at last it had the Commune over again? Nicky take my word on it the curse of God has stricken that People for ever![26]

Throughout the next few years of his reign, the Emperor often exasperated his ministers and fellow monarchs. In the summer of 1900, he made what his foreign minister, Prince Bernhard von Bülow, considered in retrospect was perhaps the most harmful speech he ever made. Resentment in China against foreign domination had culminated in the Boxer Uprising. European citizens were besieged for three months in the diplomatic quarter of Peking, and on 20 June, Baron Clemens von Ketteler, the German minister, was murdered while attempting to negotiate with Chinese officials. The Emperor saw this as a severe blot on German honour, and a military expedition was raised to rescue members of the European community thought to be at risk. As troops were about to sail from Bremerhaven for the Far East, he climbed on to a specially erected platform at the harbour and told them in ringing tones that there would be no quarter and no prisoners would be taken:

> As a thousand years ago, the Huns, under King Attila, gained for themselves a name which still stands for a terror in tradition and story, so may the name of German be impressed by you for a thousand years on China, so thoroughly that never again shall a Chinese dare so much as to look askance at a German.[27]

Even while His Majesty was still speaking, an ashen-faced Hohenlohe turned to Bülow saying he could not possibly answer for such a foolish speech in the Reichstag. Bülow sent out orders to be given to all journalists present not to publish the speech until they had been given a corrected version. When the Emperor saw it in the papers that evening, he was disappointed to find his words had been watered down, telling Bülow he had struck out the best parts of it.

In October 1900, Hohenlohe resigned the chancellorship. Now aged eighty and suffering increasingly from heart trouble, he had never been more than a rubber-stamp for the Emperor's decisions. He was succeeded by Bülow, who was quick to establish a good relationship with the Emperor by managing him judiciously with the right amount of flattery and firmness, something his predecessors had never been able to combine. Yet like them, he had concerns about the sanity of his sovereign. On at least one occasion, Bismarck had remarked that their ruler carried the hereditary burden of his descent from the English and Russian sides, both of which could number crowned heads within the last century believed to have gone mad—namely King George III and Tsar Paul. A few weeks after taking office, Bülow told Eulenburg that it would only take one false move by the Emperor for the formation of a coalition of the German princes, led perhaps by his uncle Frederick, Grand Duke of Baden, and the Reichstag against him to have him declared unfit to rule.

4

'Not a Mouse Would Stir in Europe'

Throughout the first years of his reign, Emperor William and his chancellors had been ambivalent about the question of an Anglo-German alliance. At the turn of the century, British politicians became more interested in the idea, aware that the country's days of 'splendid isolation' were over and that they needed to look either to France and Russia or to the Triple Alliance. Matters had, however, reached no further than informal talks in England between Joseph Chamberlain, the new and very pro-German colonial secretary, and the Duke of Devonshire, when their attention and that of the Emperor was diverted by the news that Queen Victoria was apparently dying.

The Emperor cancelled his engagements and travelled to England with all possible haste, arriving at Osborne House on 20 January 1901 to join the hushed vigil of anxious relatives assembled around her deathbed. When he arrived, her mind was wandering and she mistook him for his long-dead father. At first, the rest of the family had not welcomed the prospect of his imminent arrival, but his uncharacteristically subdued demeanour in their presence impressed them all. The Prince of Wales, shortly to succeed his mother as King, wrote to one of his relations in Germany that nobody could have been kinder or more thoughtful: 'He is only the grandson here & not the powerful Sovereign he is at home'.[1] He helped to support her with his good right arm as she died early in the evening on 22 January.

No admirer of England or most of her English relations, the Empress fretted from Berlin about William's intention to stay in England for the funeral at Windsor on 2 February, and asked Bülow to try and dissuade him. She asked why he could not be represented by her eldest son or her brother-in-law, Prince Henry, both of whom were going to be there, but as so often before, her wishes carried no weight. She knew the death of the grandmother whom he had always loved and respected would bring him much closer to her family and to England than he had been for a long time.

The new sovereign, King Edward VII, made Emperor William a field marshal, Prince Henry a vice-admiral of the Royal Navy, and conferred the Order of the Garter on Crown Prince William. On the last day of his stay in England, the Emperor attended a luncheon at Marlborough House given by the King. When the latter proposed his nephew's health, the Emperor replied that England and Germany should stand together in keeping the peace of the world:

> We ought to form an Anglo-German alliance, you to keep the seas while we would be responsible for the land; with such an alliance, not a mouse would stir in Europe without our permission, and the nations would, in time, come to see the necessity of reducing their armaments.[2]

For several days after he returned to Germany, the Emperor continued to wear civilian clothes in the English fashion instead of the military uniforms in which his entourage were so accustomed to seeing him. Some felt he was obsessed with 'Anglomania' and were disturbed by the sight of their supreme war lord spending his time attired like an English country gentleman.

Even so, any prospects of an Anglo-German alliance soon faded. Bülow proposed a defensive agreement between both countries to last initially for five years, by which each power would remain neutral if the other was attacked by one other European country—only if it was attacked by two states would the ally intervene. Count Paul von Hatzfeldt, German ambassador in London, was asked to enter alliance negotiations with the ministers in London, but his suggestion that Britain should join the Triple Alliance of Germany, Austria, and Italy as a junior partner (subordinate to Germany) and be prepared to guarantee the interests and frontiers of each other member against threats from Russia and France found no favour with the Prime Minister Lord Salisbury. His dismissal of the scheme effectively ended any serious efforts by either nation to reach an agreement.

There had been one notable but reluctant absentee from the family at Osborne and then Windsor. The Empress Frederick had been diagnosed with a particularly painful form of cancer, and was almost too ill to move from her bed, let alone travel. During the previous autumn, it had been thought that she might predecease her mother, but somehow she lingered on into the summer. By the end of July, it was recognised that her sufferings would soon be over. King Edward and Queen Alexandra arranged to leave for Germany as soon as they knew she was sinking, but as they were about to depart, they learned that she had died on 5 August. They reached Berlin four days later, and were reproached by the Emperor for having taken so long to arrive. The King felt his nephew was trying to take him to tasks over the behaviour of his ministers and over the lack of progress on an Anglo-German alliance. Altogether, just before and after the funeral at Potsdam on 13 August, there was an atmosphere of tension between both men, which had been absent from the period that followed the death of Queen Victoria.

Relations between King and Emperor remained uneasy, yet the year 1901—which had seen two major bereavements for them, brought the elder one to his long-awaited inheritance, and also witnessed an attempt on the life of the younger in March, when a mentally deranged worker threw a piece of iron at him, causing a deep wound under his right eye— ended on a more harmonious note. It had been a time of 'care & deep sorrow to [them] all', the Emperor wrote to him, but Queen Victoria had left him 'a magnificent realm ... and what a fine position in the world'. Their countries belonged to 'the great Teutonic race', and he looked forward to them keeping the peace, fostering mutual recognition between their people, and banishing 'everything that could part [them]'. He was the sole arbiter and master of German foreign policy:

> The Government and Country must follow me even if I have to 'face the music'. May your Government never forget this, and never place me in the jeopardy to have to choose a course which would be a misfortune to both them and us.[3]

Such friendly exchanges contrasted sharply with the ill-feeling shown by the press of both countries. It followed a speech that Chamberlain gave a few weeks earlier referring to the behaviour of the German Army during the Franco-Prussian War thirty years before, leading to an outburst of anti-British feeling in Germany and the Reichstag and bitter comments on the conduct of British troops in South Africa. Matters reached such a pitch that the King threatened to cancel a proposal to send his son and heir George, Duke of York, and recently created Prince of Wales, to Berlin for the Emperor's birthday in January 1902. However, he was dissuaded, the Prince's visit went ahead, and he made a very good impression on his hosts.

Soon after this, the young German heir, Crown Prince William, was invited on a private visit to England. At the age of nineteen, he was becoming dissatisfied with the stiff formality of the Court at Berlin, and showed little interest in anything but sport and the opposite sex, not unlike his British 'great-uncle Bertie' had at a similar age. In his bachelor days—and even in the first few years of his marriage—the Emperor had also had mistresses, but was more successful in keeping them secret.

While staying at Blenheim Palace, the Crown Prince had an affair with eighteen-year-old American Gladys Deacon. It came to the notice of the European press, which suggested he was prepared to renounce his place in the succession to marry her. One paper reported that after he returned to Germany, the Empress noticed the absence of a valuable ring that had been a confirmation present from Queen Victoria, and he had apparently given it to Miss Deacon. The furious Emperor vowed that he would never again allow his errant son so much freedom, and he was sure the bad influence of the immoral King Edward (whom the Crown Prince liked and greatly admired) must have been largely to blame for this transgression. He refused to let his son represent him at King Edward's coronation in June, and instead sent his brother, Henry, and sister-in-law, Irene, both regular visitors to England and much liked by their cousins there, in his place. In the end, the coronation was postponed from June when the King underwent an emergency operation and was given several weeks to recover, while arrangements were made for the ceremony to take place in August instead.

Throughout this time, the Emperor watched the network of European alliances with concern. As the self-proclaimed 'sole arbiter and master of German foreign policy', he considered that he did not need a Bismarck to guide his personal efforts at diplomacy between Germany, Britain, and the other powers, unlike his grandfather. He paid more attention to what he read in the newspapers, especially those from Britain, than he was prepared to admit. As thin-skinned as ever, he took all criticism of Germany as an attack on himself, and was convinced that the hostile British press was mainly under Jewish control as part of an international conspiracy involving the British, French, Russian, Belgian, and American media. To him, it was an indictment of the feebleness of British Prime Ministers who failed to control the papers sufficiently to prevent anti-German opinion. In his more paranoid moments, he believed that the British Government was bribing journalists abroad to join the ministers in casting aspersions on the Fatherland.

He also looked askance on King Edward's state visit to Paris in May 1903, and a reciprocal one by President Loubet to London two months later. A softening of Anglo-French hostility, culminating in the signing of the *Entente Cordiale* in April 1904, alarmed him considerably. Matters had been complicated, and not in Germany's favour, when war had broken out two months earlier between Russia and Japan. Britain was sympathetic to the Japanese cause, both nations having concluded an alliance two years earlier, while Germany gave token support to Russia. In July 1904, a valuable Russo-German trade agreement was signed. As the French were now allies of Russia and the English of Japan, he hoped this might prevent the *Entente* from being ratified. Bülow asked the general staff whether, should the worst come to the worst, Russia had the military strength to intervene effectively against Germany against the Polish frontier. Count Alfred von Schlieffen, chief of staff, was sure that should hostilities break out in Europe, Germany would gain rapid victory in the west, and many staff officers supported him in what seemed to be a call for a march on Paris. On the opening of a new bridge across the Rhine at Mainz in May 1904, he delivered a speech mentioning Germany's past triumphs and her present strength in the field. It pleased high-ranking army officers who had previously complained about their monarch's vacillations in world policy, but other countries saw it as a gesture of defiance against the *Entente Cordiale*.

At around this time, his obsession with naval power began to take over and he seemed determined to impress—or alarm—the British with the strength of his growing fleet. Having invited King Edward to the Kiel regatta in June 1904, he made a point of ensuring that every available warship was moored as if for a major naval review. Among those accompanying the King were his nephew, Prince Louis of Battenberg, whose brothers-in-law included Prince Henry of Prussia and Tsar Nicholas II. Louis shared the concern with several others in authority in Britain who looked with unease on the efficiency as well as the size of German warships, and soon after returning to England, he drew up a British war plan for destroyer operations in the event of hostilities at sea.

With a network of alliances taking shape across Europe, it only took one small incident to provoke fears of conflict between one great power and another. On 21 October 1904, while sailing for action off the coast of Japan, the Russian Baltic Fleet mistook a group of British fishing smacks in the North Sea for Japanese torpedo boats, opened fire on them, and killed seven British fishermen. In what became known as 'the Dogger Bank incident', British warships subsequently trailed the Russians down the English Channel and towards the Bay of Biscay. Fearful of another ignominious naval defeat and anxious not to let it escalate, the Russian Government agreed to submit the matter to international arbitration. Emperor William attempted to exploit the situation by urging Tsar Nicholas to take the initiative in proposing an alliance of the three great mainland continental powers, Germany, Russia and France, as a counter-balance to the Anglo-Japanese partnership. At first, the Tsar proved amenable, but when his ministers recommended against it, he did not pursue the matter any further.

In the spring of 1905, the Emperor was persuaded by Bülow and Holstein to pay a courtesy visit to Morocco. The Chancellor and his advisers wanted Germany to give France and Britain a reminder that they could not act unilaterally in European matters where German interests were involved. On 31 March, he spent four hours in Tangier. In a speech there, he proclaimed to a handful of German officials and merchants that the Sultan of Morocco was lord of a free and independent country, and Germany would support his efforts to keep the country open for peaceful competition in trade among all nations. His own presence there was a pledge of Germany's growing interests. He had sorely underestimated how sensitive the British were to anything that might be seen as intriguing by Germany for a naval station so close to such vital trade routes, and the cold reception he was given by the British when he stopped at Gibraltar on his way back home angered him. Throughout most of Europe, it was accepted that Morocco was about to become a French protectorate, and King Edward saw this attempt to undermine French standing as an insult to France and Britain.

To resolve the situation, Germany demanded an international conference on the future of Morocco, and refused to negotiate with the French alone. In June, Prince Radolin, German ambassador in Paris, declared that as long as Theophile Delcassé, the French foreign minister, remained in office, there could be no chance of any improvement in Franco-German relations, and unless France agreed to a conference, she risked attack. He was well-known for his dislike of Germany, and the Emperor had called him 'the most dangerous man for Germany in France'. Once he knew he no longer had the support of his fellow French ministers, Delcassé resigned, and France agreed to submit the matter to a conference. It was a short-lived triumph for the Emperor, for in retrospect, he had almost single-handedly created, or at least helped to foster, a climate of uncertainty in which the threat of European war could not be far away. King Edward was a shrewd judge of character, and his concerns about the emotional stability of his nephew and the consequences for Europe in the future had been justified by his behaviour. To Marquis Luis de Soveral, Portuguese ambassador in London, the King wrote that Emperor William was vain, cowardly, and would tremble before his circle of sycophants when they called upon him to draw the sword in earnest: 'He won't have the courage to talk some sense into them, but will obey them cravenly instead. It is not by his will that he will unleash a war, but by his weakness'.[4]

The date of Delcassé's resignation had coincided with an event that should have boded well for national and family happiness and pride in Germany, the wedding of the Crown Prince. Anxious that their eldest son should be married before he strayed too far down the path to perdition, his parents had sought a wife for him for the last two years or so. It said something for Empress Augusta Victoria's determination, not to say desperation, that she would consider an English bride, namely Princess

Alice of Albany, daughter of Queen Victoria's youngest son Prince Leopold, a haemophiliac who had died just aged thirty. Despite his pro-English sentiments, the Crown Prince refused to consider her or Princess Alexandra of Hanover, second daughter of the Duke of Cumberland, whom they also deemed as a potential daughter-in-law. He was still chafing at a fate that denied him the choice of his first love, Gladys Deacon, or another young American woman, Geraldine Farrar, an opera singer who had performed at a few concerts in Berlin and with whom he had had an affair. However, in June 1904, Princess Alexandra had married Frederick Francis IV, Grand Duke of Mecklenburg-Schwerin. The Crown Prince was chosen to deliver the wedding present his parents had chosen the bride and groom, a porcelain service from the Berlin factory. If they had had an ulterior motive of the matchmaking variety, it succeeded. The young bachelor prince was introduced to Princess Cecilie, one of the Grand Duke's sisters, and three months later, they were betrothed.

It did not bode well for their future together that the princess had shown some jealousy of her future husband's regimental friends and his evident fondness of their company. He may or may not have preferred to spend his spare time with them than with the 'suitable' princess whom he was marrying more out of family duty than anything else, but it immediately created a difference between them that would prove hard to reconcile. It also irritated him that King Edward VII, who rather liked his great-nephew, had sent him a personal invitation to come and stay at Birkhall and Balmoral later that autumn, which his father forbade him to accept. For the unashamedly Anglophile Crown Prince, the wedding day in June 1905 was overshadowed by the ill-feeling between both countries. He was disappointed that neither the King nor the Prince of Wales were representing Britain among the guests, and the relatively junior Prince Arthur of Connaught, the King's nephew, came instead. Longing for his bachelor company, on their honeymoon, the Crown Prince began to discover how little he and his wife had in common, and he told her tactlessly that she was not to interfere with his friends.[5]

Meanwhile, there were dark days ahead for the Russian empire. Since the outbreak of war, the Tsar, his ministers, and the navy had been convinced of their superiority over Japan, but the conflict culminated in almost total annihilation of the Russian fleet at the Battle of Tsushima in May 1905, forcing them to sue for peace. The Emperor was sure the Tsar would welcome any plans from Berlin to replace Paris as her main ally, with the result that France and Britain would be isolated, producing a mighty Russo-German bloc powerful enough to meet the challenge of the Anglo-Japanese alliance. In July 1905, the Emperor sailed for a meeting with the Tsar on board his yacht at Björkö, off the Finnish coast. With him he had a copy of a draft treaty prepared the previous November, providing for each country to help the other if attacked by a third power. This would come into effect once peace was signed between Russia and Japan, as it was at the Treaty of Portsmouth, Maine, in September 1905. In order to limit Germany's obligations, the Emperor added to the original draft a clause confining the scope of the agreement to Europe. Both Emperors signed it, with a counter-signature from naval aides on behalf of each sovereign. This, the Emperor had convinced himself, was a major triumph: 'a turning-point in the history of Europe, and a great relief for my beloved Fatherland, which will at last be emancipated from the Gallo-Russo strangle-grip'.[6] When the Tsar asked how it would affect Franco-Russian relations, the Emperor answered that with Moroccan difficulties out of the way, the Germans and French could be friends once more.

Once they had been made aware of the proceedings, the ministers in Berlin and St Petersburg were horrified. Following defeat by Japan, Russia saw the treaty as a poorly considered initiative that would be incompatible with the Franco-Russian alliance, and Bülow saw that for the Emperor to commit his empire to major agreements in foreign policy without consultation would leave him and the other ministers as little more than clerks. Moreover, if confined to Europe, it would exclude Russia from any action against England in Persia or Jordan. He was so angry that he threatened to resign. The Emperor begged him to remain in office, and the Chancellor later claimed in his memoirs that he was deeply moved by his master's appeal, above all by a self-pitying reference to his 'crippled left arm'. A more probable explanation was that he felt that, having read such a pathetic outburst, he had more hope of ruling supreme over German affairs from now on.[7]

The meeting at Björkö was probably the most ambitious effort at personal diplomacy the Emperor ever undertook. Had it succeeded, his power and prestige as a monarch would have been immeasurably enhanced. Instead, it was a complete failure. He had tried to rival King Edward VII as the supreme diplomat-sovereign of the age, but when faced with a ministerial showdown, he gave way at once. This climb-down was not lost on the other crowned heads of Europe, and none more than the uncle in Britain whom he had tried so hard to emulate. Imitation, as they say, is the sincerest form of flattery, and in this case, it had gone badly wrong.

By the end of 1905, the Emperor seemed to be dreading the possibility of eventual war, something he was anxious to avoid at least until Germany had concluded a formal alliance with Turkey. They could not unleash a conflict against France and England on their own, and the coming year would be particularly unfavourable for hostilities to begin. The German military chiefs had just started a major programme of artillery renewal, expected to take at least a year. Yet the greatest obstacle to war, Bülow thought, was that his sovereign was obsessed with the 'socialist menace at home', which would prevent them from taking a single man out of the country. To do so would jeopardise the property and lives of their citizens. 'Shoot down the Socialists first, behead them, put them out of action, if necessary, massacre the lot—and then war abroad!' was the Emperor's apparent wish. 'But not before, and not *a tempo!*'[8]

In January 1906, a conference to settle the matter arising from Morocco was convened at Algeciras in Spain. The German delegates were supported only by Austria, and they had hoped to drive Britain and France apart, but the net result was to isolate Germany. On its conclusion in April, the conference authorised France and Spain to police Morocco for the Sultan under a Swiss inspector general. Germany could take some comfort in the knowledge that a principle had been established whereby the country was under international, not French control. However, the *Entente Cordiale* had been strengthened, not weakened, as a result of his folly the previous year, while after the loss of prestige following her defeat by Japan, Russia could see the advantage of an understanding, leading to an alliance, with Britain. Meanwhile, Italy had been bound to Germany in the Triple Alliance since 1882, but King Victor Emmanuel III and his government had been repelled by Emperor William's high-handed attitude and his ministers' clumsy efforts to drive a wedge between them and France. They had done nothing at the conference to support Berlin, thus implying that they no longer regarded Germany as a valuable ally.

Above all, it was the first time since the end of the Franco-Prussian War that the major European powers had peered into the abyss and seen how a territorial dispute could result in war. From this date could be marked the beginning of a crisis of confidence in the Emperor's leadership of Germany, already weakened by the folly of his diplomatic *faux pas* at Björkö, a sense of growing fatalism, and, worst of all, a resigned belief in the inevitability of conflict that would culminate in the events of 1914.

At his elder brother's wedding, Prince Eitel Frederick had met Princess Sophie Charlotte of Oldenburg, and in October 1905, their engagement was announced. Like his eldest brother, the prince was a notorious womaniser and his parents had long been concerned by the rumours about him. The Empress even encouraged Oscar, who was serving in the Prussian Army, to avoid visiting Potsdam too often when he was home as she feared the elder brother could prove a corrupting influence on the younger. Once again, the only remedy, his parents were convinced, was for the young man to be married as soon as reasonably possible. Nobody was ever under any illusions that this might have been a love match. 'Lotte' had spent most of her life under the eye of her stepmother, Elizabeth, Grand Duchess of Oldenburg, from whose stifling guardianship the young and marriageable spinster was most eager to escape. The prospect of marrying into the Prussian royal family seemed a good way out. As with the Crown Prince, it was evident within a few weeks of the wedding that their union was not to be a happy one. The prince continued his affairs with other women, leaving his wife to occupy herself at her castle at Tiergarten while she painted, read, and entertained close friends, some probably more intimately than others.

The Emperor became a grandfather for the first time when the Crown Prince and Princess's first son, also named William, was born in July 1906. Although never a model of marital fidelity, the Crown Prince would follow the family tradition in ensuring heirs to the throne in the next generation. Between 1906 and 1917, the Crown Princess gave birth to four sons and then two daughters. Nevertheless, it was common knowledge from early on that husband and wife were ill-matched. According to Alfred von Mitzlaff, one of the prince's friends, both parties were to blame. Neither was prepared to consider the possible effects of his or her behaviour, and neither was ready to listen to warnings from well-meaning friends.[9]

Foreign relations with other powers were not the Emperor's only worries. At home, his prestige was about to be weakened further by scandal. For some years, since before his accession to the throne, his closest friend and confidante had been the diplomat Philipp, Count von Eulenburg. Several people who knew him well thought him either homosexual or at least bisexual, and that his diplomatic career had ended with early retirement from his post at Vienna in 1902 not due to ill-health, the official reason, but after a threat to expose his private life. His sharp tongue spared almost nobody, from the military to the business community and the Jews, and he had made too many enemies.

Among them was Bülow, who had owed his advancement partly to Eulenburg, but now feared the Emperor might be planning to replace him with his old friend, or perhaps another of his close confidantes from the Liebenberg circle, 'the inner circle of the Emperor's Round Table', who also included General Kuno von Moltke, commandant of the Berlin garrison. Anxious to protect his position, Bülow encouraged a campaign against those whom he felt might be plotting his downfall by feeding information and gossip about their dangerous political influence and suspected homoerotic (then illegal) activities to the press. These were received eagerly by Maximilian Harden, journalist, editor, and publisher of *Die Zukunft* ('The Future'), a weekly radical journal sympathetic to the cause of German social democracy. As a Jew, he had everything to gain by discrediting Eulenburg and his anti-Semitic opinions. They were assisted by the ever-vengeful

Holstein, who had his own personal scores to settle as well as a vested interest in wishing to humiliate France and destroy, or at least weaken, the Anglo-French *Entente*. Accusations and counter-accusations multiplied, Harden exposed Eulenburg and Moltke as practising homosexuals, and, in the process, further senior ministers and others close to the entourage of the Emperor and Crown Prince were also implicated and accused.

From 1907 onwards, several cases of criminal libel came before the court. Harden imagined the accusations were common knowledge throughout Germany, but the most important person of all had remained in woeful ignorance. It was apparent that the Emperor had been shielded from much of the gossip and scandal. His ministers and the members of his military circle shrank from putting even the basic facts before His Majesty and persuaded the Crown Prince to undertake the delicate task. This he did when his father came to visit him one day, and he took him for a walk so they could be on their own and he could tell his apparently innocent father something of the less palatable facts of life. Never, the Crown Prince noted later, would he forget his father's horrified face as he was told why some of the German public had been laughing behind his back at his friends' antics. He was shocked to learn of the extent of homosexuality and the involvement of several of his circle. To make matters worse for him, at one stage, it was possible that his more worldly eldest sister Charlotte and her husband, Bernhard, Hereditary Prince and Princess of Saxe-Meiningen, might be summoned as witnesses in one or more of the trials, and he dreaded the names of friends and family being 'dragged through the dirt of all the gutters of Europe' for journalists to report on in detail. Fortunately for him, this never happened, and the disgraced Eulenburg escaped justice only because his trial was repeatedly postponed and finally abandoned on the grounds of his ill-health.

The Emperor himself, it has been said, was engaged in 'a conspiracy against self-understanding'. A reasonably happily married man, he was generally ill at ease with feminine company and seemed more at ease among homosexuals, with whom he shared a taste for bizarre after-dinner pranks of an adolescent schoolboy nature and for military colleagues who would dutifully dress in drag for his amusement. However, he himself probably never went any further than homoerotic games, and his rumoured homosexuality remained repressed.[10] Sometimes the horseplay in which he was liable to indulge could have unforeseen consequences. In 1909, the amply built, notoriously thin-skinned King Ferdinand of Bulgaria paid a state visit to Berlin, bearing among other things a lucrative armaments contract that he had planned to award to the German firm of Krupps. While attending a banquet in his honour at the *Neues Palais* in Potsdam, he leant out of a window to admire the view. The Emperor could not resist giving him a playful slap on the bottom, and when the incandescent King demanded an apology for this gross affront to his dignity, none was forthcoming. That was the end of the Bulgarian visit—and the contract.

After years of mutual suspicion, the Emperor was disturbed at the apparent improvement in relations between Russia and Great Britain. Tirpitz had made it his mission to turn the German Navy into the second largest, if not the largest in the world, and was prepared to risk bad relations with Britain if required. At the same time, he saw the need to avoid Anglo-German tension while a supplementary naval law was under discussion, especially as he suspected the British First Sea Lord Admiral Sir John Fisher of planning a surprise attack on the German fleet. When King Edward visited his nephew at Wilhelmshöhe in August 1907, he said he would be glad to receive him on a state visit at Windsor later that year.

Arranged for November, it was almost cancelled. On 31 October, the King received a telegram from his nephew pleading bronchitis and requesting cancellation, postponement, or permission to send the Empress and Crown Prince instead. The King assumed his nephew had no desire to 'face the music' and had been told that he would receive a bad reception in England.[11] Sir Edward Grey, the British Foreign Secretary, was particularly keen that the visit should go ahead as planned as he wanted to avoid speculation that the Emperor had cancelled it in protest at a recent Anglo-Russian agreement. He warned Sir Frank Lascelles, the British Ambassador in Berlin, that the Emperor should be persuaded to reconsider as any alteration would be attributed to the recent scandals in Berlin. The result was a swift recovery from his bronchitis, and the Emperor and Empress arrived on board the *Hohenzollern* at Portsmouth as planned on 11 November. During the week they were in England as guests of the King, enjoying a programme of dinners, shooting parties, and gala theatre performances, the Emperor attempted to continue his diplomatic initiatives, although his uncle scrupulously avoided any political discussions with him.

Afterwards, the Empress and her ladies returned to Germany. The Emperor was keen to stay another three weeks in England, for what he called 'a short convalescence', at Highcliffe Castle, the home of Colonel Edward Stuart-Wortley near Bournemouth. The Colonel had never met the Emperor, but he and his family were very sympathetic to the German cause, distressed by the prevailing anti-German tone of the press, and welcomed any chance to try and improve relations between both countries. He agreed to lend Highcliffe to the Emperor and his entourage as long as he could remain on the estate and act as host. With the Emperor came Prince Max Egon zu Fürstenburg, a close friend and confidante. An Austrian by birth, the Prince shared the Empress's deep-rooted dislike of England and the English, and exerted some influence on the Emperor in trying to dissuade him from being too friendly with the English as well as strengthening the Austro-German alliance.

One reason for the Emperor's desire to stay there was allegedly because it was near the family home of Admiral Victor Montagu, who was not only known for his pro-German views, but also the father of Mary Montagu, who he had met in the summer of 1905, found very entertaining company, and wanted to see again. Their relationship may or may not have been purely platonic, but like his 'uncle Bertie', the Emperor still had an eye for an attractive woman, and unlike the King, he cared sufficiently about his (less than fully deserved) reputation as a faithful husband to be more discreet in covering up his traces. Around this time, he was also travelling around the Mediterranean, partly in order to be with another female companion, the Venetian Countess Annina Morosini. Some of his circle knew of his acquaintance with both women, and it led to furious outbursts from the Empress. She may have suspected him of infidelity and begun to wonder whether her husband, like their eldest son, was starting to take after King Edward VII.

There was no record of any further meeting with Mary during his three weeks in England. However, during the last week, the Colonel received a letter from an old friend asking if he could arrange for the Emperor to grant an interview to the journalist W. T. Stead, who had already asked if he could arrange one in Berlin. The Emperor had declined on the grounds that his Chancellor had advised him never to give interviews. None of his first ministers were prepared to answer for the consequences if His Imperial Majesty was permitted to grant a journalist even ten minutes of his time. However, he had already just talked freely to the Colonel about his efforts to improve relations with Britain. He said Queen Victoria had appealed directly to him during the Boer War, and after speaking with his general staff, he had recommended a certain line of military action, for which she had thanked him. He also mentioned the possibility of war between the United States and Japan, and called Admiral Fisher 'a most dangerous and overrated man', but otherwise refrained from criticism of anyone in particular.[12] The Colonel took detailed notes throughout their conversations, with the Emperor's full approval. These took place over the course of several evenings, during which the Emperor characteristically changed his mind and his opinions every other day.

He returned to Berlin just before Christmas, sure that he had single-handedly improved Anglo-German relations and Europe would soon see the benefits. Ironically, and probably without his knowledge, while he was away, Tirpitz had laid plans before the Reichstag for shortening the effective life of German battleships, speeding up modernisation of the Imperial Fleet by 25 per cent annually. Confidential reports from the British naval *attaché* warned that if the current rate of progress was maintained, the German fleet would have two Dreadnoughts more than the British by 1911.

'Like a Battleship with Steam Up and Screw Going'

The year 1908 would prove crucial for the German Emperor, and for the wrong reasons. On 14 February, without his Chancellor's knowledge, he wrote a personal letter to Lord Tweedmouth, First Lord of the Admiralty, in an effort to calm fears in Britain about any threat from Germany. The fleet, he said, was being built for the purpose of Germany's needs in relation to her rapidly growing trade. It was never intended as a threat against Britain, whose Navy he estimated was about five times as large, but even so, he defended Germany's right to build as many warships as she wanted. The letter was shown to King Edward and discussed between Tweedmouth and Sir Edward Grey, but not passed to Admiral Fisher or any of his colleagues. The Emperor had sent a courteous note to the King, informing him he had written in his capacity as an Admiral of the British Fleet. Angry that a foreign sovereign should write directly to a member of his government, the King made his objections plain, while Bülow was likewise equally exasperated by his master's conduct. In order to try and mitigate the effects of what he had done, Tweedmouth sent a polite, evasive reply, drafted and redrafted several times with Grey and members of the foreign office, including a copy of the government's statement with naval estimates for the coming year, which were about to be presented to Parliament. When a copy of the correspondence came into unauthorised hands, *The Times* asked why a British cabinet minister was sending such sensitive communications to a foreign head of state before the House of Commons was informed. Tweedmouth, who had recently had a nervous breakdown, escaped censure, but resigned shortly afterwards and died less than a year later.

The Emperor refused to accept that either he or his ministers were at fault. He told Bülow that the British must accept the existence of the German Navy, and that 'from time to time [they] should assure them that the fleet is not built against them'.[1] He was not prepared to have 'a good understanding with England' at the expense of strong German defences at sea. The German Navy law was being carried out, and stated: 'Whether the British like it or not does not worry us. If they want a war, they may start it, we are not afraid of it!'[2]

Although Emperor William could always depend on Austria as an ally, his relations between the elderly Emperor Francis Joseph were never more than formal and restrained. They were dissimilar in personality, and the latter resented his patronising, even discourteous manner to him on his regular visits to the court at Vienna. Moreover, Emperor William had been shocked, as were most of his fellow monarchs, by the events of September 1908. Emperor Francis Joseph wrote personally to inform them all of the annexation of Bosnia and Herzegovina, two states that were nominally part of the Turkish empire that had been occupied and administered by Austria since the Congress of Berlin in 1878. The Emperor was annoyed at not having been taken into the Austrian Emperor's confidence first, while King Edward suspected that Germany had encouraged Austria to make these acquisitions in order to strengthen the Austro-German grip on the Balkans and humiliate Russia.

However, in Germany irritation at the annexation paled alongside the next crisis, the results of which left Emperor William a changed man. During the summer of 1908, Colonel Stuart-Wortley, recently promoted to the rank of brigadier, had been invited to attend the German Army manoeuvres at Metz. After further meetings with the Emperor, he wrote up the notes he had taken from his after-dinner chats with the Emperor at Highcliffe the previous year in the form of an article and sent it to him. He suggested it could be used to secure 'a fair hearing' for Germany in the British press, and that publication would undoubtedly reduce Anglo-German friction. It included his comments on Queen Victoria's appeal to him during the Boer War and his submission to her of a sound plan of campaign; his refusal to join a continental coalition with Russia and France, which would save the Boer republics and humiliate England; his belief in eventual war between the United States and Japan; and his building up the German fleet, partly to protect her growing worldwide trade, partly in order to 'be ready to end a helping hand' against the 'Yellow Peril' if necessary. He was Britain's greatest friend abroad, he declared, the one man capable of holding back the anti-British sentiments of his German subjects. In spite of this, he complained he was cruelly misunderstood and regarded as an archenemy by the English. According to one recent historian, the result read like 'a particularly incoherent rant over a liquid lunch'.[3]

The finished draft of the article was passed to the Emperor for approval. He showed it to Tirpitz, who strongly advised that it should not be published as it might create an unfortunate reaction in England. Reluctant to abandon the idea, the Emperor sent it to other ministers, including Bülow after his return from holiday, who all thought certain passages 'undesirable'. A revised, supposedly more tactful draft was produced, and seen by various ministers and secretaries. Unfortunately for the Emperor, the original document was returned to him with the non-committal advice that there were no grounds for preventing publication. He made a few minor alterations, returning it to Stuart-Wortley with a letter confirming that it correctly embodied all the principal items of their conversation, and authorising him 'to make a discreet use of the article' in whatever manner he thought best: 'I firmly hope that it may have the effect of bringing about a change in the tone of some of the English newspapers'.[4]

The Daily Telegraph, almost the only English paper at the time really sympathetic to Germany, secured it as an exclusive. On 28 October, it carried an anonymous article headed 'The German Emperor and England—Personal Interview—Frank Statement of World Policy—Proofs of Friendship'. After calling the English 'mad as March hares' in their suspicion of German intentions, it listed the various defensive remarks he had made about the many favours his empire had shown to England in the face of hostility from much of the rest of Europe. He achieved the remarkable feat of insulting several nations in turn: the British, the French, the Russians, the Japanese, and even the people of Germany came under savage criticism at one point or another. Significantly, the only nation that escaped his ill-considered censure was Austria-Hungary, undoubtedly because of the presence of Fürstenburg at the conversations.

Reaction was the opposite of what had been intended. In Germany, almost everyone thought the Emperor had made himself look foolish, or in his defence, had been made to seem thus by conspiring ministers who should have persuaded him to suppress the article. He had undoubtedly betrayed national interests by secretly siding with Britain in the Boer War when the sympathies of most of Europe had lain with the oppressed peoples of South Africa. King Edward wrote angrily to Sir Charles Hardinge at the foreign office: 'of all the political gaffes which H.I.M. has made, this is the greatest'.[5] Grey observed presciently: '[The Emperor is] like a battleship with steam up and screws going, but with no rudder; and he will run into something some day and cause a catastrophe'. He did not think there would be war 'at present, but it [would] be difficult to keep the peace of Europe for another five years'.[6]

The Emperor thought he could extricate himself from the situation with another interview. In November, he spoke to an American reporter in Berlin, William Hale, saying that he was misunderstood; that his army and navy were ready for war with England, and the sooner it came the better;

that King Edward was corrupt, his country 'rotten and marching to her ruin, and ought to be wiped out'; and that the very future of civilisation depended on Germany and the US. A brief summary of these remarks was published in the *New York World*, and in London, the *Daily Mail* intended to reproduce it until asked by the British Foreign Office to desist. Although the Berlin Foreign Office issued a statement saying that these 'particulars of statements' were baseless inventions from beginning to end', everyone in official circles realised that the Emperor had opened his mouth too wide yet again.[7] Count Paul Metternich, the German ambassador in London, wrote a letter to the King's secretary Lord Knollys enclosing a categorical repudiation from the Emperor of the remarks attributed to him, but King Edward replied that he knew the Emperor hated him and never missed an opportunity of saying so behind his back, 'whilst [he had] always been kind and nice to him'. The episode was singularly ill-timed for plans were being made for a state visit by the King and Queen to Berlin early in 1909. There was no hurry to settle anything at present, the King continued: 'the Foreign Office to gain their own object will not care a pin what humiliation I have to put up with'.[8]

The man recognised by some as 'a media monarch, perhaps the first European monarch truly to deserve this epithet', with his persistent courting of attention and love of publicity, had stumbled badly.[9] His cup of humiliation was not yet full. In Germany, he was still feeling uncomfortable after the disgrace of Eulenburg. All this coincided with a farcical episode in the middle of November after a dinner party attended by the Emperor. Count Dietrich von Hülsen-Haseler, chief of the imperial military cabinet, performed his party piece as a ballerina, attired in a ballet dress, then collapsed with a fatal heart attack. Rigor mortis set in before he could be removed from his tutu and dressed in his normal clothes again. This, on top of the embarrassment of *The Daily Telegraph* 'interview', came at the worst possible time. Unable to cope with this succession of disasters, the devastated Emperor took to his bed the next month.

Discontented voices in the Reichstag demanded his abdication, and the Crown Prince let it be known that he was ready to succeed as Emperor. Family and government, who considered him even less capable than his father, thought it a case of 'better the devil you know'. After the Crown Prince called on Bülow to keep himself informed of matters, the Chancellor formed the impression that the heir, unlike his father—'modest and polite ... discreet, and somewhat hesitant in manner, a listener rather than a talker'—would not have been unwilling to reign. It reminded him of the Shakespearean scene where a medieval Prince of Wales, later King Henry V, saw the crown on the pillow beside his sleeping father and set it on his own head.[10]

On 17 November, Bülow had a private meeting with the Emperor and Empress at the *Neues Palais*. As he approached on the terrace, she asked him gently to be kind and gentle with the Emperor as he was 'quite broken up'. During a long conversation, the Chancellor tactfully advised his dejected sovereign that they would 'win through' as long as His Majesty was prepared to be more cautious in future.

Two days later, Bülow was just about to speak in the Reichstag when one of his staff came to with a telephone message to say that His Majesty intended to abdicate. As he left the building, a footman came to pass him a letter, addressed in the Empress's handwriting. It said she would like to speak to him, and the messenger would tell him the rest. He went straight to the *Neues Palais* where she received him on the ground floor, asking him tearfully if the Emperor really had to abdicate. He assured her that such an outcome had never occurred to him, and he could not see the necessity. She then told him that her husband had had 'a nervous breakdown'. It had happened before, she said, after moments of emotional crisis, but this time it was more serious and he had taken to his bed. The Chancellor replied that he was sure the storm would blow itself out, but His Majesty would have to be more careful in his general attitude in future—a piece of advice with which she readily agreed.

Over the next few days, the Empress helped to restore something of her husband's old self-confidence. Earlier in their married life, he had treated her as little more than a child, but through the years, he had come to depend on her more and more as one of the few people he could trust. Now, the transformation was complete. If he had not actually had a complete breakdown, he was perilously close to one, but her calming influence prevented him from sliding into complete dejection, as well as providing him with a shoulder to lean on. While she still occasionally bored and irritated him, she had matured from the 'poor, insignificant little princess' of Queen Victoria's exasperated description to his shoulder to lean on in times of crisis.

It was ironic that he had married a wife whom he thought 'knew her place' and would not attempt to exert the influence on her husband that her two predecessors had over the previous German Emperors; however, it was also unfortunate that she was a prejudiced, excessively pious and xenophobic woman with none of the broadmindedness or lack of bigotry of the Empress Augusta and Empress Frederick. She had always resented her husband's close friendship with Eulenburg, and she may have suspected a whiff of bisexuality in her husband. While Eulenburg had always been reactionary and anti-Semitic, he had also been a pacifist, hating the thought of war and bloodshed, and was thus one voice of reason and restraint on the Emperor to counter the sabre-rattling influence of the military chiefs over him and his ministers.

This was the crisis that had the effect of convincing the Empress that she needed to involve herself more in the political affairs of the German Empire, and she believed that Bülow should be retained as Chancellor. Although she kept her views to herself, she knew he could hardly be blamed for the Emperor's naïveté and folly in speaking so freely and therefore could not be held responsible for *The Daily Telegraph* fiasco. The Emperor himself thought differently: always ready to blame somebody else, he was angry that his Chancellor had not suppressed or edited the 'interview'. Although Bülow continued in office for a few more months, his position had been gravely weakened.

Among other family members who were gravely concerned for the Emperor was his youngest sister, Princess Margaret of Hesse-Cassel. She thought that, 'in his heart', he always remained very English, as she herself was, but he could not resist the temptation to play up to what he thought were the feelings of the German people. He had his country's best interests at heart and meant well, but she stated that 'he [would] die of men the most disappointed, broken in spirit or in health—that is, if he doesn't lose his sanity and kill himself'.[11]

Despite the increasing differences between both countries, King Edward's state visit to Berlin could not be long deferred, and it finally took place in February 1909. The Emperor spared no effort in trying to make it a success, especially in ensuring that the rooms where the King and Queen would be staying appeared as homely as possible. Yet the few days were marred by a succession of mishaps. The state coach in which the Queen and Empress rode from the railway station to the palace was delayed as the horses suddenly came to a stop and refused to move, so they had to transfer to a less ornate vehicle to complete the journey. Meanwhile, King and Emperor were both waiting apprehensively in the courtyard, fearing there might have been an attempt on their lives.

The King had recently suffered from bronchitis and was still far from well. After a reception at the British Embassy, he was sitting on a sofa chatting to Daisy, Princess of Pless, when he suddenly coughed and fell back against the seat, semi-conscious and gasping for breath. For a few dreadful minutes, several others present feared he might be dying. 'Oh! Why not in his own country?' was the Princess's immediate reaction, until they loosened his collar and he recovered. Another unfortunate incident occurred at an opera performance when he dozed off, waking up just in time to see a glowing furnace on stage and clouds of smoke—a very realistic representation of a fire in which, according to the story, the major characters all perished. He thought the theatre was alight, and angrily demanded to know why the firemen were doing mothing about it. With some difficulty, the Empress persuaded him that it was deliberate and they were in no danger.

Since *The Daily Telegraph* affair, Bülow had probably realised that his tenure of the chancellorship was drawing to a close. After being defeated in the Reichstag on difficulties in obtaining additional finance for ship construction and failure to carry a majority for imposing inheritance taxes, he offered his resignation in June 1909. A fortnight later, he and his wife were received in a farewell audience by the Empress. She told him how much she deplored and regretted his retirement, telling him that if she had had her way, he would have remained in his position for another twenty years. He replied with a smile that His Majesty would not have found an eighty-year-old Chancellor much use. Anxiously, she asked for his reassurance that he would not make any speeches in the Reichstag against the Emperor. As he kissed her hand, he promised that as a loyal monarchist, he would never create any difficulties for his sovereign. She then said that she had 'nearly always' felt in agreement with him, and that in only two matters had she been unable to share his opinion: one was his proposed Death Duties Bill, which she thought would ruin the nobility and forfeit the support of altar and throne; and the other was that she thought he had been too friendly towards England, a country she did not trust.

On Bülow's advice, the Emperor reluctantly appointed Theobald von Bethmann-Hollweg, previously State Secretary for the Interior with no experience of foreign affairs, as his successor. Neither he nor the Empress had been convinced of his fitness for office. The Emperor initially said he could not work with that 'arrogant, pig-headed schoolmaster', while the Empress thought him 'too philosophical, unworldly and ponderous'.[12] Largely for want of another suitable candidate, he took office as Chancellor in July.

Another of the Emperor's formerly most-trusted confidantes was also about to depart for good. Eulenburg's previous trial on charges of perjury arising from denial of his homosexuality had been adjourned several times for health reasons, and in July 1909, he was judged fit to return to court. The proceedings only lasted a few hours before he collapsed again and the trial was adjourned once more. From time to time over the next few years, doctors were sent by the court to check on his condition, but they always returned with the diagnosis that he was not well enough to stand trial. A broken man, he spent the remaining twelve years of his life quietly on his estates. Not once did he meet or correspond again with the sovereign whose prestige and throne his friendship had threatened.

One man who might have been able to exert a beneficial influence on affairs was Albert Ballin, the shipping magnate and director of the *Hamburg-Amerikanische Packetfahrt-Actien-Gesellschaft*, or Hamburg-America line—at that time, the largest shipping company in the world. He was one of the few commoners whom the Emperor had made welcome at court in Berlin. Very anxious as to the effect war would have on his business, Ballin was keen to build bridges between Germany and Britain. After speaking to his friend Ernest Cassel, a merchant banker who had the ear of King Edward VII and several senior government ministers, he suggested to the Emperor that Tirpitz should meet Fisher directly and that both men should negotiate on a mutually acceptable ratio of naval strength. The Emperor was receptive to the idea until the foreign office in Berlin made it plain that such diplomacy was not a business for private citizens.[13]

The events of the previous two years marked a turning point in the weakening and ultimate destruction of the German monarchy, as well as the collapse of the old European order. At one stage during the libel trials, Harden had claimed to possess evidence that, if put before the Emperor, would lead to his abdication. By now, the Emperor felt less secure at his capital and was glad to escape to other parts of his empire. Berlin court life, he wrote to Lady Mary Montagu, was 'a Society that burns to be invited on every possible occasion, and laughs at you behind your back!'[14]

The same week that he wrote this letter, Europe's other most flamboyant sovereign had only a few days left. On a last visit to Paris in the spring of 1910, King Edward VII told an old friend that he did not have long to live: 'and then my nephew [Emperor William] will make war'.[15] Although in poor health for some time, he had gone about his business as usual to the last, and the first bulletins warning that he was 'indisposed' after a series of heart attacks were issued only twenty-four hours before he died on the evening of 6 May.

When told his uncle had passed away, the Emperor went silent for a few moments then pulled himself together and announced he would leave for England at once. He inevitably had mixed feelings about the death of the man whom he had called the 'encircler', but family duties had to be done.[16] On 19 May, the day before the funeral, he accompanied his cousin, the new and rather diffident King George V, to Westminster Hall, where they laid wreaths together on the coffin and then clasped hands above it. *The Daily Chronicle* saw this as a symbol 'of the friendship that should ever unite the two great Empires they represent in the bonds of peace'.[17] Next day, he was one of the nine crowned heads who walked in the solemn procession at Windsor. Several observers, notably Count Albert von Mensdorff, the Austro-Hungarian Ambassador to London, were impressed with his appearance of quiet dignity and sympathetic self-effacement, which made a contrast with the undignified merriment of the Greek family mourners.[18] An aide-de-camp of the King, Viscount Esher, noted that of all the foreign royalty present, it seemed to him that the only genuine mourner was 'this extraordinary Kaiser'.

At once, there was a softening of Anglo-German relations. King George V and his consort, Queen Mary, both liked and respected their German cousin, and were full of admiration for the way he had overcome the handicap of his deformed arm and hand, well enough to take an active part in the shooting at Sandringham. The insular King George did not share his father's passion for foreign travel or aptitude for foreign languages, and was always much happier at home in England. Shortly before the funeral, the Emperor had told Theodore Roosevelt that the new sovereign was a thorough Englishman who hated all foreigners, but he did not mind, as long as he did not hate Germans more than other foreigners.

Perhaps more importantly, there was none of the mutual rivalry, often bordering on irritation, which had existed between the Emperor and King Edward VII. King George never attempted to become a major figure throughout Europe, knowing he was ill-suited by temperament for such a role. As a constitutional sovereign, he would never have allowed private family feelings to colour relations with a foreign monarch, something to which his father had been inclined. Possessed of shrewd common sense, he was all too aware of how Anglo-German relations had deteriorated during his father's reign, appreciated that a clash of personalities between King and Emperor had been partly responsible, and was prepared to make efforts to mitigate any possible bitterness. He was sure that Bethmann-Hollweg was more trustworthy than the devious Bülow, and that this would help to foster greater harmony between them. His liking for the Emperor did not extend to approval of Germany as a nation. It irritated him that the Germans suspected there were English spies everywhere; he personally believed that '[English] spies [were] the worst and clumsiest in the world', while German espionage was 'magnificently organised and lavishly financed'.[19]

Although the Emperor was not generally the soul of tact, he tried to intercede in one small problem that troubled his British cousins. The recently widowed Queen Alexandra showed no inclination to leave Buckingham Palace, the sovereign's official London home, and although King George and Queen Mary could not wait to move in, they hesitated to press the matter. Exercising his charm and powers of persuasion to the utmost, the Emperor—whom she had never liked—tried to persuade her that she would be far more comfortable in her old home of Marlborough House nearby. After giving every appearance of listening, she turned to him with a smile, told him that he knew he always spoke rather indistinctly, and she had not heard a single word he was saying.[20] Once he had returned to Germany, the Queen did move to Marlborough House, as she had doubtless intended anyway.

In May 1911, the Emperor and Empress returned to London, accompanied by Princess Victoria Louise, for the unveiling of a memorial to Queen Victoria in front of Buckingham Palace. In accepting the invitation on behalf of them all, the Emperor replied to King George with an effusive letter of thanks, recalling in detail how he would never forget his presence at the deathbed of Queen Victoria. Holding her in his arms for the last few hours of her life (rather an exaggeration), he said, had 'created an invincible special link between her country & its People & [him] and one which [he] fondly nurse[d] in [his] heart'.[21]

On the day of the ceremony, they were cheered in the streets and applauded by a standing audience at the theatre, and the Emperor was pleasantly surprised to find such a friendly atmosphere at Buckingham Palace. As it was strictly a family visit, he did not attempt to have discussions with any of the ministers. However, just before leaving England, he raised the question of Morocco with King George V. It was a hurried exchange, and when the Emperor was back in Berlin, he assured Bethmann-Hollweg that the King would never go to war because of Morocco, although his government might seek compensation elsewhere in Africa if the French strengthened their position there. England would be afraid to go to war with Germany for fear of losing Egypt, India, and Ireland, and 'she would not dare to risk the loss of her colonies overseas'.[22]

In spite of this, on what was his last visit to England, the Emperor was sure that the country, monarch, and government were more well-disposed towards Germany, perhaps more than they had been for a long time. Rumours even surfaced in the press about the possibility of a forthcoming engagement between the Princess, who had, it was said, 'taken London by storm', and the Prince of Wales, but the gossip soon ceased.[23]

A few weeks later, his eldest sister, Charlotte, was a guest at the King's coronation in Westminster Abbey, as was their brother, Henry, and spent several weeks in the country afterwards. She had become increasingly Anglophile over the years, as their younger sisters had always been, and from Sandringham, she wrote effusively that there was 'no place in the world like England, & if possible [she was] more English than ever'.[24]

On 28 June, Alfred von Kiderlen-Wächter, the new secretary for foreign affairs, visited Kiel during regatta week to obtain the Emperor's approval for the Morocco venture. Germany intended to use the presence of German warships to obtain colonial concessions from the French, or at least to establish a foothold in southern Morocco. The German gunboat *Panther* arrived off Agadir on 1 July, and German ambassadors accredited to countries that had signed the Algeciras agreement informed their governments of the German naval presence in southern Morocco.

In the ensuing months of international crisis, Europe seemed closer to war than at any time for several decades. There was less excitement in Paris than in Berlin or London, especially as a change of government at the end of June had brought to power Joseph Caillaux, who was known to favour closer Franco-German collaboration. Yet the Emperor and Kiderlen-Wächter were surprised by the reaction from London. They had expected the British Government to acquiesce, instead of treating the matter as a serious threat to European peace. Sir Edward Grey demanded an explanation from the German ambassador, whom Kiderlen-Wächter had left without any clear instructions. With rumours of Franco-German negotiation, the British Government adopted a stern tone, and Grey welcomed the offer of David Lloyd George, Chancellor of the Exchequer, to deliver a strong warning in a speech at London on 21 July. While he did not mention Agadir or Germany by name, he declared that Britain could not be treated, where her interests were vitally affected, as if she was of no importance. Peace at that price, he said, would be a humiliation that Britain could not accept or endure.

At the time, the Emperor was cruising on board his yacht *Hohenzollern*. He had doubts about Kiderlen-Wächter's performance, and thought he was making demands for territorial concessions in Central Africa from France that no government could possibly make. To Bethmann-Hollweg, he insisted that there must be no mobilisation of German forces while he was on his cruise, and a representative in attendance reported back to Berlin that the Emperor was unlikely to approve of any measures that might lead to war. He was dismayed to see the press in Berlin becoming aggressively patriotic, talking of 'national dishonour' and 'unspeakable shame' while portraying their Emperor as a coward, and the generals were likewise taking a tough line. Admiral Georg von Müller, head of the naval secretariat, thought it essential to postpone any conflict with England until after the completion of the Kiel Canal, so that Dreadnoughts could move freely between the North Sea and the Baltic. Tirpitz was also anxious to wait, sure that with every passing year they would be in a more favourable position. The earliest possible date for war, he believed, would be the spring of 1914.

Only a minority in Germany were prepared to imperil the peace of Europe over Morocco, and the Emperor agreed to a conference at Wilhelmshöhe. After several weeks of negotiation, in November, Germany recognised France's right to 'protect' Morocco, receiving in exchange a certain amount of the French Congo, which gave her river outlets for exports from the Cameroons. Only then could the crisis be regarded as over.

The Emperor congratulated Bethmann-Hollweg on emerging successfully from a 'delicate crisis'. Much to his disappointment the Reichstag debated the Moroccan crisis a few days later, with conservative and liberal deputies attacking the inept foreign policies of the last few months and the sovereign who had apparently tolerated such alternations of bravado and retreat. The Crown Prince was present on one occasion, on 9 November 1911, and seen applauding the attack of a conservative deputy, Ernst von Heydrebrand und der Lasa, as he struck the pommel of his sword on the railing of the loge and nodded enthusiastic approval. This show of support for one of the Chancellor's most persistent critics earned the heir a private rebuke in the form of a stern lecture from his father on the duties and loyalties of a Crown Prince. It did not escape the notice of the press in England and France, where there were disapproving comments on the future German Emperor's lack of responsibility and his open support for such jingoistic speeches, especially as he had professed himself an ardent admirer of England. King George V told Count Metternich that he thought it 'a great act of insubordination' against his father.

Nobody really disliked the Crown Prince, but most who knew him thought him a fool who lacked his father's dignity. While he and the Crown Princess were on a visit to the Quirinal in Rome as guests of King Victor Emmanuel and Queen Margharita of Italy in April 1911, it was noted that the heir made a joke of questions and matters discussed and failed to show a serious interest in anything. At a dinner, he was engaged in conversation with Heinrich Gerhard, a ninety-year-old sculptor; when asked how he liked Rome, the artist replied that he had spent the last seventy years of his life in the city and completed many of his best works there, but he was tired and hoped he would be able to rest soon in Testaccio. The Crown Prince assured him earnestly that it would do him good: 'the sooner you go there the better'. Only afterwards did he learn that Testaccio was not a local resort, but one of the best-known (to others, at least) cemeteries of the Eternal City.[25]

Count Anton Monts, a German ambassador in Rome, was unimpressed with father and son. He thought the Emperor was 'superficial, vain, without any thorough knowledge of anything', and the heir just as bad, if not worse. According to the Austrian politician and historian Joseph Redlich, Monts thought that 'the institution of monarchy is facing great dangers in Europe. The monarchs of the future promise to accomplish very little'.[26]

6

'If the Iron Dice Must Roll, May God Help Us'

In order to maintain a strong army and an ever-growing navy, the German Government needed to increase taxation. The ministers had introduced a first major reform bill of imperial finances in 1906, aiming to spend most of the additional funds raised on defence. It failed, partly as the parliamentary parties could not agree on strategy and made numerous changes, which made it ineffective, and partly as a new Navy Law of 1908 rendered its calculations obsolete. That same year, Bülow approached the matter again, intending to levy increased indirect taxes and also seeking direct taxation to be levied by central government. As indirect taxes were raised on basic items of consumption such as bread, tobacco, and beer, which accounted for the largest proportion of the lower classes' personal expenditure, further increases to subsidise armaments would affect such people more severely than a levy on wealth and property that would only hurt the aristocracy and the upper classes.

Bülow thought the latter should make more of a contribution to the nation's defences. Previously, the more centre and right-wing parties had eagerly voted for expensive military campaigns and accused the Social Democrats and other parties of the left of being unpatriotic when they spoke out against such calls on the public purse. Yet when it came to distributing the financial burden of *Weltpolitik*, or Germany's new global politics, they would eagerly vote for higher indirect taxes that would affect the masses more than themselves. Bülow, who resigned the Chancellorship not long afterwards, sought a compromise with his proposal that around 20 per cent of the 500 million Marks required should be raised by the imposition of death duties. This was rejected by the Conservative members and parties as a direct levy on inherited wealth, and they joined with the Centre Party in drawing up and passing a modified finance bill that saw a return to the old policy of indirect taxation.

The electorate delivered their verdict in the elections of January 1912, which saw the Social Democratic Party emerge as the largest party in Germany with 110 seats, a marked increase from their 1907 total of only forty-three, at the expense of the heavily defeated Conservatives. Though Bethmann-Hollweg could still count on support from parties of the right and centre to get legislation through the chamber, Emperor William was shocked by the result. Some of the Social Democrats had no love for the monarchy, and one of their leaders, Gustav Noske, had told a party meeting two years earlier that they intended to call for a republic at the next election. Nevertheless, most of the ordinary members were less fired with revolutionary zeal than their leaders. In a society with high employment and adequate wages for the working man, there was no huge undercurrent of a seething proletariat impatient to overthrow the existing order, particularly in a country where respect for authority had long been ingrained in the national character.

Even so, with potential crises at home and throughout the continent, the Emperor sometimes feared for the stability of his throne. He felt there were lessons to be learnt from the Agadir crisis, as did Tirpitz, who was convinced they had to reduce England's naval lead as soon as possible with a substantial shipbuilding programme to be embodied in a navy bill as part of the year's budget proposals. The general staff of the army, under Erich von Ludendorff, their new chief of operations, demanded a new army bill. In 1910, Germany had spent half as much on the navy as on the army, a proportion that the Prussian war ministry considered absurd as Germany was essentially a continental power. Decisive events, they said, would be on land, and her power rested on the strength of her army.

Bethmann-Hollweg was increasingly alarmed by the whole direction of German policy. He believed the Emperor was only really listening to two advisers. One was Tirpitz, who was obsessed with building up Germany's fleet until the English would not risk a naval encounter. The other was the ever-more Anglophobe Empress, who, since the events of 1908, seemed to have more of a hold on her husband than ever before. In one of his more bellicose moods, the Emperor wrote to King George of Greece that he himself did not want war: 'but apparently England does and if they do we are quite ready'.[1]

European stability was threatened further that autumn when Russian agents encouraged an alliance that would bind the Balkan states of Serbia, Montenegro, Greece, and Bulgaria to declare war on Turkey. Within three weeks, the Balkan League had gained victories in Macedonia, Thrace, and northern Albania, much to the delight of the Emperor, who saw their campaign against Turkey as a 'historical necessity'. He was reluctant to support a hard-line policy in Vienna that might lead to the outbreak of war on a wider scale, and he told Kiderlen-Wächter that he saw no threat to the prestige of Austria in a Serbian harbour on the Adriatic. To his Chancellor, he was more forthright when warned of a possible rupture of the alliance. War might mean the downfall of Germany, and he did not favour the principle of his army being called upon merely to support another nation if conflict did break out. At length, his Chancellor persuaded him that if Serbia persisted in threats to annex Albania or secure a harbour on the Adriatic, as seemed likely, Austria would feel provoked into defensive or aggressive measures. However, he and Admiral von Müller believed that Germany would only support a war if Russia put herself in the wrong and threatened to attack Austria.

In November 1912, the Emperor and his chief of staff, Helmuth von Moltke, met Archduke Francis Ferdinand, heir to the Austrian throne, at Berlin to discuss the Balkan power structure. They assured the Archduke that his empire could count on German support, whatever the circumstances. Next, the Emperor, considering war a very real possibility, asked his ambassadors in Paris and London for information on how the French and British governments might react to worsening relations between the European powers. He was particularly keen to know whether Britain would take sides if the Balkan troubles could not be contained, as any Austrian move against Serbia would surely provoke Russia. On 3 December, he approved a plan designed to ensure that if war broke out with France and Russia, any German fleet activity against France should be limited in a way that would probably allow Britain to stay neutral. Even so, regarding the word of his diplomats as suspect, he sent his brother Henry to England for a meeting with King George V. Henry had always been on excellent terms with their British cousins, and he and Princess Irene were regular visitors from Germany.

On 6 December, while staying at York Cottage, Sandringham, as a guest of King George and Queen Mary, Prince Henry asked the King whether England would come to the assistance of Russia and France if Germany and Austria went to war with them. The King replied that they would undoubtedly do so, under certain circumstances. 'You possess signed Alliances: we unsigned *Ententes*,' he said, 'We cannot allow either France or Russia to be overthrown.' After further discussions with Sir Edward Grey and others, Henry left England and duly informed his brother that England was peace-loving; if war broke out, Germany would have to reckon 'perhaps on English neutrality, certainly not on her taking the part of Germany, and probably on her throwing her weight on the weaker side'. In retrospect, Prince Henry was considered vague and muddle-headed, but it was more likely that he reported the conversations accurately enough and the Emperor chose to hear what he wanted to hear. In the margin of his brother's report, the Emperor scribbled, 'Well that settles it, we can now go ahead with France.'[2]

That same week, the British Lord Chancellor Richard Haldane had a meeting with the German Ambassador Prince Karl von Lichnowsky in which he confirmed that the British would not stand aside in the case of an Austro–Hungarian attack on Serbia, nor would they tolerate any aggression of Germany against France. On the morning of 8 December, the Emperor read Lichnowsky's report with anger, declaring that in the 'Germanic struggle for existence', the British, blinded by a sense of envy and inferiority, were joining the Slavs (Russia) and their Romanic accessories (France). He raged in his marginal comments on the document that England was 'too cowardly openly to leave France and Russia in the lurch'; he stated: '[They are] too envious of us and hates us, other nations are not supposed to draw the sword to defend their interests, as then England would go against us after all, despite all her assurances.... A real nation of shopkeepers! And they call that a policy of peace! Balance of Power!'[3]

He summoned an informal conference at the *Neues Palais*, subsequently dubbed a secret 'military-political conference', or a *Kriegsrat* or war council a few days later by the angry Chancellor, who was not invited to attend. Among those present were Tirpitz, Moltke, Vice-Admiral August von Heeringen of the naval staff, and Admiral von Müller of the naval secretariat. As well as the Chancellor, the state secretary for foreign affairs and the minister for war were deliberately excluded because the Emperor regarded them as mere civilians responsible for purely political matters and not military or naval issues. The Emperor and his military leaders agreed initially that if war was necessary, it should be launched soon. Tirpitz maintained they were not ready for 'the great fight' and would not be for eighteen months. He said the navy was unprepared for a general war that included Britain as one of her enemies, and they should wait until the U-boat base at Heligoland and the Kiel Canal were completed. Moltke opined that postponing the war was unacceptable as it would place the army in an unfavourable position as their enemies were arming more strongly. He argued that the German Army was short of finance and would be less well-equipped to fight in two or more years hence than now. For him, a preventative war—a strategy that Bismarck had often dismissed as one of 'committing suicide out of fear of death'—was to be preferred. With reluctance, he bowed to the prevailing view when the Emperor sided with Tirpitz.

Without the restraining influence of Eulenburg and the more pacifist Liebenberg circle, it has been argued that the Emperor was increasingly open to manipulation by the generals and his military entourage. Equally plausible is the theory that he was deliberately surrounding himself with hawks who, he knew, were prepared for, if not actually relishing the prospect of a war in which the German Empire would prove itself victorious yet again. Moreover, in his hostility to France, he was angered by Britain's apparent determination to defend her Gallic ally to the hilt. It was significant that the doves—such as the Chancellor, who had urged acceptance of Haldane's proposals to slow down, if not cease battleship production altogether, and not to attack Russia or France and had been overruled—were excluded. It is hard to absolve Emperor William from a major element of responsibility for the outbreak of war eighteen months later. If he neither wanted war in 1914 nor started it, he was partly to blame by letting himself be manoeuvred into a position, or a frame of mind, in which he regarded an avoidable conflict as inevitable if not actually desirable.

Prince Henry's report of his conversation with King George V reached Potsdam soon after the meeting. It gave his brother the impression that while England would not side with Germany, she might remain neutral or else throw her weight on the weaker side. Taking British neutrality for granted, the Emperor sought to collaborate with Grey to settle Balkan problems through a conference of ambassadors in London. The Prince wrote to King George V to explain what he had told his brother and assure him that Germany had no intention of going to war with anybody: 'We always were—& I am still—in hopes that England & Germany might go together, for the sake of the world's peace!'[4]

Herbert Asquith, the British Prime Minister, wondered whether the Prince was a fool or a knave. Had he been sent to England to allay suspicion, or did he know the true facts and merely pose as a candid friend to conceal his country's warlike intentions? He suspected the latter, but the King's private secretary Sir Frederick Ponsonby, who knew him and the imperial family better, believed Henry was a friend of Britain, a more reliable one than his mercurial elder brother, and a perfectly straightforward man who never gave the impression of having any Machiavellian cunning.[5]

Despite his fury with England, the Emperor still retained an exaggerated belief in the effectiveness of dynastic diplomacy. He believed that his cousins, King George V and Tsar Nicholas II, would somehow help between them to check the continent's desire for war. Yet those around him seemed to detect a deepening mood of resignation to the inevitability of a major conflict. German gossip said that he had damaged the nation's chances by losing his nerve and failing to stand firm in 1905 and 1911, and senior officers intended this should not happen again.[6]

There had been large gatherings of European royalties in England for the funerals of Queen Victoria in 1901 and King Edward VII nine years later. One more final reunion of the extended royal and imperial family, and this time on a happier occasion, was to come.

In May 1912, Prince George William of Hanover, eldest son of the Duke of Cumberland, had been killed when his car skidded off the road while he was driving to Denmark to attend the funeral of his uncle, King Frederick VIII. Emperor William sent his sons, Princes Eitel Frederick and Augustus William, with a deputation of Hussars to form a guard of honour around the bier where the Prince lay in state. After the funeral, the Emperor telegraphed the bereaved parents his heartfelt condolences. Soon afterwards, the family received a request to ask if the Duke's younger son, Prince Ernest Augustus, could come and pay his respects to the Emperor in person on behalf of his parents to thank him for the goodwill he had shown them. A visit of one of the Hanoverian family to the Hohenzollerns had not taken place since the Prince's grandfather, George, the last King, had been on the losing side of war with Prussia in 1866 and the little kingdom had been absorbed by the victor.

For nineteen-year-old Princess Victoria Louise, it was more or less love at first sight. On 10 February 1913, they became engaged. When the news was announced, there was some dissent. Certain conditions had been attached, among them was one that requested Prince Ernest Augustus enter the Prussian Army on marriage, take an oath to the King of Prussia, and swear not to make any move for the Hanoverian throne. Some partisans in Hanover of the Brunswick family declared that this renunciation should not be regarded as legally binding, and that it should not prevent him from agitating for the throne should it be restored. However, both families saw it as a reconciliation after years of bitterness.

The wedding took place at Berlin on 24 May 1913, significantly on the anniversary of Queen Victoria's birthday. The first guests to arrive were King George V and Queen Mary, the former attired in the uniform of a Prussian general. Significantly, they were not accompanied by the widowed Queen Alexandra, the elder sister of Thyra, Duchess of Cumberland. Although invited, she was as unforgiving as ever of the German imperial family who were responsible for decimating the Kingdom of Denmark half a century earlier. There were several royalties from the other German states, and Tsar Nicholas II also came, although without the Tsarina, whose health was now increasingly poor.

In addition to the ceremony itself, there were the usual trappings of imperial splendour with banquets, gala operas, and military parades. Even so, there was unease beneath the splendour. As Sir Frederick Ponsonby, who had accompanied King George abroad, later recalled, everyone went out of their way to be civil on such occasions, so one hardly had an opportunity of judging the real feeling. He was inclined to think that the visit helped towards establishing a measure of good feeling between the two countries, but it was difficult to disguise the fact that by now the states were practically rivals.[7] King George was not suspicious by nature, but he thought the Emperor was jealous of the close friendship between him and the Tsar, imagining them to be plotting behind his back and trying to ensure that they should not be left alone. On the rare occasions that they did manage a quiet few words together, the King suspected that 'William's ear was glued to the keyhole'.[8] The Emperor avoided discussing anything contentious with the King, preferring to vent his feelings instead at an officers' luncheon on Lord Stamfordham, taking him fiercely to task as his country had been 'making alliances with a decadent nation like France and a semi-barbarous nation like Russia and opposing [them], the true uplifters of progress and liberty'.[9]

The month after his daughter's wedding, the Emperor celebrated his silver jubilee. On the weekend of 14–15 June, the streets of Berlin were decorated with jubilee arches bearing the imperial cypher and flags fluttering everywhere. F. W. Wile, Berlin correspondent of the *Daily Mail* in London and *The New York Times*, recorded in glowing terms that 'under his active leadership the Fatherland has reached the pinnacle in its peaceful pursuit of commerce and industry and has become the mightiest military force in the world'. Such successes, he said, had combined to equate the name of Germany with progress and power, and that the world attributes to the Emperor 'the exceptional manner' by which his empire had been spectacularly elevated to the status of a world power: 'As Managing Director of Germany Ltd, Kaiser Wilhelm has had a difficult role to play yet has succeeded in fulfilling his duties with eminent success'.[10]

Another cause for celebration was the centenary of the war of liberation and victory at Leipzig in October 1813, marked by the unveiling of a monument on the 'battlefield of the nations'. However, the Emperor seemed unusually downcast. Friends and family thought he was suffering from depression following his daughter's marriage, but others put his low mood down to different reasons. Bishop Boyd-Carpenter, an old friend of Queen Victoria, called on him a few weeks later and found his personal moods altering suddenly from confidence to utter despair and back again. Was he somehow aware that many of those 'who had enjoyed his hospitality, and shown their friendship and affection, would soon be ranged against his Empire'?[11]

At fifty-four years old, the Emperor was a more subdued, less impulsive character than he had been some ten years earlier; he was less impulsive and less prone to making outrageous statements without thinking first. Sometimes, it was as if he had peered into the abyss of war and retreated, considering it not worth the risk. War-hungry nationalists impatient with his restraint transferred their hopes to the Crown Prince, who seemed ambitious and impatient for glory, if not to rule. Baron Constantin von Gebsattel, a retired general, bombarded the heir with calls for 'courage' in foreign policy, stricter controls on liberal and socialist newspapers, and the proclamation of a state of siege pending the introduction of repressive anti-Jewish laws. The Crown Prince passed this advice on to his father in November 1913, but the latter rejected it as 'childish', pointing out that if the Jews were forced to leave the German Empire, they would take their riches with them. The tension between father and son was no secret, and Jules Cambon, the French ambassador, thought the Emperor was jealous of his son's popularity with the more right-wing deputies in the Reichstag. While Emperor, friends, and family were on a shooting party early the following year, one begged another to aim carefully and not to shoot His Majesty, 'for the young one is much, much worse!'[12]

When Bethmann-Hollweg proposed a direct tax as a contribution to the costs of the 1913 Army Bill, which had been partly a response to tensions in the Balkans and the uncertainty of the Dual Alliance's position in that corner of Europe, there was opposition from the conservatives, but they were no longer strong enough to block the finance bill with its proposals for a wealth tax. Ernst von Heydrebrand und der Lasa, now leader of the German Conservatives, accused the government of having brought about the introduction of a property tax that had undermined the position of the federal states in favour of the democratic convention role of the Reichstag. To many on the right, the outcome of the 1913 tax battle had raised some fundamental questions about future German society. A retired general and leader of the Pan-German League sent a memorandum to the Crown Prince, who forwarded it to the Emperor, proposing a violent solution to the growing domestic deadlock. When asked by the Emperor for his opinion, Bethmann-Hollweg was appalled by the possibility that major unrest might erupt into civil war. If this came to pass, it carried the further danger that other European powers might use the internal state of the Empire as a good opportunity to declare war.

By the end of 1913, Germany was fiercely divided. Some feared a constitutional crisis similar to the army bills dispute that had brought Bismarck to power half a century earlier, while others gloomily foresaw a revolution from the large, increasingly articulate proletariat unsettled by rapid economic growth during the last thirty years. The Chancellor feared that a detachment of armed guards might descend on the Reichstag, send the deputies packing, arrest any dissidents, and shut down the opposition newspapers.

A group of staff officers believed Germany's internal problems could be resolved by a swift and victorious campaign against the French or the

Russians, as war would rally the population behind the Emperor. While he shrank from risking the lives of his men for what he saw as a frivolous cause, he felt unable to argue with Moltke and his military secretariat. They pointed to a combination of the increasing strength of Russia's armies and France's decision to strengthen her army by introducing three years of military service, which would make an outbreak of hostilities very likely. Any continental war that might thus come about had to be guaranteed the participation of Germany's only ally, the multi-national Austro-Hungarian Empire, at the right moment. As France and Russia were both increasing military spending, it was possible that within two or three years Germany might lose her military superiority over both countries. The Emperor was thus swayed into believing that conflict in Europe, a preventive war, was surely inevitable if not desirable, and he was obsessed with taunts of cowardice should he argue otherwise.

Sometimes guests could be discomfited by his behaviour. In November 1913, he entertained King Albert of the Belgians at Potsdam, and while showing him around Sans-Souci, suddenly remarked that war with France was close at hand. At dinner that evening, the Emperor and Moltke attempted to find out how Belgium might react in the event of a Franco-German conflict. Refusing to commit himself, King Albert told them firmly that the Belgians would remain neutral unless attacked. However, he was so concerned by their attitude that afterwards he sent President Poincaré and the French Government a full report on their conversation.

Early in 1914, the Emperor visited his closest allies in Austria. A brief courtesy call on Emperor Francis Joseph, now aged eighty-three, was followed by another to his heir, Archduke Francis Ferdinand, neither of much consequence. In June, he went to stay with the Archduke at his home at Konopischt. Although it was a private visit, the subject of politics could not be avoided and the Archduke asked his guest pointedly how Germany would react if the Austrian Army was forced to discipline the Serbs and crush Slav terrorists. The Emperor tried to evade the question, but the Archduke would not be brushed aside and elicited from him a reluctant, but specific declaration that Germany never could nor should engage in a war for life and death on two fronts.

At the annual regatta at Kiel a few days later, a squadron of British warships, including four battleships and three cruisers, was moored alongside the Imperial High Seas Fleet. There were several friendly personal exchanges between the Emperor, his brother Prince Henry, and Tirpitz and the British officers, who were each welcomed on board each other's ships for receptions and descriptions of recent developments on both sides. When the Emperor was welcomed aboard the yacht *King George V* for lunch by Admiral Sir George Warrender, commander of the

British squadron, he was wearing his uniform as Admiral of the British Fleet and was thus technically the senior Royal Navy officer present.

Three days later, on 28 June, the Emperor was racing in his yacht *Meteor* when Admiral von Müller received an urgent telegram from the German consul in Sarajevo, the Bosnian capital. It informed them that Archduke Francis Ferdinand and his wife Sophie had been assassinated while on an official visit to the city.

Müller caught up with the Emperor's yacht, and as the boats drew level, he called out the grim news. Outwardly calm, but inwardly horrified at the fate of two people who had become close friends as well as allies, the Emperor cancelled the race and went back to Potsdam the next morning. His immediate plan was to attend the funeral at Vienna, and was surprised when asked not to attend. Some thought it was a ruse to keep him away from Vienna so that he would not witness the inflexible Habsburg protocol, which meant that, even in death, the morganatic wife of the heir to the imperial throne could not be given due honours at her burial. The more probable reason was that, in view of the appalling lack of security that had allowed a Bosnian fanatic to claim the lives of two people who should have been guaranteed rigorous protection, it might have been tempting providence—in the shape of another passionate fanatic or anarchist with a gun or bomb—to have a parade of royalties present at Vienna on the occasion of their burial all at once.

At Kiel, the regatta drew to an orderly conclusion. Flags were lowered to half-mast, all remaining functions were cancelled, and, at a final ceremony, Warrender addressed sailors from both fleets on Anglo-German friendship, then finished by calling for three cheers for the German Navy. A German admiral responded in kind, and they cordially shook hands. On 30 June, the British squadron weighed anchor and sailed for home.

The Duke and Duchess of Brunswick, who were on a motoring holiday through the Dolomites to the Tyrol, heard news of the deaths at Sarajevo while staying in a hotel. As they left for home and reached Gmunden, the Austrian home of the Duke's parents, they met Emperor Francis Joseph. He was evidently 'no longer his serene self', and thought the murder of his heir and his wife would have a fateful impact on the destiny of the Habsburg Empire. After they had had a meal together, he took the Duchess aside and asked her to tell her father that he was counting on his 'friendship and loyalty'.[13]

Some of the family, especially the Empress and the Crown Prince, seemed eager for hostilities. Several members of the Emperor's entourage were resigned to the inevitability of war and thought such an outcome would be better than what was threatening to become an indefinite state of uncertainty, otherwise 'the war machine would rust' if it was not put to work. The Emperor was still vacillating between their view and that of his more pacifically inclined Chancellor and other ministers. Having been more inclined towards the pro-war faction eighteen months earlier, a sense of caution had prevailed since then to the extent that he had been pleased to keep Germany out of the subsequent Balkan Wars and was now giving serious consideration to withdrawing from the alliance with Austria.

Nevertheless he still wavered between one choice and the other. 'The Serbs must be disposed of, and very soon,' he wrote in the margin of a despatch from his ambassador in Vienna on 2 July.[14] He was appalled by the enormity of the crime, as he and other European crowned heads had been eleven years earlier when a palace revolution by army officers at Belgrade one night had resulted in the grotesque murders of the hapless, if much disliked King Alexander and Queen Draga of Serbia and several of their courtiers. As ever, the powers in Germany were divided on their solution to the crisis. The foreign ministry wanted to restrain Austria-Hungary, the 'sick man of Europe' that, during the reign of Francis Joseph, had twice been to war and twice been defeated, from any precipitate action. On the other hand, the general staff saw it as a perfect excuse for war at a time when Germany was more ready for a lightning campaign than her potential adversaries. The navy was still unprepared, and only nine weeks earlier, Tirpitz had warned that he needed at least another six to eight years. However, he and Admiral von Müller were disturbed by reports of a proposed Anglo-Russian convention for increased naval collaboration, and they favoured any policy that would weaken the Russians first. Russia was widely thought to be unprepared for war, and it was probably this that inclined the Emperor towards siding with advocates of firm action against Serbia. A swift campaign could probably be fought and won before Russia and probably France would have time to organise their forces.

On 6 July, he told the industrialist Gustav Krupp von Bohlen that the Austrians intended to wipe out Serbia, the 'nest of assassins', and that Germany would support them, even at the cost of war with Russia. That evening, he embarked on his annual three-week cruise on the *Hohenzollern*. Initially, he had felt he ought to cancel his holiday and stay in Berlin because of the impending crisis, but Bethmann-Hollweg and the other ministers told him that if he continued with his plans as arranged, it would help to create an impression of calm. Should the crisis develop 'into a warlike situation' after he had cancelled his holiday, he would be personally blamed for any outbreak of hostilities. In truth, his absence from the capital would spare his ministers any sudden switches of policy, which had exasperated them in previous situations. They could therefore be selective in the information they passed him, more so than if he was close at hand in Potsdam.

By 18 July, Bethmann-Hollweg and the foreign minister Gottlieb von Jagow knew Austria intended to present Serbia with a forty-eight-hour ultimatum five days later, and that the demands would be so draconian that Serbia would be unlikely to accept them. Diplomats in Berlin were confident that any resulting war could be confined to the local area and would not spread throughout Europe. The Emperor had his doubts that Russia would support Serbia, until reports of the reaction in St Petersburg suggesting otherwise reached him on the morning of 25 July. He decided to terminate his cruise forthwith, and although his Chancellor and the Foreign Office at Berlin assured him it would not be necessary, preferring to allow him to continue so that they could resolve the matter themselves without him trying to interfere, he was back at Potsdam within two days.

Cautious by nature and aware of the political risks involved, Bethmann-Hollweg hoped the crisis could be contained, at worst, to armed confrontation between Austria-Hungary and Serbia, in which Germany would be obliged to come to the defence of the former and in which the Great Powers need not become involved. Yet, as it became clear towards the end of the month that such a scenario was optimistic, military leaders relished the virtual certainty that this would lead to the European war for which they had been waiting. Most were confident that if they struck immediately, the imperial war machine would be invincible and victory would soon be theirs.

Prince Henry had been taking part in the yachting at Cowes. Afterwards, he called in at Buckingham Palace to say goodbye to King George. Much to his surprise, the latter advised him that in view of the threatening situation, he should return home as soon as possible. According to an account that the King wrote down, possibly some time after the event, when Henry asked what England would do if war broke out, he said he did not know:

> We have no quarrel with anyone & I hope we shall remain neutral. But if Germany declared war on Russia, & France joins Russia, then I am afraid we shall be dragged into it. But you can be sure that I & my Government will do all we can to prevent a European war![15]

At the end of this meeting, which lasted about eight minutes, they shook hands and agreed that even if their countries were fighting on opposite sides, they hoped it would not affect their friendship. Two days later, Henry was back at Kiel, where he wrote a report of their conversation. King George's apparent preference for neutrality, the Emperor was convinced (perhaps because he ardently wished to find it convincing), was as good as an official guarantee. When Tirpitz questioned its validity, the Emperor told him testily that he had the word of a king and that was good enough for him. It was a grave miscalculation, and perhaps the worst he ever made in his life. As the Duchess of Brunswick observed many years later, her father had failed to perceive that King George V never possessed anything like the political authority or weight that King Edward VII had done. King George considered himself a constitutional monarch or figurehead rather than a politician, and to his dying day, the Emperor would always be convinced that his cousin in England had deceived him.[16]

Elsewhere, events were moving beyond their control. Shortly before the Emperor's return, Moltke had drafted for the foreign ministry a message to be sent to Brussels, justifying a German march into Belgium to forestall an alleged invasion by the French. Meanwhile, officials in the empire drew up emergency decrees providing for mobilisation and internal security, which only needed signatures from sovereign and chancellor to become effective. By the time he was back, Austria had broken off diplomatic relations with Serbia. Jagow warned the French ambassador that he could not support a British proposal to settle the dispute with Serbia at a conference in London as that would imply recognition of Austro-Hungarian as well as Serbian responsibility for tension in the Balkans. In England, the Admiralty the First Sea Lord was sending a signal to the Commander-in-Chief of the Grand Fleet ordering him to concentrate his battle squadrons at Scapa Flow. Jagow remained confident of British neutrality, but the Emperor and Bethmann-Hollweg still believed that Britain had to be kept out of a continental war if Germany was to emerge victorious from a short, localised conflict.

The still vacillating Emperor seemed unconvinced that war was either necessary or inevitable. On the morning of 28 July, he received a copy of the Serbian reply to the Austrian ultimatum, showing that they had conceded almost everything, and he told Jagow that it was 'a great moral victory for Vienna'. He assumed that there was now no reason for war, and that any remaining differences between the Serbs and Austrians should be settled by negotiations. Any military operations, he supposed, should be restricted to a temporary occupation of Belgrade. A telegram containing these proposals was not sent to the German ambassador for another twelve hours, and even then, it was reworded in a way that seemed to be urging the Austrians on. That evening, the Emperor telegraphed the Tsar asking him for help 'in smoothing over difficulties that may still arise'. It crossed one from the Tsar asking the Emperor to hold back his allies from going too far. By the time it arrived, Austria-Hungary had declared war on Serbia.

On the morning of 29 July, the Emperor's attitude was apparently hardening towards war. His ambassador in St Petersburg was ordered to warn the Russian foreign minister that if Russia mobilised, Germany would do likewise, and if this happened, it would be difficult to prevent the outbreak of war throughout Europe. Over the next three days, Emperor and Tsar exchanged regular messages. Partial mobilisation was ordered in St Petersburg that same day, with general mobilisation following forty-eight hours later. With this, the Emperor proclaimed a state of 'imminent war' and an ultimatum was drawn up requiring Russia to cease all military preparations. This was impossible, and on 1 August, the German ambassador in St Petersburg delivered a declaration of war. Three hours later, the Emperor sent the Tsar a final message stating that only immediate orders to begin demobilisation and to prevent Russian troops from committing any act of trespass over German frontiers could 'avoid endless misery'. On this document, the Tsar wrote 'Received after war declared'. The previous day, the Emperor had tried to resist the advice of Prince Henry and most of his sons that, should Russian troops assemble on its German border, he would issue a similar order to the German Army. He still held a sentimental regard for the deathbed words of Emperor William I that he should maintain the traditional friendship with St Petersburg. The death blow to any such feelings came with the news that Tsar Nicholas had ordered mobilisation along the German border. With a heavy heart, Bethmann-Hollweg made a statement to the Reichstag, ending ominously with 'If the iron dice must roll, may God help us'.

The Emperor had to accept that war had broken out, but he still clung to the hope that it could be contained in extent and duration. It was essential for him that Britain should stay neutral, as British participation would surely spread the conflict to Africa and the Far East, as well as impose a strain on Germany's maritime commerce. After the council, Bethmann-Hollweg offered the British ambassador a neutrality agreement that guaranteed the territorial integrity of France and Belgium within Europe in any post-war territorial settlement, as long as Britain did not enter the conflict. This proposal reached the British foreign office on 30 July, and was taken to mean that Germany, determined on war, intended to violate Belgian neutrality.

The Emperor's belief that he 'understood the English' was shattered when he realised Britain would probably enter the war on the side of Germany's enemies. Grey had told Lichnowsky that London would not become involved unless the Austro-Hungarian–Russian–Serb war widened to include France and Germany, a declaration that the Emperor called 'the worst and most scandalous piece of English pharisaism' he had ever seen, totally at odds with King George V's remark to Prince Henry about British neutrality.[17] Yet he still hoped otherwise. On 1 August, after signing an order for general mobilisation, he received a telegram from Lichnowsky suggesting the possibility that Britain would guarantee French neutrality in a Russo-German war, as long as Germany did not attack in the west. When he told Moltke that they need only wage war with Russia, Moltke explained that military plans could not be improvised. German patrols were already infiltrating Luxembourg, and the Emperor ordered his principal adjutant to send a signal halting all operations in the west. A telegram from London just before midnight arrived, affirming that there could be no pledge of neutrality in the west.

The Emperor now had to admit that he no longer had the power to control or even influence events. On 2 August, an ultimatum was presented to Brussels that sought free passage of German troops through Belgium. Germany declared war on France on 3 August, and the first German units entered Belgian territory early the next day. An ultimatum from Britain was despatched to Germany a few hours later, and by midnight, Britain and Germany were at war.

As they prepared to return to their own countries, the French ambassador Paul Cambon told his English colleague, Sir Edward Goschen, that only three people in Berlin that night regretted the outbreak of war—both of them and the Emperor himself. The latter called the British 'a mean crew of shopkeepers', Sir Edward Grey 'a common cur', and King George V a liar. King Edward VII, he fumed, was even more responsible because of his policy of encirclement, that he was 'stronger after his death than [the Emperor], who [was] still alive', and that his nefarious work had been completed by his son and successor. 'To think that George and Nicky should have played me false!' he lamented. 'If my grandmother had been alive, she would never have allowed it.'[18]

'The Waves of the Revolutionary Flood Will Sweep Away Everything'

The outbreak of war coincided with the marriages of two of Emperor William's sons. As they would be going on active service, both princes who had recently become betrothed made haste for the altar.

Prince Oscar had fallen in love with a member of the nobility, Countess Ina von Bassewitz-Levetzow. Having taken an immediate liking to her, the Empress appointed her one of her ladies-in-waiting. Within a few months, she had helped to fill the void in the Empress's life that her daughter had left when she had married. The Countess was won over by the endearing awkwardness and quiet personality of Oscar, a more likeable young man than his sometimes loud and conceited elder brothers. The governess Ethel Howard had been struck by one of his comments while he was small, about how glad he was he would not have to follow the same profession as his father. 'I don't want to be an Emperor,' he told her, 'all I want is to be just a gentleman.'[1]

For princes or heirs who fell in love with ladies-in-waiting, as proved by the stormy history of the recently assassinated heir to the throne of Austria-Hungary and his morganatic marriage that had been resented by the Emperor, the road to matrimony was never a smooth one. They kept their relationship a secret at first, but one evening, Prince Eitel Frederick, probably the worse for drink, struck Ina during an argument. Oscar heard her screams, came running to find out what had happened, and knocked his brother to the floor. Having calmed Ina down, he declared to his mother that he loved the woman and intended to marry her. If he was forbidden to do so, he would make her his wife anyway and they would gladly go into exile.

The Empress was fully conscious of the family's reputation. She had once been as resolutely opposed to the Battenberg match of her sister-in-law as the rest of them, and it might have been unlike her to sanction any of her sons making a similar *mésalliance*. Yet Oscar had always been a particular favourite of hers, and she felt there was no reason to oppose the marriage for the sake of tradition. He was a younger son, with no chance of succeeding to the throne, and he had clearly made his mind up. She accordingly asked the Emperor for permission for them to marry. He told her angrily that it would be sheer folly on his part even to consider the idea and that she, his Empress, 'was a fool to think of it'. Ina, he snapped, should be 'given exactly one hour to clear out of Berlin'.[2] Ina meekly obeyed, but she was prepared to wait in the hope that her sovereign would relent. The Empress and Oscar argued and pleaded with the Emperor for several weeks to consent to the marriage, and at length, their opposition won him over, while the Duchess of Brunswick supported them. Her first child was about to be christened, and when her father asked her what she would like him to give her for a present, she said that all she really wanted was permission for Oscar, her brother, to be allowed to marry the love of his life. He conceded and the engagement was publicly announced on 26 May 1914.

When war seemed likely, Oscar was ordered to take up his army command and most of those at court, including his brother, Eitel Frederick, who had been particularly hostile to the engagement, wanted him sent out to join his regiment immediately. If the marriage was to take place, it had to be as soon as possible, and Ina was summoned back to Berlin on 31 July. Preparations were made at once, and a small private wedding was held that night at Bellevue Palace, attended by the Emperor and Empress. He gave his daughter-in-law the title of Countess von Ruppin, which allowed her greater precedence at court.

On 3 August, the day the German Empire declared war on France, the second imperial wedding within the family was held as Adalbert married his second cousin, Adelaide of Saxe-Meiningen, whom he had been courting for several years. The groom was a lieutenant on board SMS *Luitpold*, at the naval base of Wilhelmshaven in Schleswig-Holstein. When he knew that war was imminent, like his brother Oscar, he decided that he and Adelaide should be married quickly. A simple wedding was held in the chapel at the naval base on 3 August, performed by the chaplain at Wilhelmshaven and attended by a few officers.

After these happy family diversions, they all turned their minds to serving the Fatherland. Each of the Emperor's closest male relations had specially assigned roles. Prince Henry was Commander-in-Chief of the Baltic station in the Imperial Navy, largely a nominal post with fighting at sea left to other commanders and officers. He was, however, closer to the centre of action than his brother, although as the most Anglophile of the Hohenzollerns, he was the one who had most dreaded taking up arms against his relatives in England. All six of the Emperor's sons saw active service, five in the army and Adalbert in the navy.

Crown Prince William was appointed to command the Fifth Army, although with his lack of military experience, he was instructed to defer at all times to his chief of staff. In October, he gave what was to be his first interview to the press, and the first such statement from any of the German nobility since the outbreak of fighting. Speaking to Karl von Wiegand, an American press correspondent, he said grimly that although it would go on for a long time, Germany had already lost the war. Using words that probably did not please his father, and which must have made him the despair of the military staff, he said they were engaged in surely the most stupid, senseless, and unnecessary war of modern times. At the same time, he was just as hostile to the British as his father, writing to him that 'perfidious Albion' had been responsible for setting the Japanese and 'half-wild Indian hordes' at their throats. The ultimate aim of the war, he opined, was 'the crushing of England, victory over France and Russia [was] only a means to that end'.[3]

Ten months later, he was sent to command forces on the Western Front for the rest of the war. In 1916, his troops began the Verdun offensive, an attempt to try and destroy the French armies that ultimately ended in the failure he had seen coming. He had wanted to sue for peace after the Battle of the Marne in September 1914, a decisive victory for the Allies that had forced the defeated German Army to retreat towards the north-west. Deeply resenting those who had the ear of his father, he remarked in conversation with Naval Captain Albert Hopman in February 1915 that those who had the most influence over the Emperor were 'all weaklings without backbone'—always trying to save him from everything unpleasant and from making difficult decisions. His father, he knew, 'shies away from serious argument'. If (if, not when, it might be noted) he himself should ever come to the throne, he stated:

> The whole gang would be kicked out at once. I want to talk with people who tell me the plain truth. But my father doesn't ever do that, but cuts off every discussion. A conversation with him consists of his doing all the talking while the other person listens.[4]

Prince Eitel Frederick was given a senior regimental command with the 1st Foot Guards. In the front line from the start of the fighting, he was wounded during the first few weeks at the Battle of Bapaume in northern France, and he temporarily relinquished command to Count Hans von Blumenthal, but was fit enough to return to duty before the end of the year. In 1915, he was transferred to the Eastern Front and served in Russia.

Over the next two years, he commanded the 1st Guards Infantry Division, which saw service at the Battles of the Somme, Chemin les Dames, Aisne, and Argonne.

Of the three younger brothers in the army, Prince Augustus William, a front-line staff officer, was made district administrator (*Landrat*) of the district of Ruppin. His personal adjutant, Hans George von Mackensen, a close friend since his youth, was said to have 'played an important role in his life', to the detriment of his marriage. Prince Oscar, commanding the Liegnitz King's Grenadiers, saw action at Verdun in the early weeks of the war. He had a nervous breakdown in 1915 and temporarily withdrew from front-line service. Prince Joachim, a cavalry officer, received a shrapnel wound while fighting in the battle in the Masurian Lake District of East Prussia, and his father was most impressed on receiving a letter from one of the sergeants describing his youngest son's gallantry under fire.

Their cousins had also rallied to the cause of the Fatherland; within two months, the family suffered the first casualty. On 13 October 1914, Prince Maximilian of Hesse-Cassel, second son of the Emperor's youngest sister, Margaret, died in northern France of wounds sustained in action with the Prussian 1st Life Hussars, one week before what would have been his twentieth birthday. Almost two years later, his elder brother, Prince Frederick Charles, was killed in action while fighting in Romania. The Duke of Brunswick was on active service as a staff officer in Belgium and France, and during his absence, the Duchess was installed as regent, with responsibility for the administration of the state as well as her activities involved with nursing the wounded—setting part of the castle aside for use as a hospital.

Soon after hostilities began, Emperor William took care to put on a show of the utmost confidence in front of his troops, and in what he judged their ability to bring everything to a speedy and victorious conclusion. Sometimes the mask slipped. One servant who saw him a few days after the outbreak of war said he had never seen his master look so downtrodden and tragic before. From the start, it was as if he had foreseen what the diplomats, generals, and politicians had not—that anything other than a very limited campaign would probably result in the end of his empire. According to Prussian tradition, the sovereign normally left his capital in time of war to establish his field headquarters close to the battlefront. This had been the practice of Emperor William I, and the army assumed that his grandson would do likewise. Yet the situation in 1914 was very different from how it had been in the age of Bismarck. The sovereign now needed to retain responsible authorities in the capital, oversee political and diplomatic problems, maintain links with their ally Austria, and keep in touch with spokesmen of neutral governments.

In the middle of August 1914, the Emperor set up his headquarters at Coblenz, installed in the official residence of the Lord-Lieutenant of the Rhineland. Meanwhile, Bethmann-Hollweg, Tirpitz, members of the civil, military, and naval administrations, and general staff were all found accommodation within the city. Within a week, they had good news from the west, although according to the Duchess of Brunswick, her father 'never exulted in all the hurrahs despite all the mighty successes at the front'.[5] These 'mighty successes' would not continue thus for long. While it is not unnatural to assume that her recollections of her father were bound to be somewhat gilded, she recalled in her memoirs that despite all the disappointments and bitterness with which he condemned the behaviour of King George V and Tsar Nicholas II, he had no feelings of vengeance or hate towards either.

Those who were closest to the Emperor at this time were alarmed by his sudden changes in mood. One moment he demanded that his soldiers should take no prisoners, and gave orders that air raids on London should only target military objectives—avoiding Buckingham Palace, Westminster Abbey, St Paul's Cathedral, and all residential districts. The next, he would declare that if one German family was to starve because of the British naval blockade, he would 'send a Zeppelin over Windsor Castle and blow up the whole royal family of England'.[6] The Empress believed that events leading up to the outbreak of war had aged him suddenly, and insisted he should be allowed plenty of rest, with nobody interrupting his sleep unless there was urgent news. She and his adjutant, General Hans von Plessen, told his suite that their duty was to keep him in good spirits. Defeats and reverses were not mentioned to him, and he was only shown positive battle reports or told about great victories.

British and Allied propaganda portrayed the Emperor as the devil incarnate, a stereotype reinforced by cartoons in *Punch* magazine and other publications, holding him responsible for every episode of German misconduct or carnage; in person, he was much milder than generally supposed, if the testimony of his daughter—admittedly one of those bound to be heavily biased in his favour—can be believed. She would relate that whenever he went to visit the German wounded, he made a point of going to see enemy casualties in hospital as well without even asking the officers in charge whether his company would be agreeable to the men or not. One day, when he passed a train carrying French prisoners, he stopped his car and gave orders for the train to be halted. He then asked their officers to step forward before delivering an impromptu speech in French, praising the bravery of their army, offering them his sympathy, and promising them that they would be honourably treated in the prisoner of war camps.[7]

Even so, he apparently shared the common belief—initially at least—that it would all be over by Christmas. Ordinary soldiers in Germany had faith in the High Command and their supposedly foolproof plan for a swift victory that had already been decided on before the call to arms. By the middle of August, he and the Chancellor were discussing how the future of Europe would take shape once the fighting was over. Bethmann-Hollweg's preference was for an alliance of Germany, Britain, and France against Russia, an idea that found no favour with Tirpitz, who had become increasingly Anglophobic; he thought: '[They are] beating one another to death on the continent for the greater good of England, and at the same time England has managed to make the whole world believe that [Germany is] the guilty party'.[8] The Emperor took issue with them, declaring that he wanted France utterly defeated, after which he would offer the French an arrangement by which no territory would be annexed as long as they were prepared to conclude a defensive and offensive alliance with Germany.

The first signs that everything was not going according to plan came in September 1914. After the German troops had been marching on France for three weeks under a fierce late summer sun in blistering heat, they found their task more difficult than expected. The Battle of the Marne, fought over five days in the second week of September, was the result of a counteroffensive launched by six French field armies and the British Expeditionary Force against the German advance towards Paris. On the third day, Moltke, who had never completely recovered from a stroke shortly before the outbreak of war, instructed Lieutenant-Colonel Richard Hentsch, his head of intelligence, to take over responsibility of visiting each army headquarters in France. If disaster or defeat appeared likely, he must order a general retreat to defensive positions along the River Aisne, where they would prepare for another offensive. Lacking confidence both in his men and in his own ability to strike a decisive blow, Hentsch ordered them to retreat north-west.

In retrospect, some saw it as the point at which the Germany Army faltered and threw away any chance of a swift victory, or indeed victory altogether. It was a tacit admission that Germany was ruling out any prospect of an early end to the fighting, and the supreme war lord himself was not consulted. German forces were pursued by the French and British and driven back to north of the river Aisne, where they dug in, preparing trenches for what promised to be a far longer war than anticipated. Although a triumph for the *Entente*, it was the beginning of four years of trench warfare stalemate on the Western Front.

The German retreat was the end of the Schlieffen Plan, named after General Count Alfred von Schlieffen, chief of general staff from 1891 to 1905, who had died in 1913. He had envisaged a war for Germany on two fronts: violation of the neutrality of Belgium and Luxembourg in order to deliver a lightning blow against France, culminating in a pincer movement engulfing Paris by one army attacking it from the north and another from the east and precipitating French collapse—France, the German military commanders believed, could be attacked and defeated within three months; and then advancing eastwards to inflict similar defeat on Russia. The French and Russian generals had foreseen such a strategy for at least three or four years, and assumed that the first great battles of any forthcoming conflict would be fought in Belgium and Luxembourg. Schlieffen's successor, Lieutenant-General Helmuth von Moltke, a former aide-de-camp to the Emperor, was regarded as a capable administrator but lacking in self-confidence. As the troops drew back, Moltke allegedly reported to the Emperor that they had 'lost the war', at the same time writing to his wife that the campaign was not going in their favour. The Emperor ordered him to hand over the functions of chief of the general staff to General Erich von Falkenhayn, minister of war, whom he had chosen against the advice of some of his circle, hoping his appointment would allow him more influence over the course of events.

Falkenhayn did not intend to encourage the Emperor to venture south and see for himself the day-to-day conduct of battles in Flanders and northern France. Throughout the war, he witnessed little actual fighting. By the beginning of November, he was complaining to his second cousin, Prince Max of Baden—a brother-in-law of the Duchess of Brunswick—that if people in Germany thought he was supreme commander, they were mistaken. The general staff told him nothing and never asked his advice; all he did was drink tea, saw wood, and go for walks: 'then from time to time I hear that this or that has been done, just as the gentlemen [generals] think fit'.[9] Falkenhayn ordered that he must not be told about anything at the planning stage, only briefed about what had happened—and then only as long as it was favourable. It was more convenient if he merely kept away from headquarters, with the best cure for his restlessness being to keep him moving around, and he should concentrate his energy on visits to previous battlefields like Sedan, or if he needed something more sedentary, to stay at the dinner table just talking and playing cards.

Discouraged from doing any work at headquarters, although there would have been nothing for him to do, he soon sank into bored and nervous isolation, alternately depressed and stridently overconfident. In one such mood, in December 1914, he declared he would make peace with France and Russia, but not with Britain until she was brought to her knees; only amid the ruins of London would he forgive King George. Admiral Georg von Müller, head of the imperial naval cabinet, was sure he had no more understanding of military or naval strategy than most of his other contemporary sovereigns. Bloodthirsty details from the front interested him, 'but he [showed] little comprehension of the gravity of the whole situation'.[10]

His hatred of Britain was continually encouraged by the Empress. In October 1915, King Alfonso XIII of Spain, a neutral nation, appealed to her to intervene on behalf of Edith Cavell, an English nurse who had been sentenced to death by German court-martial for helping enemy soldiers to escape. She firmly refused on the grounds that women who behaved like men must be punished like men, and Cavell met her death by firing squad.

By then, not even the most optimistic clung to any hope of rapid victory. Both sides had considerable resources in terms of manpower and armaments, as well as tenacity, and it slowly became evident that an end to the war was less likely to be the result of a major victory by one side than from gradual physical and mental exhaustion on the part of whichever major power sought an armistice. The Emperor, Chancellor, and representatives of the foreign ministry had to decide whether to continue war on both eastern and western fronts or to seek a separate peace with Russia, something the Emperor personally favoured. Clinging to the authority of Tsar Nicholas II as the arbiter of the Russian Empire at war and peace, he asked his cousin, Ernest, Grand Duke of Hesse, to establish contact with the latter's sister, Alexandra, Empress of Russia, and try to persuade the Tsar to discuss laying down arms. At the same time, he tried to exploit the dynastic links of the Bavarian and Belgian royal houses in order to seek peace with King Albert of the Belgians, whose consort, Queen Elizabeth, was a Wittelsbach.

Sentimental family considerations still prevailed. While he still saw the republican French as a race beneath him, fellow empires and happier days in a more peaceful age with cousins 'Georgie' and 'Nicky' still counted for much. Sometimes he wanted the war ended on acceptable terms without delay. Heavy casualty lists and sustained blockades directed against the people of the German Empire must be avoided, and in his view, weighty matters such as war and peace were the business of Emperors and Kings. He brushed aside offers of mediation from Woodrow Wilson, President of the USA, on the grounds that he, together with the King of England and the Tsar of Russia, would make peace when the time had come. 'Mere democracies' like France and the United States could never participate in a peace conference, as war was 'a royal sport, to be indulged in by hereditary monarchs and concluded at their will'.[11]

To some of those around him, he still seemed to be living in the nineteenth century, when peace was kept or restored merely by a few friendly words between the cousins who reigned over much of Europe. 'He really believes in a tacit understanding between the monarchs to spare one another,' noted Tirpitz, 'a quaint sort of notion!'[12] By the spring of 1915, the admiral had his own secret plan for the future direction of war, one which was supported by the Empress and the Crown Prince. It involved persuading the Emperor to dismiss Bethmann-Hollweg and Falkenhayn from their posts and then temporarily withdraw from the business of government. Tirpitz greatly admired the Crown Prince, but felt he had a feeling that he would never succeed to the German throne. In the spring of 1915, he noted in his diary that the heir was very polite, but uncommunicative. He had never learned how to work, but he had good judgment, and if he should succeed to his inheritance, he would not carry on a rule of the cabinet: 'I also believe that he has a knowledge of human nature. But the Kaiser does not give him a chance'.[13]

As the war dragged on, the Emperor found himself relying on the Empress more than ever. She was increasingly the strength behind the throne. In public, he propagated the myth of a powerful, confident *paterfamilias*, and she the role of the *kleines hausfrau*, but the truth was rather different. Behind the façade was a man plagued by insecurities and prone to emotional instability. The Empress's days of hysteria and jealousy were gone, and in supporting her husband, she found a new strength and fortitude. As well as trying to make the burden of an increasingly unstable husband as light as possible—a man who had lost his status as supreme warlord, with his chiefs of staff, his military cabinet, and the generals making all the important decisions, veering between euphoria and low spirits—she kept in regular contact with his ministers. During the war, she also had to take on more tasks than ever before, such as responsibility for managing the imperial residences, including almost sixty palaces and castles in the Berlin–Brandenburg region alone.

At the same time, she continued to maintain a simple domestic routine for her family in Berlin. She spent her evenings by the fireside, knitting clothes for soldiers and making arrangements to care for the wounded or the widowed. When her husband returned from headquarters at Spa, she tried to entertain him and his entourage, keeping their spirits up whenever they appeared overtired or disheartened. Yet much as he loved her and valued her influence, it was no secret that he preferred to spend his leisure time in the company of other men, be they soldiers, ministers, or other princes. Moreover, although he was head of state and nominally commander-in-chief of the armed forces belonging to the empire's constituent states, a shift in power had come. Although slow to recognise the fact, the influence of 'the warlord of the Second Reich' had sharply diminished. For some time, power had been moving into the hands of the Chief of General Staff Paul von Hindenburg, appointed as successor to Falkenhayn in the summer of 1916, and his deputy Erich von Ludendorff. Since the outbreak of war, both had had the full confidence of the Crown Prince, who had once asked despairingly, 'how would things have turned out without those two?'[14] Later, in 1916, they threatened to resign unless the Emperor dismissed Bethmann-Hollweg as Chancellor.

Matters were made worse by a delicate problem that had to be kept secret. The Emperor had been suffering for some time from a swollen scrotum, which gave him increasing discomfort. The doctors thought it might have been caused by a riding accident, although the cause was more probably related to the trauma he had suffered at birth. Not until February 1917 did he undergo an operation to cure the problem.[15]

The Empress watched anxiously as he alternated between utter despair and deluded dreams of victory. It added to her problems, since her own health was poor and she was doing everything she could to take her mind off it, such as keeping a closer eye on her children, with her sons involved in the fighting, alongside the rest of German manhood, and her grandchildren. Adding to their woes was the behaviour of their youngest son, at a time when the last thing they needed were family distractions.

Now aged twenty-five, the weak and outrageously spoilt Prince Joachim was described by Countess Emilie Alsenborg, one of his mother's ladies-in-waiting, as not strong, 'either mentally or morally'. His military duties were not onerous, and he spent much of his time gambling for want of anything better to do, running up vast debts. He became personally involved with Erna, the sister of his equerry, Franz von Weberhardt, but his reasons were less than romantic. On her nineteenth birthday, her father had given her a magnificent collection of jewels that had been in the family for several generations, and she was wearing these when she first met the prince. His creditors were continually pressing him for payment, and he was afraid to ask his parents for financial assistance. On a visit to the Weberhardts' castle in Saxony, he begged Erna to let him have the jewellery so he could pledge it on a temporary basis to settle his debts, and on the understanding that he would return them. She handed it over, and he returned to Berlin where he immediately sold everything.

At the time, the Empress was trying to arrange a marriage between him and Marie Augusta, the daughter of Prince Edward of Anhalt, later Duke (very briefly). Count Ferdinand von Zeppelin, a close friend of the Anhalt family, informed the Empress that he would tell them about the prince's disgraceful behaviour. She feared her son would be forced to marry Erna to keep the scandal quiet. Erna would doubtless have been equally aghast at the very idea of having to marry someone who had so shamelessly reneged on his word, but as he was the son of the Emperor, she would probably have been in little position to refuse. The price of his silence, the Count stipulated, would be for the Empress to try and persuade the Emperor to allow Zeppelin airship bombing raids over London, something he was reluctant to do. She had no option but to agree, although as she now hated the British more than ever, it was unlikely that she had second thoughts on the matter.

Meanwhile, she confronted Joachim about his behaviour. The equally furious Weberhardts were duly informed where Erna's jewels had gone. Fearful of how his father would react, the humiliated Joachim was left with no choice but to visit the unfortunate Marie Augusta and propose to her. The couple were married in March 1916, at a simple ceremony at Bellevue consisting of a Lutheran service with only a few guests. The Emperor, who may or may not have been informed at this stage about his son's misconduct, insisted his duties at Spa would not let him return for the wedding. The Empress had readily forgiven Joachim, and mother and son were both wounded by his father's absence.

At around the time of his nuptials, Irish republican leaders briefly considered offering the throne of an independent Ireland to Joachim. It never progressed to an informal invitation, but any King of Ireland would surely have been required to be or become a Roman Catholic. The Catholic-hating Empress would have fiercely resented any of her children from thus changing their religion. A year later, there was talk of him being offered the throne of the independent Russian state of Georgia, but again, nothing came of this.

Throughout the months of German advances and setbacks, although the Emperor took little part in military discussions, he remained in theory the final political authority. He was, however, little more than the figurehead of an authoritarian government, still interested in any chance of a general settlement as long as the German proposal came from a position of strength and not weakness. In December 1916, the Chancellor told the Reichstag that Germany was prepared to discuss an end to hostilities in one of the neutral countries. He claimed that the German front line was indestructible, and warned that the empire had the power to use submarines to starve a persistent enemy into surrender. As a nation, Germany continued to reject President Wilson's subsequent offers of soundings towards a mediated peace. The Emperor was taken aback by the *Entente*'s lack of enthusiasm towards his Chancellor's speech, and declared Germany would have to extend her war aims against France and Belgium. In January 1917, he told them the coast of Flanders must belong to Germany, and King Albert could not be allowed to return to his kingdom. There were calls in Germany for an intensification of the U-boat campaign, or submarine warfare, which would force the *Entente* to sue for peace before American aid could have any impact in Europe. Hindenburg and Ludendorff said they could no longer take any responsibility for the further progress of military operations unless unrestricted submarine warfare was begun by 1 February. Their demand was granted. Despite harsh winter weather, 750,000 registered tons of British shipping was sunk in the first month alone, a figure that rose in succeeding months, and Britain was thought to be close to collapse.

On 3 February, the US broke off diplomatic relations with Germany, and two months later, after American merchant vessels had been sunk by German submarines, America declared war. Three months after this, the Emperor learned that the first troops had crossed the Atlantic and landed in France, ready to fight.

By then, he had lost his venerable ally, Emperor Francis Joseph of Austria. At the beginning of the war, in a moment of resignation, the Habsburg ruler had told his chief of staff that if the monarchy was doomed, at least they could let it 'go down honourably'. In dying at the age of eighty-six on 21 November 1916, he was spared the final chapter in seeing the collapse of his doomed empire. He was succeeded by his twenty-nine-year-old great-nephew, Emperor Charles.

The two allied Emperors and their consorts, Augusta Victoria and Zita, met for the first time in April 1917 at Homburg at the request of Charles, who wanted to discuss his and his wife's contacts with the *Entente* through an intermediary, Empress Zita's brother, Prince Sixtus of Bourbon-Parma. While Charles and Zita liked and respected Emperor William, they thought him completely dominated by his generals, a dreamer who still believed in eventual victory when many around him recognised it would take a miracle to avert defeat. Charles knew they were fighting a new enemy, which was more dangerous than the *Entente*—namely internal revolution, which found its strongest ally in general starvation. If the monarchs of the Central Powers could not conclude peace during the next few months, he warned, the people would go over their heads 'and the waves of the revolutionary flood will sweep away everything for which our brothers and sons are fighting and dying'.[16]

Now that the German economy had been mobilised for total war, Bethmann-Hollweg and his ministers were less powerful than the military. Their power had been eclipsed by August 1916 when Field-Marshal Paul von Hindenburg was appointed Chief of General Staff and Erich Ludendorff, Quartermaster General—and effectively his deputy. Both men were now the wartime rulers of the empire in all but name, and between them, they would have ultimate responsibility for German military operations for the rest of the war.

Although there was no obvious successor as Chancellor, the Emperor's suite expected that Bethmann-Hollweg would either soon resign or be dismissed. He was not yet ready to leave office, and hoped to stay long enough to act as a brake on some of the more irresponsible policies the military were attempting to impose on their sovereign. The third winter of war had had a serious effect on the nation's morale, and it was felt that the people should be promised a share in government of the German Empire as some recompense for their wartime sufferings once peace came.

The Emperor reluctantly accepted a proposal from Friedrich von Löbell, Prussian minister of the interior: at some unspecified time after the war, a more democratic regime would be introduced in Prussia. He did not want any sudden alteration of the constitution, which he feared would lead to democratisation in the Prussian officer corps. An army without aristocratic officers, he believed, had been the ruin of France. He also thought a parliamentary regime had proved 'bankrupt' in Britain and would be impracticable for Germany because of the large number of parties in the Reichstag. Yet a sense of urgency prevailed after news of the Russian Revolution and its effect on public opinion. The Chancellor persuaded his sovereign to give a specific assurance that all Prussians would be granted equal franchise rights in elections to the lower house, and that the composition of the upper chamber would be reformed more democratically in peacetime.

On Easter Sunday 1917, a decree was published in his name promising franchise reform after the war to bring democracy to Prussia and a complete revision of the empire's constitutional structure. It was a move with which he probably did not disagree. As he told Prince Max of Baden, who would shortly become his last Chancellor, even if Germany won the war, there would be great changes. Whatever happened in future, the monarchy must emerge strengthened, something that could probably be done only by gaining the support of all the people. Yet members of his suite were distinctly hostile, as were Hindenburg and Ludendorff, who thought that such talk during a critical juncture of the war would demoralise the troops.

By the summer, they were increasingly hostile towards the Chancellor, who they thought favoured a negotiated and 'weak' peace. Encouraged by the Crown Prince and the English-hating Empress, they presented the Emperor with an ultimatum to choose between Bethmann-Hollweg and them. He complained that never before had Prussian generals resorted to such blackmail, but he was powerless to resist. Realising his situation was untenable, the Chancellor resigned on 13 July, to be succeeded by Georg Michaelis, controller of food supplies for Prussia. A poor debater in the Reichstag, with no enthusiasm for the post, he resigned on 1 November and was replaced by the elderly Bavarian Prime Minister Count Georg von Hertling.

Two years into the war, the Emperor was spending little time on German soil. Hindenburg and Ludendorff were keen to distract him from taking too much interest in any differences between civil and military authority. He was therefore encouraged to visit various places around Europe, boosting the morale of his troops as well as of Germany's allies, inspecting regiments, and visiting other rulers, including King Ferdinand of Bulgaria and the Sultan. In November, he had another meeting with Emperor Charles and Empress Zita, both increasingly anxious for a speedy end to the war. Yet the Emperor's mood of elation made their hopes of a negotiated peace appear defeatist, and Emperor Charles hesitated to press the matter.

As ever, Emperor William's mood varied from elation to depression. Having sunk into a mood of gloom after the resignation of Bethmann-Hollweg, with whom he had been reluctant to part, he seemed to remember only successes and victories later in 1917. At one stage, he told the Reichstag party leaders that after the war, they would enter into a far-reaching agreement with France. After this, the whole of mainland Europe, under his leadership, would 'begin the real war with England—the Second Punic War'.[17]

'Rewarded Only with Betrayal and Ingratitude'

In March 1917, revolution broke out in St Petersburg, and within a few days, Nicholas II abdicated. The once-mighty Russian Empire was now no more. Emperor William's reaction to the initial fate of his cousins and their children was a heavy handed one, which outraged the Grand Duke of Hesse, the Tsarina's brother. On 13 March, his silver jubilee day in the German grand duchy, he received a phone call from the Emperor telling him bluntly of the news, and that the family had been taken prisoner. A brief 'happy anniversary' without any expression of sympathy followed before he put the phone down. Two months later, the Grand Duke received a telegram from the Emperor's headquarters stating that the Tsar and his family had all been killed. At that stage, it was no more than a false rumour. Nevertheless, the Tsarina's brother, who had never liked the Emperor, was infuriated that he should have passed on such distressing news so insensitively.[1]

Since the Tsar's abdication, the Emperor had been increasingly concerned at the implications for himself and his empire. During the eight-month rule of the provisional government, the former sovereign and his family were held in moderately comfortable captivity, but the rule of Vladimir Lenin and his Bolshevik followers posed a more sinister threat to their well-being. Emperor William sent a message through to Petrograd through Copenhagen that the provisional government was responsible for the Romanovs' welfare, and if the family decided to seek refuge in the west, German vessels would not attack any warship carrying them through the Baltic, where Prince Henry, the former Empress's brother-in-law, was still Commander-in-Chief. When the Romanovs were removed to the inner heart of Russia, ostensibly to protect them from the mounting fury of Bolshevik mobs in the capital, this plan was superseded and the former ruler, his wife, and their children were abandoned to their fate.

Above left: Emperor William I.

Above right: Empress Augusta.

Below left: Prince Otto von Bismarck.

Below right: Crown Prince Frederick William, later Emperor Frederick III.

Above: The declaration of the German Empire, Salle des Glaces, Versailles, 18 January 1871, after a painting by Anton von Werner. Crown Prince Frederick William and his brother-in-law, Frederick, Grand Duke of Baden, stand on either side of the Emperor.

Left: Crown Prince and Princess Frederick William and their family, 1875. *Children, left to right*: Prince Henry; Princesses Margaret (standing at back), Victoria (seated at front), and Sophie; Princes Waldemar and William; and Princess Charlotte.

Above left: Prince William and Crown Princess Frederick William, 1876.

Above right: Prince William, *c*. 1880.

Emperor William II and Prince Otto von Bismarck, at Friedrichsruh, the latter's home, Friedrichsruh, *c*. 1888.

Left: 'Dropping the Pilot', *Punch*, 29 March 1890, by Sir John Tenniel, on Bismarck's resignation as Chancellor.

Below: The royal family at Coburg, April 1894. *Standing, left to right*: Arthur, Duke of Connaught; Alfred, Duke of Saxe-Coburg Gotha; Emperor William II; and Edward, Prince of Wales. *Seated, left to right*: Queen Victoria and the Empress Frederick seated in front.

Above left: Count Leo von Caprivi.

Above right: Chlodwig, Prince of Hohenlohe-Schillingsfürst.

Right: The children of Emperor William II.
From left to right: Prince Oscar; Prince Eitel Frederick; Princess Victoria Louise, on lap of Crown Prince William; Prince Adalbert; Prince Joachim; and Prince Augustus William.

Above: The family at Friedrichshof, May 1900.
From left to right: Sophie, Crown Princess of Greece; Princess Adolf of Schaumburg-Lippe; Emperor William II; Empress Frederick; Charlotte, Hereditary Princess of Saxe-Meiningen; Prince Henry; and Princess Frederick Charles of Hesse-Cassel.

Below left: A marine table of battleships drawn personally by Emperor William II, 1897.

Below right: 'Appreciation, 1901', *Punch*, 30 January 1901, by George Roland Halkett.

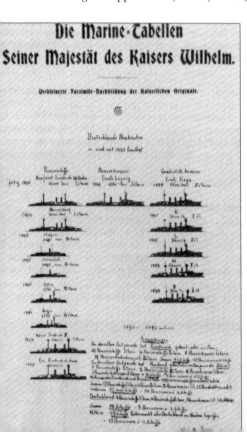

Above left: Emperor William II in British naval uniform, 1904.

Above right: Empress Augusta Victoria, *c*. 1903.

Below: Crown Prince and Princess William, 1905.

Above left: Prince and Princess Eitel Frederick, 1906.

Above right: Louise, Grand Duchess of Baden, 1906.

Below: The royal gathering at Windsor Castle, November 1907.
From left to right: Louise, Princess Royal; Arthur, Duke of Connaught; Maud, Queen of Norway; Prince Alexander of Norway; Emperor William II; King Edward VII; Mary, Princess of Wales; Princess Patricia of Connaught; Infanta Isabel of Spain (seated); George, Prince of Wales; Princess Henry of Battenberg (seated); King Alfonso XIII of Spain; Empress Augusta Victoria; Grand Duchess Vladimir of Russia; Prince Arthur of Connaught; Queen Alexandra; Grand Duke Vladimir of Russia; Queen Marie Amelie of Portugal; Queen Ena of Spain; Louise, Duchess of Connaught; Princess Victoria; Helene, Duchess of Aosta; and Prince and Princess John of Saxony.

Above: The German Emperor, Empress, their children, and daughters-in-law after a painting by Ferdinand Keller, 1906.

Below left: 'The Historic Interview: Discussing the Kaiser's Revelations in a Berlin Café', *The Graphic*, 7 November 1908, after *The Daily Telegraph* 'interview'.

Below right: Count Philipp von Eulenburg.

Left: King Edward VII and Emperor William II, *c.* 1908.

Below: Emperor William II and Tsar Nicholas II of Russia, *c.* 1910.

Above left: Princess Frederick Charles of Hesse-Cassel as Chief of the 80th Fusilier Regiment, *c.* 1910.

Above right: The Duke of Connaught, Emperor William II, and King George V in King Edward VII's funeral procession, Windsor, 20 May 1910.

Below left: Prince Bernhard von Bülow.

Below right: Theobald von Bethmann-Hollweg.

Above left: Emperor William II, *c*. 1909.

Above right: Prince Adalbert, 1908.

Below left: Crown Prince William, 1910.

Below right: Princess Augustus William, formerly Princess Alexandra of Schleswig-Holstein-Sonderburg-Glücksburg.

Above: Crown Prince William with Orville Wright at Berlin Aviation Week, 2 October 1909.

Below left: Crown Prince William and his eldest son Prince William, *c*. 1910.

Below right: Emperor William II, his brother Prince Henry, and their sisters from a postcard of 1911.

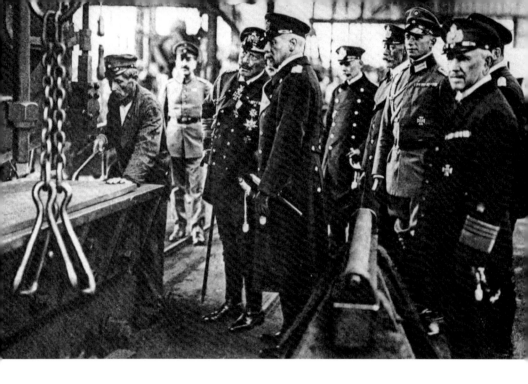

Above: Emperor William II in the shipyard at Kiel, 1911.

Left: Prince Augustus William, Princess Alexandra Victoria, and their only child, Prince Alexander Ferdinand, 1913.

Right: Guests at the wedding feast of Princess Victoria Louise of Prussia and the Duke of Brunswick at Berlin, 24 May 1913, after a watercolour by Fortunino Mascania.

Below: Emperor William II and King George V at Berlin, May 1913.

Above left: Princess Adolf of Schaumburg-Lippe, 1913.

Above right: Charlotte, Hereditary Princess of Saxe-Meiningen, *c.* 1912.

Below left: Queen Sophie of Greece.

Below right: Cecilie, German Crown Princess, 1911.

Above left: Emperor William II with Alfred von Tirpitz and Helmuth von Moltke on the battleship *Friedrich der Grosse* in 1912.

Above right: Albert Ballin.

Below: Prince and Princess Frederick Charles of Hesse-Cassel, with King Constantine and Queen Sophie of Greece and their children, 1914, shortly before the outbreak of the First World War in which Princes Maximilian (right, back row) and Frederick William (right, centre row) were both killed.

Above left: King George V.

Above right: Prince Henry of Prussia.

Below left: Princess Victoria Louise, Duchess of Brunswick.

Below right: 'Four against Eight', a postcard showing heads of state and government on both sides during the First World War.

Above left: Emperor Francis Joseph of Austria-Hungary, Emperor William's most venerable ally at the outbreak of the First World War.

Above right: The arrest of Gavrilo Princip, the assassin at Sarajevo.

Below: Archduke Francis Ferdinand and Sophie at Sarajevo, just before their assassination on 28 June 1914.

UNCONQUERABLE.

The Kaiser. "SO, YOU SEE—YOU 'VE LOST EVERYTHING."
The King of the Belgians. "NOT MY SOUL."

Left: 'Unconquerable', *Punch*, 21 October 1914, a cartoon by Bernard Partridge in which a defiant King Albert of the Belgians faces up to Emperor William.

Below: Princess Adolf of Schaumburg-Lippe, with soldiers convalescing from their wounds received during the war, *c.* 1915.

Mackensen v. Moltke Kronprinz Wilhelm v. François v. Falkenhayn v. Beseler v. Bethmann-Hollweg
                              v. Preussen   Ludendorff   v. Einem
w Kronprinz Rupprecht Herzog Albrecht   v. Kluck v. Emmich v. Haeseler   v. Hindenburg   v. Heeringen
        v. Bayern v. Württemberg Kaiser Wilhelm II.   v. Ti

Above: Emperor William II, Crown Prince William, the leading generals, and entourage during the First World War.

Below: Emperor William II with Generals Paul von Hindenburg and Erich Ludendorff at German General Headquarters, 1917.

Left: Prince Oscar, Countess von Ruppin, and their children.

Below left: Prince Joachim of Prussia and Princess Marie Augusta of Anhalt, 1916.

Below right: Crown Prince William in conversation with General Hindenburg, June 1918.

Above: Mutinous sailors at Kiel during the last few days of empire, November 1918.

Below: Crowds in Berlin at the proclamation of the German Republic, November 1918.

Above: Crown Prince William in exile, November 1918.

Below: German soldiers returning home from after the war, 1918.

Above: As the peace conference opened at Paris, speculation mounted as to the Emperor's punishment for war crimes, from *The Evening News*, 20 January 1919.

Below: Broken windows in a hungry Berlin, on the edge of revolution, 1919.

Above: The funeral procession of Empress Augusta at Potsdam, 19 April 1921. *Front row, left to right*: Prince Eitel Frederick and Crown Princess William. *Back row, left to right*: Princes Augustus William, Adalbert, and Oscar.

Left: Princess Hermine of Reuss, October 1922, shortly before her marriage to Emperor William II.

Above: Prince Augustus William, painting flowers in the greenhouse of his villa at Potsdam, 1923.

Below left: Adolf Hitler.

Below right: Crown Prince and Princess William at Oels, Silesia, November 1923.

Above left: Emperor William II and Princess Hermine on his sixty-eighth birthday, 27 January 1927.

Above right: Alexander Zoubkoff and his wife, the former Princess Adolf of Schaumburg-Lippe, 1928.

Below: Emperor William II, his gardening staff and a prized collection of logs at Doorn.

Emperor William II, Princess Hermine, and her youngest daughter, Princess Henrietta, in the park at Doorn, March 1931.

Crown Prince William and Adolf Hitler in front of the garrison church, Potsdam, March 1933.

Prince Louis Ferdinand of Prussia at his wedding to Grand Duchess Kira of Russia, 4 May 1938, with his grandfather Emperor William II at the private chapel, Doorn.

Emperor William II and Princess Juliana of the Netherlands at the wedding.

Prince Augustus William of Prussia at Ivry Cemetery, Paris, for the ceremony of the commemoration of German war dead, 12 March 1939, with Count von Welezeck, German ambassador in Paris, on his right.

Above: Emperor William II and the Wehrmacht at Doorn, May 1940.

Below: The funeral procession of Emperor William II at Doorn, 9 June 1941.

Left: Victoria Louise, Duchess of Brunswick, on her eightieth birthday, 13 September 1972. (*Marlene A. Eilers Koenig Collection*)

Below: Prince Louis Ferdinand, whose wife had died ten years previously, with his children and grandchildren on his seventieth birthday, 9 November 1977.

Following the Bolshevik revolution in November, Leon Trotsky, the People's Commissar for Foreign Affairs, formally requested an armistice with Germany. Ludendorff told the Emperor that he needed a quick settlement in the east in order to release troops for a major spring offensive to take Paris and end war in the west. Peace talks with Russia opened at Brest-Litovsk on 22 December. Ludendorff was keen to rush through a settlement, and after a clash occurred over a frontier line in Poland, he told the press that he was on the verge of resignation. Telegrams began arriving at the palace begging the Emperor to retain his services, and he gave in.

In January 1918, Hindenburg demanded the dismissal of Rudolf von Valentini, head of the Emperor's civil secretariat for the last ten years, as he had been over-sympathetic to Bethmann-Hollweg's plans for post-war reform. William was angered by Hindenburg's impertinence, but knew he could not risk the loss of either him or Ludendorff at such a critical stage in the war. If the Brest-Litovsk talks failed, the eastern armies would have to march on Petrograd. Ludendorff's staff had been preparing for a spring offensive on the Western Front to begin in about two months. To lose one man would surely mean the loss of both, and culminate in a palace revolution that would probably end with the Emperor's abdication in favour of the Crown Prince. Valentini eased the situation by offering to resign.

An increasingly weary Emperor suspected President Wilson of attempting to assume the mantle of leadership of the *Entente*, remove the Hohenzollerns from Germany, and impose peace on Europe. He complained the President was supporting the Bolsheviks, and that there was a conspiracy of 'international Jewry' against him. If Trotsky continued to procrastinate at Brest-Litovsk, the German Army would have to go to Petrograd and wipe out Bolshevism before the revolution reached Germany.

In February 1918, Russian delegates signed a treaty at Brest-Litovsk that deprived Russia of a third of her pre-war population, a third of her arable land, and most of her coalfields. The Emperor was relieved as he now felt there would be no need to bury Bolshevism; all they required was a military victory against the Allies, and the moment seemed right for a decisive breakthrough in the west. About 1½ million soldiers were still committed in the east to police the occupied territories, and there were still large contingents that could be sent to northern France to engage in a final major offensive. An onslaught on the British and French armies, which had recently been reinforced by the arrival of about 30,000 American troops, began in the third week of March. It would be the Second Reich's last chance. Although the armies on both sides sustained heavy losses, at first it seemed as if the German forces would triumph as they made a few territorial gains in the early stages and came within 40 miles of Paris. By the end of June, the Emperor and Ludendorff were confident of French collapse, but the attack soon faltered, and by July, when Marshal Foch and the Allied forces had regrouped for a counteroffensive during the summer, the Germans were driven back to their pre-March positions. A final German offensive later that month was repulsed by a combination of English, French, American, and imperial forces. Hindenburg had to admit that they had tried their best but failed, and the outlook was bleak.

From Russia, horrifying news arrived in July that plunged the Emperor into a mood of even blacker despair. The former Tsar Nicholas, his wife, and their children had been massacred in the house at Ekaterinburg where they were held for the last few months, just as their captors feared that sympathisers were about rescue them. Although he had given his cousin the Grand Duke of Hesse the impression that he hardly cared when passing on news of his abdication the previous year, he was genuinely horrified that a monarch who was family and had been a close friend, plus his wife and children, could be butchered in such a merciless manner.

Moreover, if revolution was to erupt in a war-weary defeated Germany, where people were disillusioned with the old political order and only needed a few determined agitators to persuade them to take the law into their own hands, history might all too easily repeat itself where the Hohenzollerns were concerned. Since signing the treaty at Brest-Litovsk, Russia had officially been a friendly power. Yet in June, the new German Ambassador to Russia Count Wilhelm von Mirbach-Harff was assassinated by one of the Bolsheviks, and when this was followed by the murder of the Tsar and his family, plus several more of the Romanovs during the next few months, some of the German aristocracy were uncomfortable, if not incensed by the thought of their country maintaining friendly relations with Bolshevik Russia. One, Princess Löwenstein, was angered at the German conservative press: '[They] play this down, since our intimate new friends the Bolsheviks have killed [the Tsar]. How disgusting I find the friendship with these pigs! One day this will exact vengeance'.[2]

On 8 August, in Ludendorff's words, 'the black day of the German army', Allied forces united for the first time under the command of Marshal Foch to make a decisive break through the German lines near Amiens. The German Empire's military position could no longer be maintained. It was just a month since Ludendorff had dismissed Richard von Kühlmann, the foreign minister, for saying in the Reichstag what many others had already voiced—namely that they had no hope of victory and were no longer in a position to enforce a military solution. Now Ludendorff was forced to concede he had been right, and that he and Hindenburg needed to accept that they had almost certainly lost the war. An utterly downhearted Emperor likewise believed that they now faced defeat, yet clung to the hope, which he voiced at a council in spa on 14 August: an approach for peace should be made at a point of German recovery, rather than weakness. Defeat was not yet imminent, and they had to pursue hostilities in the hope that the Allied counteroffensive might still lose momentum. It was the last ray of hope. Later that month, he went to stay at Wilhelmshöhe with the Empress, who was recovering from a minor heart attack, the stress of the war years having taken its toll on her. She now realised it was pointless keeping bad news from him, and during their three weeks together, he was told of successful offensives by British, French, and American forces on a supposedly impregnable section of the Western Front, which finally convinced him that the war was lost.

It was at this most unpropitious of times that it seemed the beleaguered Hohenzollerns might acquire a new throne. In August, the government of Finland, formerly a grand duchy under the Tsar of Russia, which had declared independence after the revolution, voted in favour of establishing a monarchy. A German prince was favoured as some guarantee of German military support against Russia, and in October, the Emperor's brother-in-law, Prince Frederick Charles of Hesse-Cassel, was elected King. He prudently declared that he could not give any firm answer regarding acceptance for two months as he did not want to place any obstacles in the way of peace. Within those months, events around them sealed the fate of the brief Finnish monarchical experiment.[3]

By September, it was a matter of how long the Emperor would still reign. Hindenburg believed that while German troops were on French soil, they could force peace on their own terms from a position of strength. Queen Wilhelmina of the Netherlands, a neutral territory, had offered to mediate with a peace conference at The Hague, and Albert Ballin advised the Emperor to approach President Wilson for peace talks before feeling hardened against the Hohenzollern dynasty. Ballin had been deeply disillusioned by the outbreak of war, and his worst fears had been realised when many of his ships were lost or suffered major damage during hostilities. It was unfortunate that he was kept away from the Emperor, which was only done because the Empress and others distrusted him because of his Anglophile opinions.

Towards the end of the month, the Austrians sued for a separate peace, the Balkan front was collapsing and British troops entered Bulgaria. King Ferdinand, the first sovereign among the Central Powers to bow to the inevitable, called for an armistice. He thus became the only one to save the throne for his dynasty, abdicating in favour of his son Boris. Turkey followed suit, and it was recognised that Austria-Hungary would not be far behind. At a conference on 29 September, Ludendorff told the Emperor, Hindenburg, Hertling, and Admiral Paul von Hintze (the new foreign minister) that with the collapse of their allies, the army's position was desperate. They had lost the war and had to seek peace urgently. Next day, Hertling resigned as Chancellor, and on 3 October, Prince Max of Baden was appointed his successor. Although seen by some as a forward-thinking liberal, at heart he was anti-Semitic, an admirer of Russian autocracy, and intent on resisting the 'democratic infiltration which [had] been spread by England and America with its tricks, hypocrisy and defamation'.[4]

The German Navy had been immobilised by the Allied blockade for much of the war. It was ironic that the armed force responsible for so much bitter Anglo-German rivalry over the last few years before the war, and which had cost the German taxpayer so much, had only been fully deployed against the British in the North Sea during the indecisive Battle of Jutland in May and June 1916. Now, just over two years later, on 30 October 1918, without consulting the government, Admiral Scheer, Chief of Naval Staff, ordered the fleet to assemble in the North Sea off Wilhelmshaven for a final operation against the British fleet. He admitted that while the course of events could not be significantly altered, and that it might even undermine the efforts of the civilian government in Berlin to agree to an early armistice, it was important to try and lay the foundations of a future navy and he planned to demonstrate that it was still capable of fighting. Earlier that month, he had been dismayed, if not angered, to learn that the cessation of German submarine warfare was one of the main preconditions for an armistice, and that Ludendorff had already agreed without consulting him. Having been poorly treated throughout most of the war with little active service, the naval ratings cared nothing for the patriotic principle or romantic notions of death with honour, and had no reason to respect their commanding officers. They refused to obey the orders of their officers who wanted to engage them in a futile, suicidal battle.

The mutiny spread rapidly to other German ports, and on 4 November, a naval mutiny broke out at Kiel. Formerly loyal sailors waved red flags, taking to the streets as they sang *La Marseillaise*, and a newly formed sailors' council took over the city, which became the centre of the revolt, with every ship flying the red flag at its mast. Gustav Noske, well-respected on all sides in the Reichstag as one of the leaders of the Social Democratic group, was sent by the Chancellor to negotiate an end to the revolt. The mutineers elected him as Chairman of the Soldiers' Council, and at length, he managed to restore the authority of the officers and persuade the naval ratings to resume normal duties. Nevertheless, unrest spread throughout north and west Germany, and by 6 November, every North Sea port and several major industrial cities were in the hands of the councils as workers joined the sailors. When the government sent troops to quell the revolutionaries, the soldiers defied them and joined their comrades in the revolt.

The Emperor was deeply distressed: 'the fact that it was [among] my navy, my proud creation, that there was first open rebellion, cut me deeply to the heart'.[5] Well aware of growing republican anger, his brother, Grand Admiral Prince Henry, was not taking any chances. Putting a red armband over the sleeve of his greatcoat and a red flag on his vehicle, he drove his wife and son at high speed through a sailors' picket line to safety. Later, it was alleged, he blamed British money, which he said was used to instigate the sailors' revolt. Public services came to a standstill in Berlin on 7 November, as monarchist and rebel forces exchanged cannon fire in the streets and railway lines were cut to prevent troops still loyal to the Emperor from sending for reinforcements. The *Stadtschloss* in Berlin flew the revolutionary flag, and the Empress was furious when her brother-in-law, Prince Frederick Leopold, hoisted a red banner above his hunting lodge at Glienicke. That same day in Munich, the Bavarian capital, the elderly King Ludwig III, alarmed by the clamour, left his palace during the night for the safety of Salzburg. It was a blow to the monarchist cause in Germany, which would gradually gain momentum.

Six days earlier, on 1 November, Dr Wilhelm Drews, minister of the interior, had arrived at headquarters with a formal plea from the Chancellor requesting the Emperor to abdicate. William rounded on him with fury, asking how, as a Prussian official and a subject who had taken the oath of allegiance, he had the insolence and effrontery to appear before him with such a request. If he did abdicate, he said, the army would collapse and return to Germany as pirates, thus leaving the way free for enemy troops to come across the borders. He insisted he could not abandon his crown just because of pressure from the Jews and the socialists.[6]

The Reichstag socialist leaders knew they would need to take the initiative if they were to remain at the head of the revolutionary movement and avoid losing the sympathy of their rank and file to the Independents. As socialist members had joined the cabinet, it was possible that soldiers and workers in revolt would turn against the party, and the outcome might be unrest on the Bolshevik scale as seen in Russia the previous year. To forestall this, they informed the Chancellor that they would withdraw from the government unless the Emperor abdicated and the Crown Prince renounced his place in the succession by midday the next day (8 November).

Meanwhile, the *Entente* powers were reluctant to conclude peace terms that did not acknowledge their full victory. Emperor William declared angrily that President Wilson wanted to bring down the Hohenzollerns and sweep the German monarchy away. He had interpreted his motives correctly, for the President argued that the power structure of Imperial Germany was still intact and he would only deal with what he called a genuine democracy. Prince Max hoped he would follow the example of King Ferdinand and offer to step aside in order to save the monarchy, but the Emperor retorted that he could not shirk his duty—a successor of Frederick the Great did not abdicate. The generals had no idea of the general public mood in Berlin and the other cities, and were unaware that the throne was as good as lost. A few days earlier, Hindenburg had suggested that in the interests of public relations, the Emperor should make a visit to his front-line troops on a morale-boosting tour of duty, but the politicians would have told him it was too late for such a gesture to have any effect on the outcome of events.

On 8 November, the Emperor left Potsdam that night on the imperial train, never to return. His family thought it ominous that he should leave his capital at such a crucial time, but most of his entourage knew it was only a matter of time before the question of abdication would be put directly to him again, and the sooner he went, the better. His daughter, the Duchess of Brunswick, was one of those who believed that before he stepped on to the train, he had come to terms with the inevitable. Nevertheless, if only to try and mask his true feelings, on his arrival at Spa the next morning, he told Hindenburg bluntly that his Chancellor and government were trying to throw him out.

Few, if any around him showed greater perception than the now seriously ill Ballin, who admitted that Germany had caused the war. Ever loyal to his sovereign and friend, he blamed the High Command and ministers, saying bitterly that if they wanted to give 'a convincing proof of the completeness of the success they have achieved, they can do no better than demand condign punishment for the man who has been held responsible for the war, and inflict it upon him'. He did not think the Emperor would be particularly saddened if given a chance to retire into private life without much loss of dignity, and suggested that the sovereign, without losing his position, could be invested with the rights and duties similar to those of King George V, who enjoyed 'all the advantages of his dignity without having to take upon himself responsibilities which he is unable to bear'. It was his belief that His Imperial Majesty Emperor William II never really derived much pleasure from his sovereign powers, and if he did, he had ceased to do so 'since this unfortunate war has been forced upon him'.[7]

The Chancellor told his cabinet that His Majesty's abdication would have to be voluntary, and done in such a way as to protect both the kingdom and the forces from harm 'and retain the honour of Germany'. Prince Max tried to enlist the help of other German princes who might be able to persuade the Emperor without being seen to put him under pressure. Prince Frederick Charles of Hesse-Cassel's credentials as an intermediary were beyond question, as the husband of the sister with whom the Emperor had always got on the best, as one who had been wounded while fighting at the front, and as the father of two princes who had been killed in action. He received a final briefing at the Chancellor's office with a draft proclamation for the Emperor announcing his intention to renounce the crown of Prussia, when news came from the High Command and the foreign office of a slight improvement in the situation at the front. When Wilhelm Gröner, deputy chief of the general staff, visited Berlin later that week and spoke to the Chancellor and other ministers, they agreed there could be no question of abdication while the army was still fighting, or discipline would break down as it had in Russia and chaos would follow. Next day, he met Friedrich Ebert, the moderate socialist leader, who proposed the Emperor should abdicate at once and entrust the regency to one of his sons, but not the Crown Prince, who was hated and despised by the German people. He was sure the nation would be willing to accept a regency under one of the Emperor's younger sons or one of his grandsons, but none of the Crown Prince's brothers was prepared 'to usurp his rights'.

As he returned to Spa, Gröner found the Emperor in no mood to compromise. Fearing that Bolshevism at home was now a greater threat than the *Entente* forces could ever be, he talked of placing himself at the head of his field army, leading the men back into Germany, and putting down mutiny and revolution wherever it reared its head. One of his commanders, Count Schulenburg, advised him to stage a military showdown and meet a hero's death fighting either the Allies or the Bolsheviks at home. Gröner was inclined to agree as, if the Emperor was wounded, he would win a hero's laurels and retain his throne, while if he was killed, the dynasty would be saved for his heirs. The Emperor had no intention of sacrificing himself *à la* Emperor Nero; suicide would be an admission of failure and contrary to his religious convictions. Yet in his wildest moments, he hoped that some of the *Entente*—especially the English, for whom he had reserved his most bitter invective over the past four years—might come to his aid and help restore law and order in Germany, thus preventing a repetition of the previous year's events in Russia. Armistice talks were beginning at Compiègne, and there was doubt as to the loyalty of many units in the army. Some of the Emperor's suite thought he was living in a world of his own, as if the destiny of his country still depended on the orders of a medieval monarch.

By the morning of 9 November, having consulted some of the commanders, Gröner knew he would have to renounce the throne and go into exile if civil war in Germany was to be avoided. The less he prevaricated, the greater his chances of saving the dynasty and the monarchy. Hindenburg accepted the logic of these arguments, but his loyalty to his master was so deeply engrained that he hesitated to recommend such a step. The Emperor's aides still thought he should hear only what it was good for him to hear. His Adjutant-General, Hans von Plessen, declared that His Majesty could not 'simply and quietly capitulate to the revolution'. Yet the general staff knew the situation was irretrievable. The Emperor said he did not want to be responsible for civil war among his people, so he would wait until after the armistice was signed and then lead his troops back into Germany. Gröner had the unenviable task of shattering his illusions by telling him that the army would march back home under its leaders and commanding generals, but not under the command of His Majesty. At this, he angrily said that he would require that statement in writing. His soldiers had taken a solemn oath of allegiance to him, and if they no longer stood behind their supreme war lord, he must have proof. Drews had to tell him that in such a situation oaths were meaningless.

The dismayed sovereign and his eldest son lunched together privately. Their meal was interrupted by a telephone message from Berlin. Faced with the threat of imminent revolution, Prince Max had taken the initiative, and at 11.30 a.m., he announced to the German news agency that His Majesty had abdicated and the Crown Prince had renounced his place in the succession. He had done so with a heavy heart, knowing that he would be 'tainted with it', but he had been under intense pressure, and the only alternative would have been to 'let the Kaiser be deposed by the mob'.[8] Immediately afterwards, the Socialists arrived at the Chancellery in Berlin and insisted that Ebert should be appointed the new Chancellor. Later that day, a republic was proclaimed on the steps of the Reichstag by the Social Democrat Philipp Scheidemann.

When told the news, the Emperor railed against this 'barefaced, outrageous treason'. He was King of Prussia, intended to remain so, and would stay with his troops.[9] If necessary, he would abdicate as Emperor but remain King of Prussia, and would cross into Holland. One day, he imagined, he would be able to return to his kingdom. He left his villa to dine on the royal train, where he was given a message from Prince Eitel Frederick telling him that the Empress was still well and in good heart. This momentarily stiffened his resolve. He turned to his suite, and said that as his wife was staying where she was, for him to go to Holland would be like a captain leaving a sinking ship. Then Gröner rang to report that the situation was deteriorating rapidly, with mutinous troops said to be marching on Spa. Hindenburg arrived, and told him firmly that he could not accept the responsibility of seeing his sovereign taken to Berlin by mutinous troops and handed over as a prisoner to the revolutionary government.

The Emperor did not need to be reminded of the fate of Tsar Nicholas II. The only road open to him, it had been made clear, was the one that would take him to safety across the border with Holland. It might not remain open for much longer, and nobody could answer for the consequences if he did not avail himself of it as soon as possible. Convinced at last that there was no alternative, the Emperor agreed to leave but not until the following morning. He wrote to the Crown Prince, telling him that he had decided, 'after severe inward struggle, to leave the collapsed army'. He asked him to remain at his post and hold the troops together until they began the march back home, then retired to bed.[10]

Berlin was now in the hands of the socialists. For four years, the people of Germany had made sacrifices in a land where one-quarter of their food had been imported before the war, and had been in short supply as a result of the naval blockades that sent prices rising rapidly—and defeat was their reward. That night, shattered by the catastrophic turn of events, Ballin took a fatal dose of sleeping pills.

Back at Potsdam, on the eleventh birthday of the Crown Prince's second son, Louis Ferdinand, the Empress phoned the Crown Princess that morning with a request to bring the children with her to the *Neues Palais* as soon as possible. The Crown Princess stated: 'Grossmama believes we shall be safer over there'. Yet she herself saw no danger if they stayed where they were. Shortly after lunch, they drove there through ominously quiet, almost deserted streets, to be met outside the palace by a bravely smiling, but obviously tearful Empress. She assured them that they would have a little birthday party, though she apologised in advance for not having much of a present for her grandson. As their mother followed their grandmother into her boudoir while they went to their bedrooms for a short rest, they realised something was very wrong. Shortly before teatime, their mother entered their room. In a voice 'thick with tears', she told them that the revolution had broken out, their grandfather had abdicated, and the war was lost.[11]

In Brunswick, as in several other cities, soldiers and other armed demonstrators rampaged through the streets. The prison was forced open, prisoners were released, and public buildings were occupied. The Duchess lay in bed, having caught the Spanish influenza that had affected so many throughout a war-weary continent, and at intervals, the Duke came to keep her informed. Some convicts entered the castle guardroom in the evening, and early next day, a group broke into the castle and demanded to speak to the Duke. After listening to their complaints about lack of food, those in authority, and anything else they could think of, he made it clear to them that he had no military authority and was in no position to redress their grievances. This surprised them, but they accepted his word, asked if they could come to him again if there were any further problems with which he might be able to help, and left. One helped himself to a cigarette box, but another told him to leave it alone. After that, their possessions were left touched.

Back in England, as he contemplated the downfall of his cousin, King George V could not resist a note of triumphalism in his diary, on what would have been his father's seventy-seventh birthday.

> 'How are the mighty fallen'. He has been Emperor for just over 30 years, he did great things for his country but his ambition was so great that he wished to dominate the world & created his military machine for that object. No man can dominate the world, it has been tried before, & now he has utterly ruined his Country & himself.[12]

At 2 a.m. on 10 November, the Emperor's chauffeur at Spa was woken and asked to prepare His Majesty's car, stripped of its imperial insignia, for a long journey. Some five hours later, a party containing William Hohenzollern, several officers, and a modest suite arrived at Eysden, on the Dutch border. When stopped by the guard, the driver told him his passengers were a German general and his staff. They were allowed to pass, and when the former monarch's identity was known, the town mayor received him with courtesy, asking him for his assurance that he would not attempt to leave Holland, to which he acceded with a handshake. He gave notice of one of his intentions at a meeting later that day with Friedrich Rosen, the German minister to Holland, who had been informed that the Emperor was on his way. When he said despairingly that he was a broken man, there was no hope for him, and nothing left except despair, Rosen suggested he could vindicate himself by writing his memoirs. The 'broken man' looked delighted for a moment, as he vowed, 'I'll start tomorrow!'[13]

The next day, he did indeed put pen to paper, as he wrote bitterly to the Empress in Potsdam that his reign was ended, his dog's life was over, and he had 'been rewarded only with betrayal and ingratitude'.[14]

'And Then Heads Will Roll'

Nobody in Holland had been ready for the arrival of the former monarch and his suite. When a Dutch sergeant on the border with Germany asked members of his entourage to produce their passports, none of them could do so, and he telephoned his commanding officer who received the Emperor's request for asylum and his sword, and gave orders for the Eysden frontier station to be sealed, pending official instructions from The Hague. The German cars remained at the frontier all morning, and the Emperor paced up and down to keep warm until he was allowed to accompany the officer to a railway station and sit in a waiting room. Soon afterwards, the imperial train arrived. He lunched and dined in his restaurant car, still unaware of his eventual destination. Shortly before midnight, word came from the German minister at The Hague that Queen Wilhelmina had agreed to grant him sanctuary. As they had nowhere to stay, while they were having lunch, Count Godard Bentinck was asked on the telephone if he could accommodate the former sovereign and his suite of fourteen officers, plus a number of functionaries and servants, for three days in his seventeenth-century house at Amerongen.

The train left Eysden at 9.20 a.m. on 11 November, arriving at Maarn six hours later. As William stepped down from his saloon coach for the last time, he was met by the provincial governor of Utrecht and Count Bentinck, and taken to Amerongen, thirty minutes away. It had advantages as a place of refuge as the region was little known and the house isolated behind double moats—a deterrent to zealous journalists and other intruders. Tired and confused, the Emperor said barely a word until they were almost at the front door, when he turned to the Count and asked for 'a cup of real good English tea'. Here, his quarters would be comfortable enough, even though he was under house arrest. His post and telephone calls were censored, and he was not allowed to leave the grounds of the house without a Dutch escort.

That evening, the German party was treated to dinner, with several courses and the best wine. The Emperor wrote to his wife, still at Potsdam, to tell her of the excellent hospitality. Still weak after a stroke and heart trouble, she longed to be reunited with him. A few days later, she was joined by most of her sons, daughters-in-law, and grandchildren. Though she was comforted by their presence, she was increasingly worried about his state of mind. When warned that hostile troops were on their way to the palace, she refused to leave on the grounds that to do so would be cowardice, despite her fear of what might happen. Those still loyal to the monarchy advised her to stay in Germany as there had been no immediate threats against her life, mainly because she was far more popular than her husband. She had never forfeited the respect of their subjects, and many hoped that if she remained where she was, she might serve as a rallying point for the monarchists, or even possibly pave the way for an eventual restoration of the monarchy.

When asked what she would do, she said without hesitation that her place was by her husband's side as she could not bear to be apart from him at a time when he needed her more than ever.[1] The newly formed Council of People's Commissars allowed her to cross the German border into the Netherlands now that her husband had given his word to abdicate. Queen Wilhelmina was likewise anxious that she should join him to give his stay in her country 'a more private character'. Once she had made the decision to do so, she packed as much as she could take away—gathering up everything from clothes and jewels to cutlery and knick-knacks— as she could not face the idea of thieves misappropriating her private possessions. She advised the Crown Princess and her children to join them as they would be vulnerable if they stayed in Germany. To this, the wife of the former heir answered defiantly that if the revolutionaries wanted to kill them, they could do so right there in their own house: 'but I do not want my children to grow up as exiles if I can help it'.[2]

As the revolution gathered apace and the spectre of events in St Petersburg under the Bolsheviks a year earlier loomed large, with Marxist Communists fighting the more moderate elements for government control, it became impossible to protect the *Neues Palais* and those still there. There were attempts on the lives of the Emperor's brother, Henry, and on some of the other princes, and while nobody was harmed, it was enough to make the imperial family realise they were in danger. Bands of rioters tried to break into the palace, and a detachment of guards sent to defend the Empress found it impossible to defend the premises adequately. Eitel Frederick persuaded his mother to come and take refuge nearby in Villa

Ingenheim, his home at Potsdam, which was thought to be safer from the red menace. She left just in time, for shortly after her departure, crowds broke in, ransacked the ground floor, and helped themselves to antiques, furniture, and clothes.

Ingenheim was hardly more secure. The guards assigned to protect her proved that they supported the revolution by wearing red cockades, although they too had great respect for their Empress and did what they could to protect her. Some held true to their new republican ideals, and on the first night that she was there, a group of drunken sailors broke into the building and overpowered the guards. They went through the rooms to look for her diaries and letters, and when they found her, she was interrogated by an officer. Although still unwell, she faced them bravely and when they suggested that she might like to sit down, she stood defiantly, saying she was accustomed to sit down only when she felt like it. By sheer force of character, she managed to subdue them, and afterwards she was left in peace. The rest of the time she remained in seclusion, still suffering from continual heart pain and fatigue, exacerbated by stress, spending much of her time in bed. Her only comfort was the presence of her sons, Eitel Frederick, Oscar, Augustus William, and their wives and children, as well as the Crown Princess. Two sons were elsewhere, the Crown Prince in Wierigen Island, and Adalbert, a naval captain, still in Kiel.

On 26 November, she completed packing her jewels, clothes, and personal items. Most of the crown jewels had been spirited away to safety in the care of her cousin, Queen Victoria of Sweden, daughter of the Dowager Grand Duchess of Baden. Next morning, she left Potsdam for the last time. Escorted by soldiers from Eitel Frederick's regiment in civilian clothes to safety outside the German border and, accompanied by a small group—including her ever-faithful friend Countess Mathilde von Keller, her dachshund, Topsy, and one or two attendants—she and was driven by the Crown Princess to Charlottenburg Station where she left Germany in a specially prepared black train and was provided by the government with an escort from the First Guards Regiment to accompany her to the border and then disembark. They did not wear traditional dress uniform, but were attired in civilian clothes. The journey through German territory was performed at breakneck speed to ensure she left the former empire while public opinion was still in her favour. While her companions chatted and passed the time by playing cards, she sat in isolation at the back of the train, attended only by Countess Keller. She would never see her country again.

On 28 November, husband and wife embraced each other as they were reunited at Amerongen. That same day, he formally signed a document of abdication as German Emperor and King of Prussia. As the Crown Prince had also sought asylum in Holland, the Emperor appointed Prince Eitel Frederick, still in Germany, to represent him in any family and financial matters that might arise. Three days later, the Crown Prince signed a similar document renouncing the throne.

Within days of his leaving Germany, British authorities were discussing how he should be held to account. King George V's private secretary Lord Stamfordham told him that most people had 'lost their balance' about the former warlord. Some advocated sending him to the Falkland Islands without trial: 'But sending Napoleon to St Helena did not prevent his nephew becoming Emperor and the Kaiser's sons cannot all be hanged!'[3] The Northcliffe Press, publishers of the *Daily Mail*, led a campaign calling for the Germans to be brought to their knees and for 'the arch-villain of Europe' to stand trial. A British General Election was about to take place, and the wartime Prime Minister David Lloyd George tried to ignore such hysterical outbursts and demands for retribution, but popular opinion prevailed on him to think otherwise. Jurists concluded unanimously that the former Emperor was guilty of an indictable offence for which he should be held responsible. Yet most other British politicians, members of the British diplomatic service, and leading statesmen from the British Empire and the US agreed that demands to 'Hang the Kaiser' should not be pursued.

The Dutch Government insisted there could be no question of extraditing a former ruler who had sought asylum, although the Dutch socialist party wanted him to leave their soil so they would not be asked to hand him over or be confronted by force. William said he was willing to leave to avoid embarrassing the government, and neutral Sweden— where his first cousin, Victoria (wife of King Gustav V, and described by her critics as a 'little Prussian soldier') was Queen consort—or Switzerland were thought the most suitable lands where he could settle. This came to nothing, but the Dutch Government had every right to refuse requests to hand him over on condition that the former Emperor should abstain from political activity as long as he remained in their country, a pledge he gladly gave. Queen Wilhelmina kept her distance from him, partly for diplomatic and political reasons, and partly because of protocol. They never met once during his twenty-two years there, although the Emperor received several other members of the Dutch royal family at various times.

Nevertheless, for several months, speculation that the former sovereign would be put on trial continued. When the peace conference at Paris began deliberations in January 1919, one of the French delegates, Ferdinand Larnaude, produced a letter from the Emperor to Emperor Francis Joseph of Austria in August 1914 in which he made his objectives clear:

My soul is torn, but everything must be put to fire and sword; men, women and children and old men must be slaughtered and not a tree or house left standing. With these methods of terrorism, which are alone of affecting a people so degenerate as the French, the war will be over in two months, whereas if I admit humanitarian considerations, it will last years. In spite of my repugnance I have, therefore, been obliged to choose the former system.[4]

To France and her allies, this was the proof they required that the man they would like to arraign had been prepared to sanction the worst crimes against humanity possible. When the Treaty of Versailles was signed in June, Article 127 stated that the Allies and associated Powers 'publicly indict Wilhelm II von Hohenzollern, former Emperor of Germany [*sic*.], for the gravest violation of the international moral code and the sanctity of treaties'. A special court was to be set up, with five judges nominated from Britain, the US, France, Italy, and Japan to form the court and 'address a request to the government of the Netherlands to deliver the former Emperor for the purpose of his judgment'. Other 'war criminals' named in the treaty included Crown Prince William, Prince Rupprecht of Bavaria, Bethmann-Hollweg, Hindenburg, and Mackensen. At Westminster, Lloyd George announced confidently that 'the ruler who, for thirty years spoke only of his pride, his dignity and his power, is now a refugee who will soon be arraigned before the Court'.[5]

For a while, the Emperor lived in fear of the prospect of being captured and either executed after a show trial or even lynched. The *Entente* requested the Emperor's extradition, and public opinion in the country was divided. The Duchess of Brunswick felt he should flee rather than let himself fall into the hands of the *Entente*. He refused to consider doing so, although he did briefly contemplate whether he would be doing the Fatherland a service by giving himself up. Against this, he had to recognise that a fair judgment could hardly be expected from a court composed of men who would be judge and jury. If there had been the slightest prospect of obtaining any improvement of the situation in Germany through such a step, he admitted, then there would have been no possibility of doubt regarding his 'surrender'. He did not wish to play the role of a Vercingetorix, the Gallic chief and contemporary of ancient Rome who had deliberately allowed himself to be delivered into the hands of his enemies as a sacrifice on behalf of the defeated Gauls, only for his victorious captors to renege on their word and execute him after keeping him in captivity. In view of the behaviour of the Allies during the war and the peace negotiations, he thought it unlikely that they would 'show themselves any more magnanimous than Caesar'.[6]

At length, the other European nations made it plain that they had no intention of pursuing him, and he became less worried by any physical threats. Consideration was given to banishing him to various remote places around the globe, among them the Falkland Islands, the Dutch East Indies, Devil's Island, or one of the countries of South America, while it was said that the French wished to banish all the Hohenzollerns to Algeria. None of the *Entente* powers could agree, and he remained in Holland.[7] The Empress had been more anxious about their fate as a couple than her husband appeared to be, and at Christmas in 1918, she wrote a farewell letter to their children in case they should never see each other again. A couple of clumsy, poorly planned attempts to kidnap them were easily foiled, and afterwards, they were left in peace, if not necessarily in a good peace of mind.

After the abolition of the German monarchy, a national assembly was convened in Weimar. A new constitution was drafted and adopted in August 1919, hence the name Weimar Republic. One of its first actions was to abolish all legal privileges and immunities of the nobility, appertaining to an individual, a family, or any heirs. The Emperor's brother, Henry, and his family had remained at Hemmelmark, their home near Kiel, and were accordingly deprived of their titles. The postal service refused to deliver them any letters addressed to 'Your Royal Highness', and only the forms '*Herr* von Preussen' or '*Frau* von Preussen' were deemed acceptable.

Prince Henry undertook to live quietly as a citizen of the German Republic and not to cause any trouble by his continued presence within its borders. Nevertheless, he was not prepared to forego old family loyalties. At the beginning of December 1918, he issued a statement in which he declared that despite the new state of affairs that he was compelled to recognise, he would 'strive to help an orderly, legal, and constitutional Government to attain tolerable conditions. On the other hand, he considers himself bound to the person of the King [of Prussia, ex-Emperor William] till the end of his life, and will do all in his power to protect him from danger'.[8] For the rest of his life, Prince Henry would always come to the defence of his brother as best he could, and prove steadfastly protective of his good name, such as it was.

One month later, the *Hamburger Nachrichten* published Henry's statement concerning the future of Germany. It said that he defined his standpoint as the restoration of Germany's power and prestige, and the rebuilding and strengthening of the economic life. He looked forward to the return of the monarchy under the Hohenzollern dynasty, Prussian leadership, and that of the dynasties in the federal states. At the same time, he demanded the removal of the 'costly and parasitical Soldiers' and Workers' Councils, and the formation of a well-disciplined war power by land and sea on the old tried model', as only then would Germany have a weighty voice in the so-called Peoples' League. In conclusion, he said that events since November 1918 had proved that the unqualified return of the monarchy was the first condition for Germany again to grow strong and healthy.[9]

Three of their sisters stayed in Germany. Charlotte, Duchess of Saxe-Meiningen—whose husband, Bernhard, had been deprived of his grand ducal title as had the other German sovereign princes—was in failing health, a victim of the porphyria that had blighted the life of her great-great-grandfather King George III of Britain. She survived the declaration of the German Republic by less than a year, dying in October 1919. Victoria's husband, Prince Adolf of Schaumburg-Lippe, had died after a short illness in July 1916, and she remained at the family home in Bonn. Margaret, her husband, and surviving sons lived at Friedrichshof, which she had inherited from the Empress Frederick on the latter's death in 1901. Sophie, the only one to marry a foreign prince, had become Queen of Greece on the accession of her husband, Constantine, to the throne in 1913, but after differences with their chief minister, Eleutherios Venizelos, and the Allies over their neutral stance during the war, they were forced to abdicate in 1917 in favour of their second son Alexander and go into exile. His tragic death in October 1920 from blood poisoning after a monkey bite saw them recalled to the throne. After a disastrous war against Turkey, they abdicated and were sent away from Greece a second time.

Even though he might have been glad to lay down his crown, the Emperor did not rule out the chance that, like King Constantine, he might be recalled. Total anarchy had been avoided in Germany. Ebert, elected leader of the Social Democratic Party in Germany in 1913, represented the more moderate, less pacifist view that even socialists had to accept that the war in which they were engaged was a necessary patriotic, defensive measure, especially when their enemies numbered the Russian autocracy. He also knew what it meant for his family to make sacrifices for the Fatherland, having lost two of his four sons in action during the space of three months in 1917. While some of his more left-wing colleagues rejoiced at the opportunity to declare a republic, he dreaded the thought of his country following the Bolshevik example of Russia and was among those who personally favoured retaining the monarchy under one of the princes, but not the Crown Prince. Prince Max thought him the most level-headed of the Social Democrats, and the one who could maintain some control of the situation to prevent the far left radical revolutionaries from taking over.

When he resigned, Ebert was his choice as Chancellor and Minister-President. His first action was to issue a series of proclamations asking the people of Berlin to remain calm, stay out of the streets, and restore peace and order. While lunching with his colleague, Philipp Scheidemann, at the Reichstag, he was asked speak to the crowds outside the building. When he refused, Scheidemann seized the chance, hoping to forestall any initiative the Communist leader Liebknecht might be planning in an effort to seize power on behalf of the revolutionaries, such as declaring Germany a Soviet Republic. He walked to the window, threw it open, and made a spontaneous speech ending with the words that the monarchy had collapsed: 'Long live the German Republic!' On his return to the dining room, a furious Ebert told him he had no right to do so. Whether Germany retained the monarchy or became a republic was a matter for an elected national assembly to decide.

The Emperor had not actually abdicated on 9 November, and Germany legally remained a monarchy until he signed a formal deed of renunciation of the throne on 28 November. However, once he had handed over supreme command of the army to Hindenburg, he had effectively left the country without a head of state. The price of Ebert's saving the country from the threat of revolution and possible civil war, and assuming power with the Social Democrats, was one of sharing power with members of the more left-wing parties in the Reichstag, particularly the Independent Social Democratic Party. Against his personal convictions, he agreed to compromise by cooperating with workers' councils and forming a fully socialist government, and a power-sharing agreement was reached. The loyalty and cooperation of the military was secured by an arrangement with Gröner, in exchange for a commitment to a firm stance against Bolshevism, a national assembly, and a return to a state of law and order. This was not good enough for the Spartacist League, an anti-war body formed in 1915, which had founded a German Communist Party under the joint leadership of Karl Liebknecht and Rosa Luxemburg.

A mass demonstration by workers in Berlin during the first few days of January 1919 threatened to turn into an uprising that aimed to overthrow the government and put the communists in power. Ebert called on the *Freikorps* or German volunteer units to restore order, with over 150 civilians and seventeen soldiers killed in the fighting that ensued. Liebknecht and Luxemburg both went into hiding, but were captured, questioned under torture, and executed on the orders of Waldemar Pabst, one of the *Freikorps* commanders and a staunch opponent of Bolshevism. A *Nationalversammlung* or constituent assembly convened in Weimar on 6 February, and five days later, Ebert was elected provisional President of the German Republic. He remained in post after the new constitution came into force and was officially sworn in on 21 August 1919. As Germany's first-ever democratically elected head of state, he was the first commoner, the first socialist, the first civilian, and the first person to hold the position. Subsequent history would also recognise him as the only German head of state in power between 1871 and 1945 unequivocally committed to democracy.

One of the major issues facing the new government was its acceptance or otherwise of the Treaty of Versailles. Its provisions included territorial changes to German borders that amounted to depriving her of 25,000 square miles (65,000 square kilometres) and 7 million of her population, renouncing sovereignty over former colonies in Africa, demobilising a sufficient number of soldiers by March 1920 to leave her with an army of 100,000 men or less, abolishing conscription, a reduction in the size of her navy to a manpower of no more than 15,000, prohibited from having an air force, and accepting full responsibility for the war, requiring her to pay a heavy indemnity in gold, commodities, ships, securities or other forms, and 20 billion gold marks in reparations to cover civilian damage caused during the war and to compensate the Allied powers. To ensure compliance, the Rhineland and bridgeheads east of the Rhine were to be occupied by Allied troops for fifteen years, with provision for a staged programme of withdrawal if Germany committed no act of aggression. It was denounced by members of the Weimar assembly across the political spectrum. Scheidemann, who had succeeded Ebert as Chancellor in February 1919, spoke for many of the government when he called the terms unacceptable, resigned rather than sign the treaty, and in a passionate speech before the National Assembly, deemed it unacceptable. As President, Ebert was similarly angered by the treaty, but knew the government was in no position to reject it. If they refused to sign, the Allies would invade Germany from the west, and there was no guarantee that the army would be able to make a stand in the event of an invasion. Hindenburg warned him that the army could not resume the war, even on a limited scale. Scheidemann was succeeded as Chancellor by Gustav Bauer. He told the *Entente* powers he would sign if certain articles were withdrawn, and in response, the Allies issued an ultimatum stating that Germany would have to accept the treaty within twenty-four hours or face an invasion of Allied forces across the Rhine. On 23 June, Bauer capitulated and sent a second telegram to confirm that a German delegation would arrive shortly to sign. The National Assembly voted in favour of doing so by 237 to 138, two ministers travelled to Versailles to sign the treaty on behalf of Germany on 28 June 1919, and it was ratified by the National Assembly on 9 July by a vote of 209 to 116.

They had been reluctant signatories, and reaction came early the following year. In March 1920, a right-wing *putsch* in Berlin was led by Wolfgang Kapp, a civil servant and journalist with strong pro-monarchist sympathies who had been elected to the Reichstag, and General Walter von Lüttwitz, the commander of the Reichswehr district, which included Berlin. They were supported by Ludendorff, who had just returned to Berlin after having fled to Sweden where he spent several months in exile, as well as various military, conservative, nationalist, and monarchist factions. With major reductions in the German armed forces, several of the formations recruited the previous year to uphold internal order or to protect the eastern frontiers feared they might be disbanded and therefore out of work. The result was increasing hostility and anger directed at the government. The aims of Lüttwitz, Kapp, and their supporters were to overthrow the Weimar Republic and establish a right-wing autocratic government in its place. When Gustav Noske, now Minister of Defence, tried to disband two naval brigades stationed near Berlin in compliance with the treaty, they refused to obey orders, took the law into their own hands, and marched into the city unopposed overnight. Noske and General Walther Reinhardt, Minister for War, wanted to offer resistance, but their military colleagues refused to support them. General Hans von Seeckt of the Defence Ministry spoke out firmly against the army involving itself in what appeared to be a political battle, saying that the interest of the army had to come before his duty to defend the government. It left Ebert and most of his cabinet with no choice but to flee the city, first to Dresden and then to Stuttgart.

From his exile the Emperor followed events with great excitement, telling his aides that they would soon be toasting a return to the old order with champagne. His guests in Holland had been astonished by his bitterness against those who had betrayed him, including Tsar Nicholas, Emperor Charles, the Italians, the Romanians, and, above all, his own people. Even a year or more after his abdication and journey into exile, his anger seemed to know no bounds. His physician, Dr Alfred Haehner, noted in his diary in April 1920 that the Emperor thought it was only right that the Germans were threatened with being starved into compliance with the Treaty of Versailles by the Allies; after everything they had done to their former sovereign, they deserved no better fate. Only a few weeks earlier he had told his brother-in-law, Frederick Charles of Hesse-Cassel, that he would certainly return to Germany, but only if he was begged to do so on bended knee, 'and then heads would roll'.[10]

If he had hoped that the result of the Kapp *putsch* would be to see him welcomed back with open arms, disillusion was not long in coming. The disturbance was all over within a week. Showing solidarity with the legitimate government, the trade unions called on the people to join a general strike, which was endorsed by the ministers; Kapp, Lüttwitz, and their supporters were unable to govern, and most of the commanders were invited to support a military dictatorship but refused. Within a week, Ebert and the government had returned to Berlin and the strike collapsed. Significantly, none of the conspirators had ever mentioned a word about attempting to bring back the Hohenzollerns. The Emperor's widowed brother-in-law, Bernhard, former Hereditary Prince of Saxe-Meiningen, had never liked him as a person, and claimed that not even the most blue-blooded conservative in Berlin would welcome him back.

The Emperor's sojourn at Amerongen as the guest of Count Bentinck was never meant to be more than temporary. In August 1919, with the consent of the Dutch Government, he bought a country house at Doorn, about 5 miles west, and they moved in there on 15 May 1920. While he was making the final arrangements, the Empress eagerly took charge of furnishing their new home. For a while, as she threw herself with enthusiasm into the task, she seemed almost her old self again. Two months earlier, the Duchess of Brunswick had come to visit her parents, a journey made difficult by fighting in the streets of Berlin and Potsdam between monarchists and republicans. Delighted as she was to be reunited with her parents, she was concerned by the change in her mother's appearance. The Empress's health was failing, she was too weak to climb the stairs, and a lift was installed to allow her to move between floors. The presence of her daughter as well as the joy of finding and placing furniture in Huis Doorn allowed her to focus on something other than their problems. Yet heart trouble, arthritis, and high blood pressure had aged her badly, and she was confined to a wheelchair for most of the time. The loss of their throne was one thing, but perpetual anxiety over the possible fate of the husband whom she had loved devotedly for all his faults for nearly forty years, and who remained a potential victim of kidnappers although no longer the processes of law, was telling on her even more.

A few days after they had moved in at Doorn, they were visited by the Crown Prince, who had fled to Holland at the time of the armistice and was interned on Wieringen Island in the Zuiderzee as an officer serving in a belligerent army, his movements were carefully monitored, and he could only leave the island and come with the permission of the Dutch Government. He evidently needed financial assistance from his father, as borne out by correspondence from the latter to Prince Fürstenberg at the beginning of January 1920:

> Wilhelm is often complaining by letter or verbally about restrictions because everything is expensive and he has to be economical owing to Cecilie's loss in Russian shares. I have repeatedly assisted him, but I am decidedly in favour of his moving to Oels, where life is cheaper.[11]

The paternal wish for his son to return to the Fatherland would be granted during the next four years. In the same letter, the Emperor declared that he had no inclination ever to return to Germany: 'The sight of collapse through one's own fault is too painful'. Ever ready to blame others, he complained bitterly about being 'deceived and deserted', particularly by Bethmann-Hollweg, Ludendorff, and Tirpitz.[12]

By the time this letter was published in the English press, almost four weeks after it was written, its ever-mercurial writer had had a change of heart. Fear of Bolshevism throughout Europe, he had decided, would be beneficial for manipulating public opinion, especially with regard to a reversion to monarchy in his homeland. On his birthday at the end of the month, he wrote of his belief that '[his] people' would soon be faced with the question of whether to fight again. The Bolsheviks would soon overrun Poland and, in concert with the Spartacists, would 'suppress Germany as they carried Bolshevism across the Rhine and into England': 'Then the *Entente* will have to unite with Germany. Then our time will have come!'[13]

The Crown Prince returned to Doorn a few months later, staying over Whitsun, and the family was joined by his youngest brother, Joachim. To help the Empress feel more at home, her husband had had an elaborate garden planted near her rooms, and then a small greenhouse built so that fresh roses could be grown and delivered daily to her room. Yet she never ceased to miss her beautiful gardens at the *Neues Palais* in Potsdam, which she had tended for so long. When her eldest son commented on the glory that surrounded them, she commented sadly how lovely it was, but alas, it was not 'her' Potsdam, not 'her' home, which she always longed to see again.

Each of the sons came to Amerongen at various times. They could always count on an affectionate welcome from their mother, if not their father. He had never enjoyed a good relationship with them as children or young men, and as the diary of his physician Dr Alfred Haehner noted, in exile, nothing changed. On the other hand, the Empress's warm feelings towards them never wavered, although as a firm believer in the sanctity of a couple's wedding vows, she was distressed at the collapse of several of their marriages.

That of the Crown Prince and Princess had been in trouble from the early days. By the end of the war, Princess Cecilie was unofficially separated from her unfaithful husband. Eitel Frederick and Charlotte, who had no children, were shamelessly indulging in extramarital affairs, although they remained married to each other, largely out of respect for his mother's feelings. The hard-drinking Eitel Frederick was not known for his tact or patience, and as he represented his father as head of the family while he was the eldest son still living in Potsdam, he had his differences with the elderly Count August zu Eulenburg, Minister of the House of Hohenzollern, whom he referred to freely as a 'totally senile old ass'. The Prince's visit to Doorn in July 1920 ended in 'a violent set-to with his father, so that it is even being said, and in fact by his siblings, that he will never come here again'. The Emperor was infuriated with his son's 'repulsively obese figure', the result of alcoholism that had 'softened his brain'.[14]

Prince Augustus William and Princess Alexandra Victoria had one son, but the prince's 'homophilic tendencies' had exacerbated the problems between them. She left him for one of their servants, they were divorced in March 1920, and he was awarded custody of their son. About three months before the divorce was finalised, he came to Doorn on a visit, and the Emperor was disgusted with him. Dr Haehner was unimpressed as well, thinking he looked 'like a foppish young hairdresser or shop assistant', with what struck him as a thoroughly effeminate display of rings on his fingers and bracelets on both wrists.[15]

The shining exceptions to this chronicle of sibling disharmony were Adalbert and Adelaide, who had settled down with their two children in Switzerland, and Oscar and Ina, with three children, also content with their lot. Although the Emperor hardly cared for these sons any more than he did their elder brothers, the Empress adored her grandchildren, and she always seemed happier when they were with her. The Emperor had reluctantly given his consent to Oscar's morganatic marriage, but as head of the house of Hohenzollern, even though no longer a reigning sovereign, he bestowed upon his daughter the style and title of Her Royal Highness the Princess of Prussia in June 1920. Even if little more than an empty gesture, it was one that pleased the family.

Of all their sons, the one that caused the Emperor the most annoyance was Joachim. Having always been publicly critical of King Edward VII's passion for betting and cards, it was not surprising that he took a firm line with his youngest son's gambling obsession. Joachim had been a sickly youngster, and unlike her husband, the ever-forgiving Empress was always particularly protective of him, ready to make excuses for his misdemeanours. He became a neurotic adult and a bad husband, although the latter could also be said of three of his brothers. Having bought a villa in Switzerland after the war, he was unable to settle down there, a prey to depression while gambling his money away for want of anything better to do. It was alleged that he beat his wife, who had fled their home at least once, and he filed for divorce and won custody of their son. While the Empress was delighted to see him, the furious Emperor ordered him out of the house. Mother and son had a last tearful embrace as they said goodbye, leaving them both in a mood of gloom. Soon afterwards, on

13 July 1920, she had a heart attack and was confined to her bed. When the Duke and Duchess of Brunswick arrived later that week, the doctor warned them that she would have to greet them from her bedchamber.

Joachim did not return to Switzerland, but visited one of their old homes in Potsdam, Villa Leignitz. On the afternoon of 18 July, three days after his sister arrived at Doorn, he shot himself, was taken to hospital, and died of his wounds a few hours later. When his father was told, there were two versions of how he reacted. One said he collapsed in a chair, utterly shocked, then pulled himself together, another said that he was beside himself with rage that 'the oaf' should have done such a thing to them, and especially to his mother. He and Dr Haehner warned the household that the Empress must never be told the truth. She was already in poor health, and they feared the shock might kill her. When he told her their youngest son had been killed in an accident, she immediately interrupted him, asking whether he had shot himself. She had evidently prepared herself for such an outcome, and sensed everybody was trying to shield her from the worst.

Rather irrationally, and ever ready to look for scapegoats, the Emperor maintained that the betrayal of the German people in November 1918 by 'a rabble of Jews' was what had brought about Joachim's death, and was thus responsible for the decline in his wife's condition. Both were denied permission to travel to Germany and attend their son's funeral at Potsdam. While three of their sons attended, with Hindenburg and Ludendorff also there, all his mother and father could do was to send a large wreath. The ex-Crown Prince went to Doorn to comfort his mother in 'the first and severest hours of her sorrow'. According to her sister-in-law, Victoria, the widowed Princess Adolf of Schaumburg-Lippe, Joachim's death was the blow that finally broke her spirit.[16]

After Joachim's funeral, the Emperor declared that the childless Eitel Frederick ought to have sole custody of Charles, the dead prince's three-year-old boy, who was often brought to Doorn to visit and stay with his grandparents. A year later, a German court ruled that the ex-Emperor had no legal authority to issue such an edict, and the boy was returned to his widowed mother. Yet while he was at Doorn, he brought something of an atmosphere of gaiety to what had become a very gloomy residence, and as a living link with his father, he had a special bond with his grandmother. Yet she was now too ill to play with him, and could only watch him in the garden from her wheelchair or sit with him at lunchtime. In the autumn, he was joined by his elder cousins, the children of the former Crown Prince. The Emperor and Empress loved entertaining all their grandchildren, and the former felt invigorated as he heard them laughing while they played together in the halls or outside in the fresh air.

When the Crown Princess came to visit her mother-in-law in August 1920, she was shocked to find her looking so delicate and frail. She was as kind and affectionate as ever, and the younger woman thought that 'she had grown perhaps even more tender-hearted in her foreign environment'. Yet she was obviously suffering immeasurably from being cut off from her own country. Cecilie took her leave of the Empress and looked at her in the doorway of the house: 'my heart told me that I would never see this devoted mother here on earth again'.[17] The family came to celebrate her sixty-second birthday in October, while she spent the day in bed, from which she had hardly been able to move for several days. The Crown Prince sat beside her while she held his hand, listening to him telling her little anecdotes about his household as he saw her features light up every now and again with just a flicker of former times. On the rare times that she was strong enough to get up, she would walk painfully through the rooms as 'her tired eyes' wandered caressingly over all the old furniture and memories from Berlin and Potsdam. To her family, it seemed 'as though she were bidding them all a silent farewell'.[18]

By the end of November, she was only semi-conscious during the day. Her sons came to see her for what they knew would surely be the last time, but even in the face of such overwhelming sadness, their father was just as irritable and unforgiving as ever. When Prince Augustus William arrived in December, the Emperor would not allow him to stay in the house with them; Dr Haehner noted in his diary: 'because he thought him too much of a softy and could not bear to see him walking around the house all day'.[19] Prince Adalbert and Princess Adelheid also came, but there was likewise a mutual antipathy between them, their father, and his entourage. Adalbert was considered cold, arrogant, and the most stupid of the brothers, his wife highly strung, and the Emperor could hardly wait for them to leave again. The seriously ill Empress remained shielded in her bedroom from the hostility between her husband and their children. At Christmas, she was surrounded by family and especially her little grandchildren, as she had specially requested, but she made few appearances during the festivities. She could no longer even leave her wheelchair to walk unaided, and spent her days in bed, rarely sleeping, semi-conscious much of the time.

The Duchess of Brunswick returned to Doorn in January 1921 for five weeks, torn between the needs of her husband and four small children at home and her ailing mother in exile. While she was there, the Empress told their daughter—the only one of the family whom her father still really liked to have with them—that it was her dearest wish to be laid to rest in Germany. As she realised, the time was fast approaching. She lingered on pitifully over the next few weeks, but had plainly lost the will to live. Shortly after midnight on 11 April 1921 there was a change in her breathing for the worse. Her husband and Prince Adalbert were summoned to her bedside, and early next morning she passed away.

The Republican Government agreed to let her be interred in the royal mausoleum at the *Neues Palais*, but the train carrying the coffin and its caretakers was required to travel without any official ceremonies at any point on German soil until it reached Potsdam. Her widower was not allowed to attend the funeral or even accompany her coffin beyond the Dutch–German border. To their four younger sons fell the duty of escorting her to her final resting place at the ceremony eight days after her death. The Crown Prince was still not allowed back over the border with Germany, while the Duchess of Brunswick, who had been returning to Doorn when she learnt of her mother's death by seeing an announcement on the newspaper placards, stayed to comfort their father.

He was stricken with grief at the death of the woman who had gradually become his rock throughout the increasingly difficult years. In the depths of his misery, he went down with bronchitis, and a nurse was summoned to look after him. The Duchess of Brunswick also came to assist. She found his expression 'painfully blank', as if he had almost lost the will to keep going: '[he seemed] timid and embarrassed, and I believe he did not wish the world to see the dreadful despair which had overcome him'.[20] Among the letters of condolence he received, only one came from the British royal family—from his aunt Beatrice, Queen Victoria's youngest daughter.

After visits from his brother, Henry, and his family, as well as various friends, he gradually recovered his old spirits. Among those were his youngest surviving son, Prince Oscar, and his wife, Countess Ina, who came in August. The Emperor seemed to get on better with his daughter-in-law than before, although there was still little warmth between father and son. One of his adjutants, Sigurd von Ilsemann, thought there was 'something cold, something military in their relationship to one another'.[21] Another visitor was Baron de Radowitz, a former Prussian officer who had attended university with the Emperor's sons and served on his staff during the war. He was struck by the change in his former sovereign, now looking comparatively unkempt with his untidy hair and beard, initially grown as an effort at disguise to keep would-be kidnappers at bay, the moustache no longer pressed into a sharply defined letter 'W'.

It was rumoured that he would soon take a second wife. Before her death, the Empress had urged her husband that once she was gone, he must marry again. His entourage suspected that he was not likely to remain on his own for long, and thought that his choice as a second wife would probably fall on his old childhood friend, *Frau* Gabriele von Rochow, who was only a year younger than him. In fact, he was about to look elsewhere.

Among the letters he received on his sixty-third birthday in January

1922 was one from the little son of Prince Schönaich-Carolath, who had died two years previously. As he knew the family, William invited the boy and his mother, Princess Hermine, to come and stay at Doorn. The daughter of Prince Henry XXII of Reuss and one of the late Empress's godchildren, twenty-eight years younger than him, she was only seven months older than his youngest son. A dark, vivacious woman with a five children aged between fifteen and three years, she came to visit him at Doorn in June. Within a month, they were engaged. While his children had expected him to remarry, they thought it was too soon. His three elder sons respected their father's decision, without enthusiasm, but the two younger princes and their sister were utterly dismayed. Oscar and the Duchess of Brunswick wrote and jointly signed a letter asking him to reconsider. He answered that he understood and respected their feelings and did not take them badly as he still loved them too much, but it would be yet another pain for him 'if [they] were to turn [their] back on [their] lonely father, so there can be no question of [their] departure or even of shaking the dust of Doorn from [their] feet'. The Crown Princess asked her outright what her intentions were, and Hermine admitted that with children of her own and so many different interests she was 'hardly the wife' for the Emperor, but they suited each other, they were mentally compatible, and she would do her best 'to ease his severe loss'. Such words did not convince the Duchess of Brunswick, when the conversation was reported to her: 'they seemed to flow just that bit too facilely'.[22]

A deputation of monarchist supporters in Germany came to ask him not to remarry so soon; if he did, it would probably discredit him in the eyes of those who were attempting at a restoration of the monarchy. Some suspected that Hermine, who was known to be deeply in debt as her estates had been badly mismanaged and eager to provide well for her children, was an opportunist. He told everyone who objected that as a private citizen he was free to do as he wished, and that their interference was 'unwarranted and impertinent'.[23] They were married at Doorn on 5 November, and he created her Her Royal Prussian Highness The Princess Liegnitz—the same title his great-grandfather King Frederick William III had given his second wife. The Emperor's siblings fully understood and respected their brother's decision to remarry, with Prince Henry and Princesses Victoria and Margaret among guests at the wedding. The Crown Prince was also there, as were Princes Eitel Frederick and Adalbert, but their younger brothers and sister, and the Crown Princess, all stayed away.

In some ways, Hermine was good for her husband. Less placid, less prone to violent prejudices than the Empress, she encouraged him to take up his old interests, especially his archaeological studies and writing. She made him take a pride in his appearance again, and shared his enthusiasm for gardening. Careful to treat her stepchildren with tact, she suggested he should hang a portrait of the Empress in her boudoir next to one of her late husband. However, his children found it difficult to like her. The Crown Prince and his estranged wife resented her regal pretensions and referred to her coldly as 'the new wife', while the Duchess of Brunswick felt she lacked her mother's goodness and quiet ways: 'she was lively and industrious, liked to argue and was ambitious'.[24] The retinue at Doorn found her grasping, full of bogus dignity, and disliked having to refer to and address her as 'Empress'.

Though the marriage was initially happy, at length, it proved less than idyllic. Soon, husband and wife were complaining bitterly about each other, he about her nagging, domineering manner, she about his childishness and impetuous behaviour. While she was able to travel freely to and from Germany, and in so doing declared that this would enable her to meet people who could help restore either him or one of his family to the throne, she was annoyed when the German Government inscribed her passport 'wife of the former German Kaiser'. She and her husband insisted that it was a German tradition for wives to bear their husband's titles, and that everybody should address her as Empress. Much as she promised her stepchildren that she would honour the memory of her husband's late wife, she was irritated when on occasion he would absent-mindedly use the phrase 'my wife' when referring to the late Empress.

'A Crown Is Not
the Only Worthwhile Aspiration'

Aided by journalists acting as ghost-writers, the exiled Emperor occupied himself as author of memoirs and histories. A first volume of reminiscences—published in Germany in 1922 as *Ereignisse und Gestalten in den Jahren 1878–1918*, and in England as *My Memoirs*—was largely a one-sided account of relations with his chancellors. A second volume four years later, *Aus Meinem Leben 1859–1888*, published in England as *My Early Life*, was regarded as superior as it seemed less concerned with trying to exonerate himself from the verdict of history. A brief volume of pen portraits of his predecessors, *My Ancestors*, followed in 1929.

Over the years, he had gradually become resigned to his fate. He could consider himself more fortunate than the other two Emperors who had lost their thrones: alongside Tsar Nicholas II, who was held in captivity and then butchered in cold blood with his wife and children, and Emperor Charles, who had made two abortive efforts to regain his throne, fallen ill in exile, and died at the age of thirty-four, he had been mild indeed. Having given up riding and shooting, two activities he had always found difficult with his deformed arm and poor sense of balance, he enjoyed sawing wood up for logs, distributing the surplus among those who lived nearby, and feeding the ducks in his moat.

Much as he may have found peace of mind and contentment as the squire of Doorn, he never forgave Prince Max of Baden for having announced his abdication as Emperor and King without his express orders. He said that when (not if) he returned to power in Germany, Max would have to leave the country within twenty-four hours or he would end up on the gallows, as a bullet was 'too good for that man'.[1] While they might not all have agreed with the medieval solution of a summary execution, others broadly shared his view. At the funeral of the Emperor's aunt Louise, Dowager

Grand Duchess of Baden in 1923, several officers shunned Max, one turning his back and refusing to shake hands.

At least two of the Emperor's children came to Max's defence, knowing he had done his best in the face of impossible odds. The Crown Prince, who still disagreed with his father on so many things, tried to intercede but in vain. The Duchess of Brunswick, whose husband was the younger brother of Princess Marie Louise, Max's wife, likewise remained good friends with him. The Emperor resented this, telling his daughter that she must surely have sufficient tact 'not to consort with him further', and that she must discontinue her association with him. Although she could understand his point of view, the Duchess was bitterly hurt, but she refused to break off contact with the brother-in-law whom she thought was being unjustly treated. He died in 1929, broken in health, having taken over the thankless task of the last Imperial Chancellor, his sister-in-law wrote, 'knowing that he would personally be sacrificed'. There was never any doubt in her mind that he had made the supreme sacrifice for his Fatherland.[2]

Rather optimistically, the Emperor continued to believe that there was a growing movement for a restoration of the throne, and he asked a retired naval officer, Admiral Magnus von Levetzow, to become his agent in Germany in charge of promoting his return. A fervent monarchist, Levetzow had supported Kapp's abortive *putsch* in 1920, but he could not arouse or even detect any desire for the return of his ever-optimistic master. By the mid-1920s, such prospects looked increasingly remote, whether they were for reinstating the former monarch himself or for one of the other princes. According to General von Cramond, a senior cavalry officer during the war, 'the father has no prospects, the eldest son damages [the cause] too much through his own faults, and his son is still too young'.[3] The Emperor had not helped himself with his rude and overbearing behaviour to many who had served him in the past; by his memoirs, which were regarded as self-serving and critical of everyone but himself; and, above all, by what was seen by almost everybody as an undignified remarriage to an unsuitable and ambitious woman. On her return to Doorn from Germany in the summer of 1923 to find out for herself what the chances were, Hermine had to admit that there was no enthusiasm for recalling the monarchy, and that it was partly due to their marriage. She knew better than to share such negative opinions with her husband, and everyone around him, including her, tried to ensure he never found out. In one sense, he had not changed at all since his reign, as he still refused to read anything about him that was critical and his entourage refrained from telling him unpleasant truths.[4]

While he followed events in Germany from a distance, it was noted that he had a limited interest in public opinion and internal affairs. Perhaps he found it less frustrating to treat them with detachment, as he no longer had any say in them. Sometimes, he would bitterly denounce the republic and its leaders, angered by the drift of what was happening to the land that had been his empire for thirty years. Yet the Duchess of Brunswick noticed that when she was there they never discussed politics, and 'it was extraordinary' how he got round the subject, 'an observation also made by others who talked to him'.[5] His bitterness against his old enemy state remained. To an English friend, he wrote that when Britain was 'on the verge of losing the unjust war which she had for many years engineered against [him] and [his] country, she led America into the fight and bought the subversive part of [his] people with money to rise against their ruler'.[6]

In addition to his own books, during the 1920s there was a regular outpouring of published reminiscences, biographies, and diplomatic documents relating to the imperial era. Many were written with a sense of self-justification and often at the expense of their contemporaries' reputations. The Emperor read several, annotating them in the margins with amusement and irritation in equal measure. One that annoyed him most of all was *Letters of the Empress Frederick*, which her godson and King Edward VII's secretary, Sir Frederick Ponsonby, had edited from correspondence with Queen Victoria with which she had entrusted him on a visit to Germany with the King in 1901 when she was dying. When he was informed out of courtesy prior to publication, he maintained that his mother's letters belonged to the house of Hohenzollern and should have been placed in the family archives instead of being taken to England. Ponsonby's 'clandestine removal of these letters [was] next to theft', he insisted.[7] Some legal wrangling took place before it was accepted that she had conferred on Ponsonby the deed of gift, and it was up to the Emperor to prove that in so doing, she had not transferred the copyright to him at the same time. It was argued that under the Act of Settlement, he could have sued as a British subject.[8] As he could not prevent the book from appearing, he purchased the German publication rights on condition that he could write the preface, and therefore present an insight into her character that, in the eyes of more indulgent biographers, justified his unfilial behaviour to some extent.[9] His former Chancellor, Bülow, died in 1929, leaving four large volumes of memoirs that had long been ready for publication but withheld during his lifetime. They appeared two years later and the Emperor faithfully read each one right through, remarking drily afterwards that it was the first case he knew of a man committing suicide after he was dead.

Within a period of three years, he lost three of his siblings, all in their early or mid-sixties, leaving only the eldest and the youngest children of Emperor Frederick III still alive. Prince Henry had lived peacefully with his wife at Hemmelmark, regularly corresponding with and sometimes visiting his brother, generally bringing as gifts copies of new German books that he read with great interest. In the spring of 1929, he fell ill and died in April. Among the messages of condolence Irene received on the loss of her husband was a message from King George V. Their sister, Victoria, who had made a disastrous marriage with Alexander Zoubkoff—a confidence trickster and liar thirty-four years her junior, who had deprived her of her savings and disappeared, leaving her almost penniless—began proceedings for divorce, then lost the will, to live and died that November. In January 1932, the former Queen Sophie of Greece, having settled in Florence, succumbed to cancer. That same month, the Emperor had a minor heart attack, brought on by bronchitis and accompanied by swelling in his legs. Having been careful to take regular exercise, he was very fit for a man of his age and made an excellent recovery.

If he did not exactly nurse the hope that the Germans or their leaders would turn to him, he still seemed to think they might call someone from the Hohenzollern dynasty to resume the throne. There was never any chance that the Crown Prince would be recalled. Not only had he renounced his claim to the throne in writing, but he had never been liked or respected by the German people as a whole, and his father made it plain he had little time for him. Unofficially separated from his long-suffering wife, the Crown Prince was now leading an aimless life, drifting from one affair to another, drinking and smoking more than was good for him.

Prince Augustus William and his wife had also separated after the end of the war, and were divorced in March 1920. His friend Mackensen having married, he was now leading a reclusive life in his villa in Potsdam. Having always been interested in and shown some talent for art, he took drawing lessons with Professor Arthur Kampf, one of the leading history painters of Germany and supplemented a modest income with the sale of his pictures.

Prince Eitel Frederick had remained at Potsdam since the establishment of the republic. His marriage had long been one in name only, and his wife obtained a divorce in October 1926 on the grounds of his ill-treatment, neglect, and incompatibility of temperament. She promptly married Harold von Hedemann, a Potsdam police lieutenant eight years her junior, to whom she had long been close. He had meanwhile formed a liaison with Countess Madeleine von Mellin, a divorcee, and wanted to take her as his second wife, but she did not meet the approval of his father due to her lower aristocracy background and her past. They remained close friends until his death.

Throughout the unsettled two decades after the war, the Hohenzollerns never completely gave up hope of a restoration. The former Emperor might in retrospect have been glad to lay down his burden, and realised that relinquishing his imperial and royal responsibilities to lead the life of an English country gentleman had been all for the best; he probably knew that his eldest son would have cut a poor figure as monarch. Even so, there were several other sons and grandsons, younger, fitter, and with more of an appetite for such a calling, should it come. The Greeks had abolished their monarchy in 1924, only to recall King and royal family eleven years later, while the French Kings and finally an Emperor of the French had been at the centre of a chequered existence in their own country for much of the nineteenth century. It was by no means a foregone conclusion that the German Republic would be anything more than a brief interlude.

After Ebert died suddenly in February 1925 after an operation for appendicitis, Hindenburg, who had remained a staunch monarchist, refrained from becoming a candidate for the vacant presidency until the Emperor had given him his permission to stand for election. He declared that it was a position that ought properly to belong to the crown, and if he was elected, he declared that he would hold the office as a trustee for his sovereign. Two other ministers from the Weimar assembly, Hans Luther and Walter Simons, served successively as acting Presidents during the ensuing ten weeks, until Hindenburg took office on 12 May. He said the monarchy should be restored, and that the former Emperor, not his son or one of his grandsons, should wear the crown. Furthermore, he realised that any premature efforts to bring back the Hohenzollerns by means of anything as untoward as a coup would fatally undermine the cause.

However, once installed in office, he made no effort to recall the monarchy and showed little patience to those who tried to persuade him otherwise. To him, the most important thing was to make Germany great once more and press for revised terms to the Treaty of Versailles. If they were to bring back the Emperor, he argued, the Allies would be antagonised and it would make the process of revising the terms of the Treaty of Versailles much more difficult. He was more loyal to the nation than to the house of Hohenzollern, he said; on sentimental grounds, he would personally like to see the monarchy restored, but the needs of *Realpolitik* mattered more than any sentimental feelings about a reversion to the days of empire. What really mattered was that Germany should achieve the status of a world power, and whatever form of government followed, be it monarchist or republican, was largely an irrelevance.

The Emperor was furious with Hindenburg, whom he felt had already betrayed him in 1918 when his throne hung in the balance and was doing so again, refusing to defend him now in the face of republican-inspired resistance. Far from inviting his former sovereign to return and resume his position as Emperor, the new President was signing the Reichstag law for the protection of the republic and continuing to forbid him to set foot in Germany again. When, not if, the day came for him to reclaim the throne again, he declared, he would never again allow any officer the supreme command that Hindenburg had had from 1916 until the end of the war. Instead, he would insist that his royal headquarters would be in charge of running the army.

A few members of the Emperor's entourage at Doorn were content to flatter him and Hermine, and even blandly assure them that a restoration was imminent, even if they did not believe it themselves. Never was this more apparent than at the festivities at Doorn for his seventieth birthday in January 1929. They started with a gathering of his former generals, who presented him with an address read by Mackensen. In thanking him, the Emperor declared that, lest any doubt still existed, he was the rightful head of the Hohenzollern family, and asked the officers whether they would still follow him faithfully. Their collective response was a rather unenthusiastic '*Ja*'.[10] It was followed by his birthday dinner, attended by several members of his family. They were doubtless relieved that Hermine, confined to her room with measles, was unable to join them.[11]

While it would be exaggeration to suggest that the National Socialist Party under Adolf Hitler would not have come to power had it not been for the German princes and aristocracy, they played a role in helping him to achieve supremacy. Having been in politics since his discharge from the army in 1920 and his beginning to work full-time for the *Nationalsozialistische Deutsche Arbeiterpartei* or National Socialist German Workers' Party (NSDAP), Hitler opposed everything the traditional German conservatives represented or espoused, including Christianity and the aristocracy, as well as the monarchy. He saw himself as a revolutionary and a national socialist, as opposed to the communists who professed to be international socialists. Born and raised in Austria, where he lived until the age of twenty-four, he had nothing but contempt for the imperial house of Habsburg. As a militant member of the working class, he resented those with what he considered any status or privilege that they had not earned. It was said that he had a lifelong hatred of the upper classes since, as a young man, he had watched members of the house of Habsburg dancing in their palaces while shovelling snow outside in midwinter. Members of the dynasty who had accorded preferential treatment of the Slavic races over the German-Austrians were anathema to him, and in his view, the pro-Slav Archduke Francis Ferdinand had got his just desserts when he was shot dead at Sarajevo. Austro-German friendship was to him an unholy alliance, and on the outbreak of war in 1914, he refused to fight for the country of his birth, but instead went to Bavaria and joined the German Army.

On 8 November 1923, Ludendorff and Hitler attempted an armed *putsch* against the Munich government. Gustav von Kahr, head of the Bavarian security forces, was holding a public meeting in the Bürgerbräukeller, a beer hall in Munich, attended by 3,000 people, which was stormed by the *Sturmabteilung* (Storm Detachment), the paramilitary wing of the Nazis. Interrupting Kahr's speech, Hitler jumped on to the stage, waving a pistol, and told the assembly that the national revolution had begun. The hall was occupied by armed men while he announced that he would lead the new government, and Ludendorff would command the army. When the latter arrived, he addressed the apparently supportive audience, and then spent the night in the War Ministry, trying to obtain backing from the army. Next morning, 3,000 armed Nazis drew up outside the hall and marched into central Munich. Their route was blocked by a police cordon, and in the subsequent firing, four police officers and sixteen Nazis were killed. The ringleaders were put on trial for treason in January for their roles in what became known as the 'Beer Hall Putsch'. Ludendorff was acquitted, largely on the strength of his military reputation, but Hitler was sentenced to five years' imprisonment, serving just over one year, including time on remand.

While in captivity, Hitler dictated the first part of *Mein Kampf* ('*My Struggle*'), a book of memoirs and political ideology, published in two volumes in 1925 and 1926. In his blueprint for a Nazi Germany, there would be no monarchs, aristocrats, or traditional religion. He wrote:

> [If the value of such an institution lay in the momentary person of the monarch,] it would be the worst institution that can be imagined; for monarchs only in the rarest cases are the cream of wisdom and reason or even of character, as some people like to claim. This is believed only by professional lickspittles and sneaks, but all straightforward men—and these remain the most valuable men in the state despite everything—will only feel repelled by the idea of arguing such nonsense.

Later, he extended his republican hostility to monarchs beyond the German borders. While in Rome, on one of his rare visits abroad, he insulted King Victor Emmanuel, whom he dubbed 'King Nutcracker', and issued express orders to ladies of the German Embassy in Italy to refuse to curtsey to the King and Queen. A suitable bow, he said, would suffice. One, the wife of a counsellor, refused to obey such an order on the grounds that she 'was brought up differently and would behave accordingly'. Her husband was immediately recalled.

Yet while Hitler had told an American military officer as far back as 1922 that monarchy was 'an absurdity', made fun of sovereigns and their families in private, and regarded them as fools and degenerates, he appreciated the value of exploiting royalist sentiment by cultivating them as long as it was expedient for him to do so.[12] The Germans as a race might have fallen out of love with their last Emperor, but there was still much traditional support if not actual affection for the glamour, institution, and respectability of monarchy. Winning over the aristocracy could give Hitler and the Nazis a veneer of respectability in conservative circles. Even once in office, he still needed the tacit support at least of well-connected German families to help him on an international level. Nowhere was this more important than among the British royal family and aristocracy. Since the Russian Revolution, the Bolsheviks and the 'red menace' had suggested between them that the house of Windsor was not completely safe from the threat of republicanism, and that National Socialism could be the lesser of two evils.

The first of the Hohenzollerns to contact Hitler personally was the Crown Prince. In 1926, Hitler sought him out in the Cecilienhof and told him that he intended to restore the monarchy. The Prince recalled that Hitler had proclaimed himself an ardent monarchist at the time of the Kapp *putsch*, but the Crown Prince thought there was something false about him and gave him the cold shoulder.

In June 1926, a referendum on expropriating the former ruling princes of Germany without compensation failed and the financial situation of the Hohenzollern family improved considerably. A settlement between the state and the family made Cecilienhof the property of the state but granted a right of residence to the Crown Prince and Princess, limited in duration to three generations. They were also allowed to retain possession of Monbijou Palace, Berlin, and two other properties until 1945.

There had been no social revolution in Germany during the Weimar Republic as in Russia after the overthrow of the Tsar. Parliamentary democracy was dominated as ever by the old aristocracy, which included the *Junkers*, a powerful wealthy landowning class descended from the old military minded Prussian nobility; they controlled over one-sixth of the total arable area of the country. As a group, they could be expected to consider National Socialism as a force for good as well as a bulwark against communism.

In 1929, the Wall Street Crash added further to the financial burdens of the Weimar Republic, already dogged by the reparations demanded in the Treaty of Versailles, rampant inflation, falls in industrial production, and rising unemployment. Millions of people who were struggling led to further radicalisation of the masses, and the middle class that had formed the basis of the republic and its government lost control. Although he had undertaken to refrain from public comment on political issues, the

Emperor, who continued to follow events, mainly from newspapers, was increasingly dismayed by what was happening to his country and left his family in no doubt as to his views. 'Political idiocy is celebrating a veritable orgy in our poor Fatherland,' he wrote that year to the Duchess of Brunswick, 'To have to witness all this chaos from abroad is frightful.' In common with many others of his generation, he thought that Germany 'was now ripe for a strong man, for only such a man could rescue the country'.[13]

The Emperor doubtless recalled the parallel case during his own childhood, the appointment of his grandfather's saviour Bismarck. There was also the example of Italy to consider. In 1922, King Victor Emmanuel III had appointed Benito Mussolini his prime minister, and within three years, *Il Duce* progressively dismantled almost all constitutional and conventional restraints on his power. The Emperor was impressed with the way in which Mussolini had brought post-war chaos in the country under full control and made a stand against Bolshevism, with state power stronger than ever and with his sovereign's full approval. When asked in December 1929 what he thought of the Italian leader, the Emperor had nothing but praise for him for bringing discipline to the country. Thanks to him, he declared, Italy had 'become a land of peace and of work under the united concentration of all the forces of the nation'.[14] He felt there was no reason why Hitler should not be able to do the same in Germany—and why he should not be able to recall the last German sovereign, or failing that, one of his sons or grandsons, at the same time.

According to historian Jonathan Petropoulos, German princes and princesses played important roles in helping Hitler come to power, and among the 270 members of royalty he identified as members of the National Socialist Party, the majority joined after he became Chancellor in January 1933.[15] By joining the party, they helped legitimise and confer respectability on the organisation. Hitler and his circle were sometimes viewed as uncouth upstarts, and for the traditional ruling elite to give their backing to the Nazi Party sent a powerful message in class-conscious Germany. The princes assisted with fundraising by making substantial donations and helping to cultivate the support of other rich backers. Prince Augustus William and his cousin, Prince Philipp of Hesse-Cassel, both attended parties at Hermann Göring's Berlin home, attended by leading industrialists who supported them, such as Fritz Thyssen, and in doing so, they lent a certain sparkle as key members of 'Nazi high society' at balls, dinners, and similar functions.

For a while, all of the Emperor's sons were members of the *Stahlhelm* ('Steel Helmet'), an ultra-right-wing paramilitary organisation for ex-servicemen committed to upholding and promoting order, discipline, and national fellowship. Clinging to the hope that Hitler would restore the monarchy and put him or his son, Alexander, on the throne, to the discomfort of his family and in defiance of his father, Prince Augustus William joined the Nazi Party on 1 April 1930.

That same year, Oscar wrote to the Duchess of Brunswick that he thought the Nazis were important, 'but their manifesto does really need to be altered'. As the party manifesto did not change and in practice became more radical, his reservations and those of all the brothers except Augustus William increased. Augustus William, the Duchess considered, was the *bel esprit* of the family with his love of art, music, and science. Ironically, his close friends included many Jewish families. As the one whom his sister called 'the only true civilian' among them, she found it surprising that he should have been the one to became most interested in politics, involving himself in the movement with enthusiasm and relishing the camaraderie of the combat units.

Like his cousin, Charles, who had been Duke of Saxe-Coburg Gotha until 1918 and also embraced the Nazi cause with an enthusiasm, which later became a source of embarrassment to many of his family, Augustus William was totally at home in the organisation. He wrote regularly to the Duchess of how much he enjoyed being with the *Stahlhelm*, saying it was 'wonderful, so exalting', carried away particularly with the enthusiasm of the spectators one day as they watched 'a splendid tattoo'. As a member of the Nazi Party, he travelled around Germany at his own expense from meeting to meeting, making speeches, giving lectures, bringing chocolates to hand out to supporters, and even putting up meekly with beatings from the police. Before long, his support created severe conflict within the family, with his father and siblings all expressing lack of interest at best and outright disapproval at worst. At this, he was mildly disheartened, but unapologetic, defending his involvement to his sister in a letter in which he told her he had 'always considered resentments and grudges quite absurd', but was determined never to quarrel with her about politics. He put up with the hostility of their father after visiting him at Doorn in the early 1930s and being treated 'as if [he] did not exist!' The prince made the mistake of lifting his arm a little, 'quite unintentionally, out of custom, and was snapped at terribly'. It also annoyed Augustus William that the Crown Prince's sons were critical of him and made public statements critical of the Nazis, on the grounds that it was making his position in the movement difficult 'and creating only bad blood against the family—just what [he] wanted to avoid'.[16]

In 1933, the Duke and Duchess of Brunswick met Hitler for the first time after being invited by Joachim von Ribbentrop, his trusted adviser on foreign affairs, to a meeting in Berlin to discuss Anglo-German relations.

They found Hitler very polite and friendly, as the Duke explained that he strongly believed an understanding with England should be the foundation of German foreign policy and that an Anglo-German rapprochement needed careful preparation. Hitler showed himself an attentive listener, and then gave them his own observations on the matter, which struck the Duke as being less than precise, more 'a general, overall picture which seemed to have been directed at people who were not at all acquainted with the subject'.[17] They left with grave doubts about having achieved anything. There were further meetings between the couple and the Chancellor, although never as extensive as their first discussion together. As guests in England of King George V later that year, they had wide-ranging talks with him, the Prince of Wales, and Prime Minister Ramsay MacDonald, and all agreed on the importance of Anglo-German friendship. The Duke never gave up hope, convinced that if no understanding between them could be achieved, war was inevitable.

Hitler and his henchmen considered 'Auwi' the most important princely member, believing that as a representative of the Prussian royal and German imperial dynasty, his membership gave them some prestige, no matter how much they personally despised the concept of monarchy. It did not matter that he was an object of mockery by press and politicians alike, being known as *Braunhemdchen Auwi* or 'Auwi the Little Brown Shirt', *Hanswurst* or 'Hans the Brown Sausage', or by Nazi leaders such as Joseph Goebbels, Hitler's minister of propaganda, as a 'good-natured but slightly gormless boy'. He may have been too naïve to realise that he was only tolerated as a token royal supporter, disparaged as 'a chinless wonder' behind his back while being deliberately used by the Nazis to gain votes in elections, as a candidate for the Prussian *Landtag* in April 1932, and as a speaker in election campaigns alongside Hitler, whom he often accompanied.[18] Through his appearances at mass rallies, he addressed himself to the crowds who were not yet convinced by the rightness of National Socialism, telling them Hitler was not a threat, but a benefactor and a positive force for good. In 1933, he briefly became a member of the Reichstag. Once Hitler had established himself as dictator, he had served his purpose. Before long, he was denied direct access to the Führer altogether, although it did not lessen his admiration of the regime to which he had committed himself so pathetically.

Two of the Crown Prince's sons served in the Wehrmacht (the German armed forces). William had been his father's heir, but while studying at Bonn, he fell in love with a fellow student, Dorothea von Salviati. His grandfather could not approve of the marriage of the second in line to the German throne with a member of the minor nobility. Although the throne was still in abeyance, he still genuinely believed in the possibility of a Hohenzollern restoration, and any marriages that might tarnish the standing of those in direct line of succession were forbidden. The Hohenzollerns, he told his grandson, were thoroughbreds, and he could not allow such a marriage as 'it produces mongrels'.[19] The smitten prince waited for two years, then, in 1933, he renounced his rights to the succession for himself and his future children, and in June, he and Dorothea were married. They had two daughters and in 1940, the ex-Emperor recognised the marriage as dynastic and the girls were accorded the style of Princesses of Prussia, though their father was not restored to his former place in the line of succession. He lived on one of his grandfather's estates as an administrator, maintaining that he had only renounced his rights to the inheritance of the family fortune, but considered himself the legal pretender to the non-existent German throne.

The Crown Prince's second son, Prince Louis Ferdinand, was elevated to the position of his father's heir. He had also broken with family tradition by not pursuing a military career, or even joining the armed forces. Having always been fascinated by engineering, he went travelling overseas, settled in Detroit, and worked on the assembly line of the Ford Motor Company. He would have preferred to stay on the other side of the Atlantic, but his elder brother's marriage 'meant farewell to an independent life in the world's most independent country'. On his return home, he decided to learn to fly and obtained a transport pilot's licence in 1935. He was anxious to maintain what he called his 'connections with the great outside world' and keep away from the family administration as far as possible. After several years of paid employment, he found the prospect of exchanging such a life for the existence of a country squire 'utterly disconcerting'. When he came to write his memoirs about fifteen years later, he realised this 'was a prejudice which experience corrected', and by then, he knew that if given the choice, he would prefer the country to the city. Nevertheless, he felt uneasy at Doorn, where the only person who accepted him in his new capacity as heir apparent was his grandfather. The rest of the family had a problem 'in getting used to the thought that such an eccentric person with Americanized ideas' would eventually become head of the house.[20]

Soon after returning to Europe, Prince Louis Ferdinand spent a few days in London under the tutelage of Robert Bruce Lockhart. While there, he met Edward, Prince of Wales, and two senior politicians, the former Prime Minister David Lloyd George and former minister Winston Churchill, a future Prime Minister then out of office and going through what were later termed his 'wilderness years'. Having tea on the terrace of the Houses of Parliament at Westminster, all three naturally made themselves very pleasant to their guest. Lloyd George also invited the prince to his home at Churt, Surrey. As they and his other guest, the South African politician Jan

Smuts, sat talking on the terrace, the former Prime Minister said that they had neither expected nor intended the downfall of the Hohenzollerns at the end of the war. He admitted that in the face of public opinion, it would have been impossible for him to conclude peace with either his father or his grandfather, but they all thought a regency for his elder brother under his mother and one of his uncles would have been established. Had the family remained in power in Germany, he was sure that Hitler would not have been causing them any problems.[21] The remark was significant, for Lloyd George was notable for his dislike of inherited privilege and never at any time a natural supporter of the institution of monarchy, either in his country or overseas.

At the time, Churchill was writing a series of short biographical studies, *Great Contemporaries*, published in 1937. In his ten-page account of the former Emperor, he commented:

> [He has] reached a phase when the greater part of Europe, particularly his most powerful enemies Great Britain and France, would regard the Hohenzollern restoration they formerly abhorred beyond expression, as a comparatively hopeful event and as a sign that dangers were abating. If it were accompanied by constitutional limitations, it would be taken throughout the world as an assurance of peace abroad and toleration at home.[22]

It was not just politicians who looked back wistfully on the era when monarchs reigned over much of Europe. A former diplomat and Member of Parliament, Lord Frederick Hamilton, noted in his memoirs:

> [There is a] feeling of regret that this prosaic, drab-coloured twentieth century should have lost so strong an element of the picturesque, and should permanently severed a link which bound it to the traditions of the medieval days of chivalry and romance, with their glowing colour, their splendid spectacular displays, and the feeling of continuity with a vanished past which they inspired.[23]

Crown Prince William strongly believed that the anti-Semitism of his father and uncle was too indiscriminate, considered it was wrong to fight or attack the Jews in general, and thought it would be better if they all tried to win over the nationally inclined Jews and make use of them. Prince Adalbert, the other surviving son, had long since dissociated himself completely from family and country. Uniquely among his brothers in having nothing to do with the Nazis, being far more hostile to the regime than they were, and disillusioned with his father, he found salvation in complete independence. Taking the name Count Lingen, he and his wife settled as private citizens in La Tour de Peilz, on the shores of Lake Geneva.

The rest of the Hohenzollerns took some interest in the cause of National Socialism. The Duke of Brunswick was one of those who never officially joined the party, but donated funds and was close to several of the leaders. He and his wife were keen for a rapprochement between England and Germany. Ostensibly desiring to pursue an alliance with Britain, Hitler asked them in the mid-1930s if they would arrange a match between their daughter, Princess Frederica, and the Prince of Wales, who as a future King and nearing the age of forty was Europe's most eligible bachelor. They refused to consider it, believing the age difference of twenty-three years was excessive and said they would not put pressure on her daughter, who should be free to make up her own mind as to whom she took as a husband. In 1938, she married Prince, later King, Paul of Greece.

If the Führer had nothing but contempt for the Hohenzollerns, the feeling was reciprocated by some, not least the Emperor himself, who soon came to see through him, although Hermine and some members of the suite at Doorn were sympathetic to the cause of National Socialism. This was partly motivated by self-interest, as she and her husband found it prudent to maintain amicable business relations with the regime, especially where negotiations concerning Hohenzollern properties in Germany were concerned. As William was forbidden to enter the country, she had to act on his behalf and meet Nazi leaders from time to time.

Sometimes, the Nazi hierarchy came directly to Doorn. Hermann Göring, Prussian Minister-President and one of Hitler's closest associates, stayed there in January 1931 and again in May 1932, and gave the Emperor and his wife Karin the impression that he favoured a Hohenzollern restoration. The Emperor received Göring coldly, finding his crude and outspoken manner objectionable. Karin thought that both men, who had 'flown at one another', were both excitable and like each other in so many ways: 'The Kaiser has probably never heard anybody express an opinion other than his own, and it was a bit too much for him sometimes'.[24] With his instinctive distrust of Hitler, it did nothing to help William warm to their cause and he pointedly kept his distance, advising the Crown Prince to do likewise. Heinrich Brüning, Chancellor from 1930 to 1932, also favoured re-establishing the German Empire with Hindenburg as regent for one of the Emperor's grandsons. Yet the Emperor and Crown Prince both believed their chances were better with Göring than with Brüning or Hindenburg. Hitler declared that Emperor William I had been 'a grand seigneur', but called his grandson 'a strutting puppet of no character'.

Göring was apparently prepared to help. In September 1932, he said he intended to see Hitler 'in order to discuss with him the question of the monarchy in the Kaiser's interests'.[25] Whether Hitler would have been prepared to do anything for a man for whom he evidently had as little liking or respect as he did for the institution that he represented is another matter, but whatever the situation, the Emperor wrecked his chances with a letter to the Crown Prince in which he was very scathing about the Führer, saying among other things he was 'wholly devoid of any political flair or knowledge of history', and calling him 'no statesman'. The letter fell into the hands of the Nazis, and after it had been circulated, Göring said that any meeting was now quite out of the question. Even so, he was prepared to give financial aid. In the summer of 1933, he and Friedrich von Berg, the Emperor's comptroller, signed an agreement that would confer a substantial annual allowance on the Emperor, the Crown Prince, and remaining princes from the Prussian state. If any of them was to criticise the Nazi regime, payments would cease forthwith.

The Crown Prince had been visited in 1921 by Gustav Stresemann, a faithful monarchist who went on to serve successively as Chancellor and Foreign Minister between 1923 and 1929 during the Weimar Republic, and said he was interested in coming back to Germany. He had made the best of his exile on Wieringen, where he was on good terms with the locals and helped the blacksmith with his work. He told his sister that an American journalist had offered the blacksmith twenty-five guilders for a horseshoe wrought by the Crown Prince. It greatly appealed to his sense of humour that people would even pick up cigarette butts he had thrown away: 'now a snob buys a bit of iron that I've hit with a hammer—and at what a price!'[26]

After Stresemann took office, the ministers allowed the Crown Prince to return in October 1923 as long as he could assure them that he would no longer engage in politics. Significantly, he chose 9 November, the fifth anniversary of the date on which his father had been told he would have to abdicate. Anxious that the Dutch Government might actively prevent him from leaving, he made his preparations in secret. On receiving a farewell letter from his son and learning that he had already left Wieringen, the Emperor was infuriated. While pleased that the Crown Prince was reunited with his wife and children, he wrote to the Duchess of Brunswick that he had chosen 'the wrong moment', and 'the fact that he left [him] completely in the dark regarding his plans has wounded [him] deeply'.[27]

The Crown Prince was now settled at Oels, where he spent most of his time, although he stayed in Cecilienhof on occasion. Husband and wife spent a certain amount of time in each other's company, but they had grown too far apart and been separated too long for there to be any chance of a genuine reconciliation. A friend of the Crown Princess, *Frau Marie Sarre*, also stayed in Oels at about the time of his return, largely at the request of her friend who was rather nervous about the reunion with her husband who had become almost a stranger to her and needed support. *Frau* Sarre, who had known him since the early days of his marriage, was struck by the change in the man she had known. He now appeared strangely lethargic, almost broken, and apparently unable to find his way around in old, but unaccustomed surroundings. Hour after hour, he would sit at the window looking out sadly into the castle park. Living in Germany, he was in a better position to gauge the mood of the country than his father, and under no illusions as to the slim chances of a restoration. To his sister, he seemed more or less resigned to his fate, saying that as long as he could live in his own country, he could be happy:

> A crown is not the only worthwhile aspiration. To be one's own master on one's own soil also means a great deal. We must not allow ourselves to be robbed of one's belief in a better future for our Fatherland, for we Germans are still a capable, intelligent and hard-working people through and through.[28]

He also told her that he had decided to lead his life more independently of his father, as he had done in the past. Father and son, he said, were often completely different in character, temperament, and nature. His father and grandfather would surely have concurred with the view.

Soon, he reneged on his undertaking to dissociate himself from politics. Sensing the advantages of associating with Hitler, he invited him to Cecilienhof three times—in 1926, in 1933, and in 1935. In 1931, he joined the *Stahlhelm*, which merged in 1931 into the Harzburg Front, a right-wing organisation formed by opponents of the Weimar Republic. He was said to be interested in the idea of running for the presidency as the right-wing candidate against Hindenburg in 1932, until his father forbade him to consider it. Thereafter, he supported the rise to power of Hitler, but rapidly became disillusioned. He had been a friend of Kurt von Schleicher, who served briefly as Chancellor until ousted by Hindenburg who replaced him with Hitler in January 1933.

Schleicher was regarded as a rival to Hitler, and like many others, he paid for it with his life in Hitler's purge of his opponents, the 'Night of the Long Knives', in the summer of 1934. The Crown Prince's adjutant, Louis von Müldner, was arrested for allegedly making statements criticising Hitler, and he was imprisoned for six weeks before his release was secured by the Crown Prince's son, Frederick. Two of the other princes also received a stern wake-up call. Prince Eitel Frederick underwent a gruelling interrogation from the Gestapo, although it was probably more a gesture to frighten him than anything else. Prince Augustus William was told by

Göring that his name had been on the regime's proscription list, and it was only his personal intervention that saved him from execution. Although shocked, the Emperor was pleased that his fourth son had now 'finished with his National Socialism', and forbade him to have any further connection with the party. His fanaticism, he told Ilsemann, was 'almost pathological' and in addition to getting no thanks for his misguided efforts to help, he had achieved absolutely nothing.[29] With this, the Crown Prince finally realised Hitler had no intention of restoring the monarchy, their relationship cooled markedly, and he returned to private life.

By the early 1930s, Hermine was spending more of her time in Berlin, mainly because husband and wife were getting on each other's nerves and could only take so much of each other's company. Perhaps even more than her husband, she clung to the idea of a crown. Oblivious to Hitler's refusal to have anything to do with her, either through grim determination or naïveté, she sent word from Berlin that the monarchical cause was making steady progress under the Nazis. The Emperor was already disillusioned with the National Socialist regime and deplored his wife's apparent eagerness to run around after its members, vainly soliciting their support and goodwill on his behalf.

11

'Great Harm Will Come
from Them'

After seizing power as Chancellor in 1933, Hitler dropped all pretence of
any sentimental attachment to the institution of monarchy. Hindenburg
died in August 1934, allegedly with the words '*Mein Kaiser*' on his lips.
Emperor William, who had sent a message to the man elected President
of Germany in 1925 as he lay dying, received this news with scorn, calling
the dead man 'the traitor of Spa'. Some monarchists in the officer corps
had considered restoring the crown, but the Nazis acted quickly, with
Hitler proclaiming amalgamation of the presidency and chancellorship.
The Emperor expected to see the Hohenzollerns recalled, if not for himself
or his son, then one of his grandsons instead.

Such dreams had been dealt a death blow earlier in the year. Hitler
and other leading Nazis knew celebrations would be held on 27 January
1934 to honour the Emperor's seventy-fifth birthday, and an order was
issued that Nazi workers must not take part. The official Nazi newspaper,
Völkischer Beobachter, warned 'those incorrigibles who cling to yesterday
to abstain from tasteless comparisons if they do not wish to draw upon
themselves a shattering judgment of themselves and their achievements'.[1]
At Frankfurt University, the students held a demonstration condemning
the activities of 'monarchist reactionaries', with their leader issuing a
statement that the youth of Germany refused to celebrate the birthday of
a man who had crossed the national frontier in the country's worst hour
of distress. Elsewhere, Hitler ordered small-scale celebrations on behalf of
the Emperor to be broken up by anti-monarchists, using itching powder
and stink bombs.

A few days later, legislation was passed outlawing all monarchist
organisations. During the 'Night of the Long Knives', a purge that took
place between 30 June and 2 July, when the Nazi regime carried out
several political extrajudicial executions intended to consolidate Hitler's

hold on power in Germany, Prince Augustus William was placed under house arrest and ordered to refrain from any political statements. The display of imperial images and memorabilia in Germany was now officially prohibited.[2] Hitler no longer needed to pay lip service to the Hohenzollerns and the institution of monarchy that he had always held in contempt.

The Emperor now had to resign himself to the likelihood of dying in exile, and the probability that not only would he never set foot in Germany again, but also that it would never be a monarchy, certainly not in his lifetime. At seventy-five, he had spent fifteen peaceful years in Holland. Had he been recalled to the throne, he would have bowed to what he saw as a dynastic duty rather than embrace once again with any great enthusiasm the crown that he had worn for thirty often-turbulent years.

In Britain, King George V had had no contact with the Emperor since the latter's abdication. Despite comments in his diary at the end of the war, he felt sorry for him, as did Queen Mary, and they thought he behaved with exemplary dignity and restraint in exile. However, when the King died in January 1936, William wrote the Queen a message of condolence, and in acknowledgement, she sent him a gold box from the King's desk as a keepsake. The Emperor despatched an aide to Berlin to ask that he should be officially represented at the King's funeral. The new monarch, King Edward VIII, suggested the Crown Prince should do so, but the foreign office in London thought this inadvisable and instead recommended the Crown Prince's fourth son, Prince Frederick, who had recently been a guest at Cowes.

Emperor William thought it would be the dawning of a new age in Anglo-German relations. He had long since been disillusioned with King George V, whose absence of personal communication with him since the outbreak of war had made his feelings plain, but he remembered the new King as a youth, and was particularly impressed when Frederick reported to him that King Edward had personally told him 'all this enmity nonsense between the two families must now cease'. Whether the Emperor was aware of the close diplomatic and personal relationships between the King, his future wife, Wallis Simpson, and Ribbentrop, recently appointed German Ambassador to the Court of St James, is unknown, but he inevitably took a keen interest in what was happening in Britain at the time.

In February 1936, he invited the British journalist and diplomat Robert Bruce Lockhart to Doorn. During their conversations, the former sovereign said Britain and Germany should unite to prevent war from breaking out in Europe again. He maintained that Bolshevism was the greatest danger and found Britain's policy incomprehensible. How, he asked, could Britain trust Russia or back Russia against Japan, and he thought it 'very foolish' to break her alliance with the latter, which was 'a bulwark against Bolshevism'. Although he did not consider himself pro-Italian, he thought the economic sanctions against Italy because of the latter's invasion of Abyssinia were 'madness and the League of Nations [which had imposed the sanctions] as worse than futile', on the grounds that more than once Britain had given tacit encouragement to Mussolini to cross the borders of Abyssinia. Their talk also touched on the question of a possible restoration, about which the Emperor still seemed optimistic, although most of those around him had more or less given up hope. If it did happen, he said, the British people must not assume that the new German Parliament would be like that in Britain, for much of Europe was not yet ready for universal democracy. The new German model, he predicted, would be one in which patrician, burgher, and apprentice were members of the same guild, with representatives selected from the best men in all professions.[3]

The Foreign Office in London kept an eye on the Emperor's activities. In February 1938, senior officials in Whitehall had learned from two sources of a plot thought to have been devised by Karl Goerdeler, the former mayor of Leipzig. There would be a naval coup at Kiel, and a warship would broadcast a recorded message from the Emperor calling on royalists to support one of his grandsons in restoring proper democratic government to Germany. Later that year, Major Ewald von Kleist came secretly to England, met Churchill at Chartwell, and told him a group of generals were hoping to establish a new regime in Berlin, probably of a monarchist character.

The Emperor may not have been aware of these projects, but he and his sons had long since become increasingly disenchanted with the Nazis, if not hostile to them. They realised Hitler had nothing but contempt for the dynasty and the monarchical principle, and despite their resentment of the Jews, they were disgusted by the violent attacks on them. Ten years earlier, the Emperor had been vitriolic in his outbursts against them as a race, and wrote to his childhood friend Poultney Bigelow: '[Jews and Mosquitoes are] a nuisance that humanity must get rid of in some way or other.... I believe the best would be gas!'[4]

Although like his father he was often inconsistent in his stance, the Crown Prince had generally distanced himself from the Nazis. In 1937, he had broken off all connections with Hitler after pointing out to him in writing what he called his 'destructive policies', and had tried but failed to seek an audience with him so they could have a frank discussion of their views. It was only beginning to dawn on the princes that the Führer no longer needed to court members of the former ruling dynasty for his own ends, and that once he had no further use for them, he had no respect for them or for the institution of monarchy either.

During the European crisis of 1938, after the German annexation of Austria and the threat to Czechoslovakia, by mid-September, many people throughout Europe feared another war was imminent. Consequently, there was general relief in September when Hitler agreed to see Neville Chamberlain, the British Prime Minister, at Munich with Mussolini and the French Prime Minister Édouard Daladier in an effort to reach general agreement. Chamberlain returned from the meeting positive that war had been averted and that it was 'peace in our time'. Among those who were convinced that all would be well was the Emperor, who wrote to Queen Mary how pleased he was that they had all been saved 'by the intercession of Heaven' from 'a most fearful catastrophe'. He was sure, he continued, that Chamberlain 'was inspired by heaven & guided by God who took pity on his children on Earth by crowning his mission with such relieving success'.[5] Queen Mary replied graciously in kind, passing the note on to King George VI, who had succeeded his brother Edward VIII after the abdication crisis almost two years earlier. 'Poor William,' she wrote on a covering note, 'he must have been horrified at the thought of another war between our 2 countries'.[6]

For once, the Emperor and Crown Prince were in full agreement, and the latter also wrote to Chamberlain later that month on similar lines, saying how thankful they were that Europe had been saved: '[During the days before the Munich agreement,] we felt as if we were awaiting our own execution'. Chamberlain replied that his words confirmed his personal conviction that 'what was achieved was only made possible by the determination of the people of all countries to avoid the folly and tragedy of another war'.[7]

After Hitler and the Nazis unleashed anti-Jewish attacks, culminating in *Kristallnacht* on the night of 9–10 November 1938, with a large number being killed, dying later from maltreatment after arrest, or suicide, and several thousand Jewish businesses and synagogues destroyed, the Emperor was horrified. Although he had never ceased to rail against the Jews, such wanton physical violence against them was a step too far. It was 'pure bolshevism' and 'an infamous blot' on Germany's reputation; he further stated that 'every decent person' would surely condemn such behaviour as 'gangsterism'.[8] For the first time in his life, he felt ashamed to call himself a German.[9] Such events 'at home', he wrote to the Duchess of Brunswick, were a scandal, and it was high time the army intervened: 'All the old officers and upstanding Germans should have protested, but they witnessed murder and arson, and no one lifted a finger'.[10] Much to his disgust, Prince Augustus William fully approved of the attacks.

Some suspected the Hohenzollerns might be next on the Third Reich's list. Colonel Don Luis Ruiz de Valdivia, a former military *attaché* at the

Spanish Embassy in Berlin, told Prince Louis Ferdinand of his despair at what was happening in Germany. He could not understand what had happened to the German people since Hitler had come to power. During the years he had lived in Germany, he had never noticed any real anti-Semitism: 'I think it is all inspired and commanded from above. They [the Nazis] want some scapegoat. Maybe you and your relations will be next after the Jews have been liquidated'.[11] Louis Ferdinand was inclined to agree, having found the country of his birth increasingly abhorrent under the new regime. Over the years, Doorn had become a second home for the family, and 'especially after Hitler turned Germany into a huge dungeon, [he] always deeply relished the moment when the train crossed the Dutch border'.[12]

Earlier that year, in the first week of May, Louis Ferdinand had provided some happiness for the family when he took himself a wife. Some years earlier, he had caused concern after a short fling with Hollywood actress Lili Damita, but after realising that an ambitious young movie star would not be the right wife for him, he fell in love with Grand Duchess Kira of Russia. Both of them were great-grandchildren of Queen Victoria, the latter being a granddaughter of her second son, Alfred, Duke of Edinburgh and later of Saxe-Coburg Gotha. Kira always said that they were married three times: at a civil ceremony at Potsdam, a Russian Orthodox service at Cecilienhof on 2 May, and then at another, according to the German Evangelical Church rites at Doorn, two days later.

Even in his last years, the Emperor remained as inconsistent as ever in his attitude towards Hitler and his party. Some of his utterances could perhaps be put down to journalists' licence, but not all. On 8 December 1938, *The Daily Telegraph* (ironically, in view of the controversy thirty years earlier) reported an alleged interview in an American magazine in which he had denounced the Nazi movement and regime. Two days later, a statement from Doorn called it a fabrication, saying that he always observed silence over current political questions. As a result, the British Foreign Office showed no enthusiasm for a proposal by John Boyd-Carpenter (whose family had known the Emperor before the war) that he should visit him and obtain a statement from him intended to ease the general situation in Europe.

At around the same time, Prince Louis Ferdinand inadvertently fell foul of the regime in Germany. During their honeymoon trip around the world, he and Kira had been house guests of President Franklin D. Roosevelt and his wife, during which, among other things, they discussed at length the dangers of Nazism and its threats to peace. Before the newly married couple left, the President entrusted the Prince with sounding out Ribbentrop, appointed Foreign Minister by Hitler earlier that year, with a view to a meeting that would bring the President, Hitler, Mussolini, and Chamberlain together—probably on some neutral territory such as the Azores. On their return to Germany, the Prince prepared a memorandum for Ribbentrop, setting forth without revealing any details that he was charged with communicating certain information from the American President unofficially to the German Government. Ribbentrop did not have the courtesy to acknowledge receipt of the message, and despite being pressed for an answer, he did not send one.

The reason why became clear when the Prince and Princess sent a Christmas message to the Roosevelts, and to other statesmen and their wives throughout the world, who had provided them with hospitality. Not long after the cablegram had been handed in, a Luftwaffe officer appeared, telling the prince that he had been sent by Marshal Göring to ask how dare he communicate with the Führer's greatest enemy. Unless he could provide a satisfactory answer, he would be discharged from the Wehrmacht, with possible further consequences. Only the fact that their greeting to the Roosevelts had been one of several saved the Prince from an accusation of deliberate intent to commit an affront against the German Chief of State. That was the end of any effort to press Ribbentrop for a reply to his memorandum.[13]

In January 1939, the Emperor celebrated his eightieth birthday. He was delighted to receive telegrams of congratulation from King Gustav V of Sweden, King Christian X of Denmark, King George II of Greece, and from King George VI, Queen Elizabeth, and Queen Mary in England. Having been ignored by the English court between the end of the war and the remainder of King George V's reign, he now felt he was one of the family once again. Hitler showed his hostility to the former sovereign by forbidding all active and reserve officers to send good wishes to their former Commander-in-Chief. It did not prevent Mackensen from joining celebrations at Doorn, where the imperial standard and the flag of Prussia fluttered from the tower as members of his family and about fifty representatives of the German nobility assembled in the Grand Hall to greet him, attired in the uniform of a German general. Prince Bernhard of the Netherlands arrived later to join the assembled company for luncheon, although on this occasion there were no speeches.

Although the Emperor and his family knew the international situation was deteriorating, the Duke and Duchess of Brunswick still hoped for a rapprochement with Britain. The Duke attempted to warn the German Government that they were heading for a calamity and that Chamberlain's policy of appeasement was not to be mistaken for a lack of toughness or determination, but he feared that his words were falling on deaf ears. He was aghast at Hitler's total lack of experience of foreign affairs, and considered his lack of travel abroad a severe handicap for a head of state as much as his lack of knowledge about foreign affairs and other countries' policies. When the Duke offered his services as mediator, Hitler did not reply.

In August 1939, he gave an audience to Robert Bruce Lockhart and another representative of the London Foreign Office in London, John Wheeler-Bennett, later known for his official biography of King George VI. To them, he confided his convictions that they were unlikely to avoid another major war. Hitler was the slave, not the master of events: 'the machine [was] running away with him as it ran away with me'. Even Hermine was becoming disillusioned. She suspected that some of her husband's household at Doorn were spies who reported everything to the Nazis, and warned visitors to be on their guard at all times. While she conceded that the regime had done some good, 'they are evil, and great harm will come from them'.[14]

Some, but not all, members of the family shared their grave concerns as they realised that the Munich agreement had been no more than a brief postponement of the inevitable. In July 1939, the Duke and Duchess of Brunswick had attended the wedding in Florence of Princess Irene of Greece to Aimone, Duke of Aosta. They were anxious that peace was in jeopardy, but the Duchess's aunt Margaret disagreed. She thought it impossible that Hitler would provoke a conflict as she could not bring herself to believe that a statesman who had done so much for his people could risk such a gamble.[15]

However, on 3 September, Germany and Britain were at war for the second time in twenty-five years. While some members of German royalty had gradually become dismissive of Hitler, they took up arms at once, not out of any love of or admiration for the Nazis, but merely to defend their homeland. Needless to say, it did nothing to change Hitler's view of royals, aristocrats, or monarchists.

Within forty-eight hours, the Hohenzollerns suffered another loss with the death of Prince Oscar, son of the Emperor's youngest surviving son, Oscar. A lieutenant with one of the infantry regiments, he was killed fighting on the Polish front. His distraught father wrote to the Duchess of Brunswick: 'I don't need to tell you what I'm going through. The dear, good, faithful boy. Now he is gone from me.... It's too dreadful— and for what!'[16]

The Emperor's loyalties were divided, for his greatest debt was to the country that had afforded him sanctuary, even though it was at war with Germany. Through the German ambassador at The Hague, he sent Hitler a message expressing relief at his survival of an assassination plot in Munich on 8 November. A few days later, the British Embassy in The

Hague was informed that if the Emperor's future was to be questioned by the Dutch authorities, the Foreign Office in London would seek to have him transferred to Sweden or Denmark, and only in the last resort be permitted to settle in the United Kingdom.

In the small hours on 10 May 1940, gunfire was heard in Doorn, and later that morning, the Dutch commandant sent orders that the Emperor, his wife, and their suite were to consider themselves interned. All but four of their German servants were requested to leave, their radios were confiscated, and their telephone wires cut. The grounds of the estate were patrolled, and there were orders to shoot anyone moving outside the house after 8 p.m. The Emperor was asked to sign an undertaking that he would do nothing to harm the Dutch Government or the country.

That same day, Chamberlain resigned as Prime Minister in England, and his successor, Winston Churchill, recommended the Foreign Office to advise William privately that he would be received with consideration and dignity if he wished to seek asylum in England. King George VI and his Foreign Secretary Lord Halifax both approved, but reaction from Whitehall was hostile, and it was pointed out that the public would surely object to his presence in Britain at such a time. After asking for time to reflect, the Emperor decided to reject the offer. He had no desire to travel by aeroplane, something he had not done before; he did not feel the British could regard him as anything other than an enemy; he could not accept hospitality from any country that was at war with Germany; and, above all, he would rather be shot in Holland than be photographed with Churchill in England. On no account, he said, did he wish it to be known that he had even had any contact with the British Prime Minister. To Bigelow, he wrote that he 'considered the British offer as a temptation of Satan therefore [he] refused it placing [his] whole confidence & trust in God alone'.[17]

On 14 May, the Wehrmacht entered Doorn, his servants were freed from internment, and a German patrol came to guard him. Excited as he was at German progress on the European mainland, he was careful to do nothing to embarrass or compromise the Dutch Government, and maintained a dignified silence as an observer of events from afar.

A few days later, the Crown Prince's eldest son, another William, was severely wounded in fighting near Valenciennes, and died three days later in a military hospital. His funeral cortege at Potsdam attracted a crowd of around 50,000 pro-monarchist sympathisers, and Hitler was so angered by this display of sentiment that he ordered every remaining Hohenzollern on active service to be removed from the army list and accept civilian employment. Any further princes killed in combat, he knew, would only increase admiration for the dynasty and, combined with popular discontent with the Nazi regime, would possibly promote the aims of the resistance in furthering a counter-revolution in favour of restoring the monarchy. He had long since ceased to pay lip-service to the institution of monarchy or pretend to have any respect for the dynasty. To him, German princes were the root cause of unrest and division throughout the country's history, and he declared that the Social Democrats, having 'done away with this ferment', meant that they should now rid themselves 'of the influence exercised by the Hohenzollern brood'. As far as he was concerned, 'hardly anyone is as stupid as a King', and the Third Reich could 'do without Royal defenders of the Fatherland'.[18]

In spite of this, Emperor William's loyalties never really wavered. When German troops entered Paris in June, he called for champagne and telegraphed his congratulations to Hitler whose victories, he declared proudly, were comparable only to those of Frederick the Great in the eighteenth century and of his grandfather Emperor William I in the nineteenth. Despite the British offer of hospitality, he could not resist another attack on his Francophile uncle, as he wrote to the Duchess of Brunswick that 'thus is the pernicious *Entente Cordiale* of Uncle Edward VII brought to nought'.[19] Even so, the Duchess of Brunswick was convinced that the war against England 'distressed him'. Perhaps there still remained some affection in his heart for the country with whom he had had always such a turbulent relationship. In previous years, much of his hatred had been directed against France, now it was the huge state towards the east; he wrote to Bigelow that he believed every country in Europe had to unite and fight against Soviet Russia, as she would 'soon threaten not only Europe but the whole world'.[20]

The Crown Prince followed his father's example in telegraphing to the Führer, not once but twice. On 7 May, he sent Hitler his sincere thanks as he offered his 'admiration and congratulations for the genial execution of the military operations in the north'.[21] About six weeks later, and a month after the death of his son, he did so again, praising his 'genial leadership', which had succeeded in forcing Holland and Belgium to capitulate, in driving the remnants of the English Expeditionary Corps into the sea, and in defeating decisively the bravely fighting French Army, leaving the way free 'for a final reckoning with Perfidious Albion'. In the final sentence of the letter, he said that, as an old soldier and German, he would 'like to shake [Hitler's] hand in complete admiration'.[22] It was almost as if he still hoped to ingratiate himself with Hitler and persuade him to grant the Hohenzollern heir a military position.

Despite his lack of admiration for Hitler, the Emperor was thrilled by every German success. To his recently widowed sister, Margaret, he wrote that the hand of God was creating a new world and working miracles:

'We are becoming the U.S. of Europe under German leadership, a united European Continent, nobody ever hoped to see'.[23]

The Landgrave and Landgravine had both joined the Nazi Party in May 1938, or in the words of their son, Prince Philipp, some years later, they were made members without much choice in the matter. Although they had invited Hitler for tea at Friedrichshof in 1931 and 1932, they initially declined to join. However, six years later, Philipp, who had been a member since 1930, spoke with Hitler in Berlin, mentioning that he was visiting his parents as it was his father's seventieth birthday. When Hitler asked whether they were party members too, he said no as he knew that they had 'put this off' more than once. When he arrived at Kronberg, a confirmation notice of their party membership had just reached them. Philipp said it was the Führer's birthday present, suggesting it would have been rude, if not impossible to decline. Nevertheless, the Landgravine wrote Hitler an effusive letter on 3 June, a few days after the death of her husband, thanking him for the memorial wreath he had sent and testifying to her husband's intense admiration for the dictator: 'not a day passed when the deceased did not speak of you.... Time and again, when we came to him, he would use his hand to refer to you'.[24]

In September 1940, when German intelligence suggested that the RAF was close to defeat by the Luftwaffe, Hitler and Göring ordered the German air fleets to attack London. From 7 September 1940, the capital was systematically bombed for a period of almost three months, and Buckingham Palace was repeatedly under fire. Two days later, a bomb struck just below the King's study, and on 12 September, six bombs hit the Palace. King George VI and Queen Elizabeth were standing at a window in Buckingham Palace when two exploded in the courtyard. They realised afterwards that they were fortunate not to have been killed or at least maimed by flying glass. For some years, it was believed that this raid had been planned or carried out by the Landgravine's son, Prince Christoph of Hesse-Cassel, intent on avenging the death of his brother Maximilian in the previous war, and having 'frequently been heard declaring how much he would like to bomb Buckingham Palace'.[25] His poor eyesight had prevented him from becoming a pilot, and the theory that he would have done so personally seems untenable. The assertion that he bore any responsibility for the attack was dismissed by members of the British and German royal families, among them Philip, later Duke of Edinburgh, whose elder sister, Princess Sophie of Greece, was married to Christoph at the time.[26]

Despite his abhorrence of the events of *Kristallnacht*, the Emperor's anger at the Jews had resurfaced once more. England, he fulminated, must be 'liberated' as it was 'thoroughly contaminated' by Jews and

Freemasons and therefore by the hand of Satan. With England's help, Jews and Freemasons, he was sure, had in 1914 and 1939 unleashed a war of destruction against Germany in order to erect the *Weltrech* (World Empire) of Juda. It was now the turn of Europe to consolidate and close itself off from British influence after the *Entledigung* (elimination) of the British and the Jews.[27]

12

'Without England, We Cannot Endure'

In January 1941, Emperor William quietly celebrated his eighty-second birthday. His health was beginning to fail and his activities were limited after a stroke and heart trouble. After a dizzy spell while cutting wood at the beginning of March, he realised he could no longer work in his garden, and he spent more time in bed or in a wheelchair. The Duchess of Brunswick came to care for him in the spring, and the Crown Prince also joined them. The Emperor had repeatedly told others that he was still suffering because of his eldest son's way of life with his extramarital affairs. Coupled with the fact that the Crown Prince had never got on well with his stepmother, this cannot have made the visit much of a pleasure for anyone.

In May, he was diagnosed with an acute intestinal complaint, and though he rallied afterwards, the doctors warned his family that he could not live much longer. The Duchess of Brunswick and Prince Louis Ferdinand remained at Doorn. To the end, the ailing Emperor passionately wanted to know what was happening around them in Europe, and as ever, his love-hate relationship with the nation over the North Sea endured. During one of his last conversations with his daughter, he asked whether Germany was still going to attack England. Perhaps forgetting the bombing raids to which London and other cities had been subjected night after night during the previous few months, of which he must have been well aware, or maybe visualising an invasion by land and sea, he stated: '[Should "we" win,] we must immediately stretch out our hand to England and go together. Without England we cannot endure'.[1]

On 3 June, he had another heart attack and realised the end was near. After saying farewell to Hermine, his daughter, and his grandson, he fell into a coma, and without regaining consciousness, he died at 11.30 a.m. the following day. In London, *The Times* commented in measured terms on the passing of 'a man essentially weak, a leader only by accident, set at the head of forces which he could stimulate but not control'.[2] It echoed the verdict of King Edward VII almost forty years earlier that he would unleash a war, not through strength, but through weakness.

In a codicil to his last will, written and dated 25 December 1933, the Emperor had left instructions that if allowed to return to Germany during his lifetime and die in Potsdam, he wanted to be buried in the mausoleum there. Otherwise, he wished to rest instead on his estate at Doorn. There he lies to this day, although as the millennium approached, there were moves to have his remains reburied in Berlin. The obsequies were to be simple, unpretentious, quiet, and dignified, with no 'delegations from home', no swastika flags, and no wreaths.[3] Unaware of these instructions (and probably not really concerned even if he had been informed), Hitler had intended to arrange a state funeral for him in Berlin.

All the Emperor's five remaining sons were present at Doorn on 9 June, where a battalion of honour consisting of contingents from the army, navy, and air force marched in the garden at Doorn under the command of Colonel Rudolf von Gersdorff, Mackensen's adjutant. Now aged ninety-one, Mackensen was there to pay his respects, kneeling in silent prayer at his former sovereign's grave. Among others who attended were some of those who had served the Emperor in years past, such as his former adjutants Captain Wilhelm von Dommes and Count Carl von der Goltz, representatives of the Wehrmacht, and, as Hitler's representative, Arthur Seyss-Inquart, *Reichskommissar* for the occupied Netherlands. To the latter, in defiance of the deceased's wish, was entrusted the duty of taking a swastika-decked wreath inscribed '*Der Führer*' to be placed on the bier. At a brief service in the chapel, the Rev. Bruno Doehring sprinkled the coffin with earth taken from before the Antique Temple of Sans Souci Park, Potsdam, where Empress Augusta Victoria had been buried. In accordance with the Emperor's instructions, he refrained from pronouncing a eulogy. Goebbels informed the papers to report the funeral as a minor event. In his own journal, *Das Reich*, he wrote of the Emperor as 'one who only floated on the highest crest of a surging surf ... a floating particle, a distinguished particle, to be sure, but nothing more'.[4]

Hermine returned to Germany a few months later, leaving Huis Doorn empty. On the first anniversary of the Emperor's death, his body was transferred to a chapel built in the gardens. Later, the house was converted into a museum, and his papers were sent to regional archives in Utrecht. Well into the twenty-first century, some considered him 'an embarrassing figure whom most prefer to forget'.[5] Nevertheless, the building was still attracting around 25,000 visitors per year.

Crown Prince William, aged fifty-nine, the same age as his father had been when he abdicated, was now head of the house of Hohenzollern.

Even then, some pro-monarchist members of the German resistance still harboured faint hopes of getting rid of Hitler and recalling one of the princes as Emperor. One of the leaders of the movement, such as it was, was Johannes Popitz, a former state secretary in the finance ministry during the Weimar Republic. A fervent conservative, who found the Nazis' anti-Semitism deeply abhorrent, and a supporter of the Crown Prince, he met the latter in July 1941 and readily endorsed him as right person to assume the crown in the event of a restoration. Popitz praised 'his clear vision, his intelligence, and what is more important, his earnestness; also his judgment about certain individuals'.[6]

The leading pro-monarchist politician Karl Goerdeler and several others agreed with him, but their view was not widely shared. Among other members of the resistance and those who might have been expected to welcome a return to the German monarchy, there was little love or respect for the Crown Prince, whose inconsistent attitude towards the Nazis and his reputation as a womaniser had alienated many would-be supporters. One who argued most strongly against his credentials as a sovereign was Count Fritz von der Schulenburg, son of the former Chief of Staff during the First World War, who had died in 1939. The late Count had asserted that the Crown Prince's conduct during the November 1918 crisis and at other times had made him quite unfit for such an honour. At around the time of the armistice, he had warned the heir to the tottering throne not to follow his father into exile in Holland, and the heir had given his word not to do so, then vacillating and doing just that. Moreover, at around the same time, he had asked General Roeder von Diersburg, one of his aides, to 'free him from this woman' (the Crown Princess) and take him to a neutral country with the latest love of his life, a French tennis partner.[7]

Prince Eitel Frederick had long since ceased to take any interest in political or military activities. Plagued by increasing heart trouble, perhaps exacerbated by alcoholism, he did not serve during the Second World War and died after a short illness at his home at Potsdam in December 1942. Hitler prohibited attendance in uniform at his funeral because of his known opposition to the regime, and his surviving colleagues from the previous war attended in plain clothes.

Of the Emperor's other surviving sons, Adalbert had withdrawn completely from public life and from his homeland, Augustus William was tainted because of his membership of the Nazis, and the only possible choice was Oscar. The candidate preferred above all was Prince Louis Ferdinand, who was well-known, liked, and respected by members of the resistance. They were impressed by the open-minded young man who had, it was said, 'radically rejected the traditions and prejudices of his princely class' and was known for his affability and lack of pomposity.

His spell as a factory worker with the Ford Motor Company in America had given him a taste of everyday life, and he enjoyed excellent relations with President Roosevelt. However, it was considered that a Hohenzollern Emperor would meet with strong resistance in Austria and Bavaria.

Prince Louis Ferdinand was reluctant to take any steps against claims to the throne from his father and grandfather. For all his faults and unpopularity, the Crown Prince was still seen as the monarch *de jure*. To circumvent this, a plan was devised whereby he should issue a proclamation to the German people and the army and assume supreme command of the Wehrmacht. It would then be his aim to secure an honourable peace for Germany, acceptable to other European nations and the United States, and then abdicate in favour of Louis Ferdinand.

After the German military defeats of 1942 onwards, Hitler and other Nazi leaders distrusted the princes even more, calling them 'internationally connected men'. Hitler believed their assurances of loyalty to him as Führer could no longer be relied upon as they were too susceptible to the influence of relatives in hostile countries abroad. Prince Philipp of Hesse, a former member of the Nazi Party, and his wife, Princess Mafalda, were among the first to suffer when they were sent to different concentration camps in September 1943. Philipp was held by the Germans, and after the end of the war for two more years by the Allies before being released. His wife, whom Hitler was convinced was working against the German war effort and whom he called 'the blackest carrion in the Italian royal house', was less fortunate. She had been in Buchenwald for less than a year when she was wounded in a bombing raid and suffered severe burns to one arm, which became so badly infected that it had to be amputated. Bleeding profusely, she died without regaining consciousness.

On 20 July 1944, a month before her death, there had been an attempt on Hitler's life. Of the many, this was the one which came the closest to succeeding. Had it done so, the man who would have subsequently become Chancellor was Goerdeler, who was increasingly disillusioned with the Nazi regime and had been involved in several plots against the Führer and in helping right-wing dissidents, many of them monarchists. He favoured the prospect of a post-Hitler Germany becoming a constitutional monarchy, similar to that in Britain, with Prince Louis Ferdinand on the throne. When the latter was approached by members of the group, he expressed surprise that he should be their choice. They told him they needed a stabilising and unifying figure to rally around before the execution of their plot and during the period following what they hoped would be its successful outcome. He would, they said, be acceptable to both the army with its conservative attitude and to the labour organisations with their progressive, forward-looking outlook.[8]

As head of the house of Hohenzollern, Hitler had the Crown Prince placed under supervision after the plot by the Gestapo and had his home at Cecilienhof watched. Also under suspicion, Prince Louis Ferdinand was interviewed by the Gestapo. He allegedly plied his interrogators with fine wines from the estate cellars, and they were soon so drunk that he was able to write and sign their report himself.[9] Among those identified as conspirators were Goerdeler, Claus von Stauffenberg, one of the ringleaders of the plot, Count Heinrich Dohna-Schlobitten, another fervent opponent of the Nazis and former adjutant of the Crown Prince, and Johannes Popitz, who had been watched by the Gestapo since conducting secret talks with Heinrich Himmler, Hitler's *Reichsführer* or Chief of German Police, for a *coup d'état* or for meeting representatives of the Allied powers for a peace settlement. They were arrested and hanged, while several hundred members of the aristocracy, many of them princes, ended up in concentration camps.

In January 1945, the Crown Prince left Potsdam for treatment of gall and liver problems. Three months later, the Third Reich collapsed. Having named Admiral Karl Doenitz as his successor as president, Hitler committed suicide on 30 April, and a week later, the German instruments of surrender were signed. From Potsdam, Prince Oscar wrote to the Duchess of Brunswick of his despair and sadness at the state of war-torn Berlin and how glad he was 'that dear Papa did not live to see the destruction of all he held so dearly'.[10] Soon afterwards, he left the city with a rucksack containing all the possessions he still had left, and made his way through the heavily guarded American lines to his sister's home at Blankenburg.

At the end of the war, the Crown Prince's home, Cecilienhof, was seized by the Soviets and subsequently used by the Allied Powers as the venue for the Potsdam Conference. He was captured by French Moroccan troops in Austria and briefly interned as a war criminal. A pathetic figure, he complained about the lack of anywhere acceptable to live to General Jean de Lattre de Tassigny, commander of the French forces in Germany. The general told him that he had lost his sense of dignity, and had no other interest than his own comfort and the women of his pleasure: 'You are to be pitied, monsieur, that is really all I have to say to you'.[11] For a while, he lived in Hohenzollern Castle under house arrest, and then moved to a modest five-room house in Hechingen, with only a shepherd dog for company. There was one last happy occasion for him and the family when his younger daughter, Cecilie, married American interior decorator Clyde Kenneth Harris in June 1949. Less than a year later came sadness when his third son, Hubertus, who had settled as a farmer in South Africa, died from appendicitis, aged forty.

In the spring of 1951, the Crown Prince had a serious heart attack and his wife came to visit him while convalescing. He passed away, aged sixty-nine, after a second on the night of 20 July. According to Prince Louis Ferdinand, he had died of a broken heart after losing the throne he had been born to occupy and seeing his country collapse twice during his lifetime.[12] Despite poor health, he had outlived all his brothers but Oscar, the youngest. He had left a wish to be buried at Potsdam, 'as soon as it is freed', but it was at Hohenzollern Castle where he was laid to rest in the presence of Oscar and the Duchess of Brunswick. His estranged wife, Cecilie, died on 6 May 1954, the date that would have been his seventy-second birthday. Apart so much during their lifetimes, they now lie side by side.

Hermine, the Emperor's widow, spent the rest of the war years on the estate of Saabor, Lower Silesia, which had belonged to her first husband. During a Red Army offensive on the Eastern Front in January 1945, she fled to her sister's estate in Thuringia. After peace was declared, she was held under house arrest at Frankfurt in the Soviet occupation zone, and later in the Paulinenhof Internment Camp. On release, she settled in a small flat in Frankfurt, still under strict guard by the Red Army occupation forces. On 7 August 1947, she died of a heart attack, aged fifty-nine, and was buried at Potsdam. She was followed to the grave a year later by her stepson, Adalbert. Grateful for the chance to lead a more remote existence than his brothers, he died at his Swiss home in September 1948, aged sixty-four.

Prince Augustus William had been the only member of the family not to dissociate himself completely from the Nazis. After making derogatory remarks in 1942 about Goebbels, he was banned from any further public speeches. In February 1945, with Crown Princess Cecilie, he fled the approaching Red Army, and went from Potsdam to Kronberg to take refuge with the widowed Landgravine of Hesse-Cassel, his last surviving aunt Margaret. In May 1945, at the end of the war, he was arrested by American soldiers and imprisoned at Ludwigsburg. At his *Spruchkammerverfahren* or denazification trial at Ludwigsburg in 1948, he was judged 'incriminated' and sentenced to two and a half years' hard labour, but as he had been confined since 1945 in an internment camp, he was considered to have served his sentence. After his release, new proceedings were instituted against him with an arrest warrant against him from a court in Potsdam in the Soviet zone. His health seriously weakened by imprisonment and loss of weight, he died in a Stuttgart hospital in March 1949, aged sixty-two, and was buried in Langenburg.[13]

Prince Oscar had served with the army again briefly during the Second World War until Hitler's edict on retiring the Hohenzollerns from active service, and then lived a relatively peaceful life in Germany. In January 1958, he was admitted to a clinic in Munich where he died of stomach cancer, aged sixty-nine, on the anniversary of his father's birthday.

Their sister, the last-born and by that time the sole survivor of the seven siblings, was the longest-lived of all. The Duke and Duchess of Brunswick lived at Blankenburg Castle until the expropriation of their property in 1945. After the war, the Duchess spent much of her time supporting palace restoration projects, high-society parties, hunting, the showing of horses, and helping with philanthropic causes, including the support of a holiday estate for poor children, supported ably by the Duke until his death in 1953.

The year after Oscar's death was the centenary of the Emperor's birthday and Prince Louis Ferdinand, now head of the house of Hohenzollern, invited surviving family members to a commemoration service in Berlin. The Duchess was moved at the sight of her father's old capital as, over the last few decades, it had inevitably changed, in some places beyond recognition, and she could only find her way around some districts with great difficulty. Standing by the Brandenburg Gate and at the Glienicke Bridge, she looked across and saw the other part of a now divided Germany. Yet she could take pleasure in the survival of the Viktoria Luise Platz, named after her, as well as the cheers of the crowds who had gathered for a sight of some of the remaining Hohenzollerns.

She was also present at the celebration of subsequent anniversaries in Berlin, most significantly the 250th anniversary of the birth of Frederick the Great. Another memorable occasion for her was a visit by Queen Elizabeth II and the Duke of Edinburgh in May 1965, the first time a British sovereign had visited Berlin since the Duchess's own wedding fifty-two years earlier to the week and the year before the outbreak of war. As she spoke to the Queen and the Duke, they were able to talk about common family ground, notably the wedding of the Duchess's grandson King Constantine II of Greece to Princess Anne-Marie of Denmark in Athens the previous September, at which she and the Duke had both been guests.

During her widowhood, the Duchess wrote three books of memoirs, edited to a single volume and published in English translation in 1977. Two years previously, one of her granddaughters, Sophia, had become Queen of Spain after the death of General Franco and the accession of King Juan Carlos. As one who had seen monarchies come and go, and in this case return, she allowed herself a few thoughts on the crown and its relevance to contemporary society. Where monarchies still existed, she wrote, it was because people saw themselves represented by the institution and by the monarch himself or herself. Such convictions 'have their roots in tradition, are fed by ethical considerations, and originate in the integral role of the Crown, which is above party'. However, when looking at what she called the landscape of ruined European monarchies, it had to be recognised that large international conflicts, 'with their massive and subversive methods of power-extension, have left deep traces behind them, and it [seemed to her] that [they had] not yet reached the culmination point in this sphere'.[14] The last of her generation from Imperial Germany who could recall the closing years of the nineteenth century, she died in December 1980, aged eighty-eight.

After the death of the Crown Prince, the head of the family, and *de jure* German Emperor, was his second son, Prince Louis Ferdinand. Like the other princes, he had been excluded from taking active part in German military activities, and had never shown any enthusiasm for the Nazi regime. As his two eldest sons both renounced their place in the succession, his third son, also Prince Louis Ferdinand, became his heir. He died at the age of thirty-two in 1977 from injuries sustained in an accident on military manoeuvres in Germany after being pinned between two vehicles, losing a leg through amputation, and succumbing several weeks later from the trauma.

Like his contemporary, Archduke Otto of Austria-Hungary, eldest son of Emperor Charles, Prince Louis Ferdinand the elder accepted his position as one of the senior would-be sovereigns of Europe, saying with a shrug of the shoulders that failing to become a monarch was 'all right with [him]'. In 1952, he published his memoirs, *Rebel Prince*. As well as reminiscing on his life from birth to the death of his father, he commented on the state of the modern world as he found it, his views on monarchy, Europe and America, and on Hitler, 'a frenzied corporal who began his career in the guise of a saviour but turned out to be a megalomaniac and satanical tyrant'. To him, it was a tragedy that such a man should appear on the political scene just as an ageing former war hero, Hindenburg, unable to restrain him, was at the helm.[15]

Hopes of any kind of German monarchist restoration had long gone, though the accession of King Juan Carlos of Spain after the death of Dictator General Franco in November 1975, thus bringing an interregnum of forty-four years to an end, was a reminder that it could never be completely ruled out. As journalist Hugh Montgomery-Massingberd observed in 1990, whereas politicians could be seen in general as exhibitionists and careerists out for themselves, 'monarchs can be shown, at the very least, to be conscientious and upright; at their best, to be an inspiration to their people'.[16]

Towards the end of his days, Prince Louis Ferdinand was happy to be recognised as 'politically a European, albeit envisaging a Europe with Germany at its heart' as his grandfather had done, saying it would be '*Deutschland und Europa*'.[17] He and Kira had four sons and three daughters; he outlived her by twenty-seven years, and died in September 1994, aged eighty-six. Prince George, the only child of their son Louis Ferdinand, aged twenty-eight, succeeded him as head of the house of Hohenzollern.

The former kingdom of Prussia did not long survive the war. Since the early years of the twentieth century, several historians, politicians, philosophers, and others had equated the German kingdom with Nazism. Prussia's history, one opined, had been 'an almost uninterrupted period of forcible expansion, under the iron rule of militarism and absolutist officialism'. Another described Hitler, Austrian by birth, if not in temperament, as 'the Arch-Prussian', and the whole structure of the Third Reich as based not only on the material achievements of the Prussian state, but 'even more on the philosophical foundations of Prussianism'.[18]

After peace was declared in 1945, the western Allies, or rather the Allied Control Council—the military occupation governing body of the Allied Occupation Zones in Germany and Austria formed after the end of hostilities in Europe, consisting of Britain, the United States of America, the Soviet Union, and France to determine plans for post-war Europe—were intent on removing the name. 'Prussia', they declared, should be obliterated from the map for ever. During the last weeks of the war and throughout the ensuing months, there was a systematic campaign to destroy or remove many historical buildings, victory monuments, and statues in Potsdam and Königsberg as part of a plan to bury the culture of the old and now-tainted nation state. On 25 February 1947, the Council formally proclaimed the dissolution of Prussia. The Hohenzollern family still remained, but their kingdom had been expunged from history.

Endnotes

A   Prince Albert, later Prince Consort
CPW   Crown Prince William (son of Emperor William II)
E   King Edward VII
F   Emperor Frederick III
G   King George V
N   Tsar Nicholas II
QV   Queen Victoria
V   Victoria, Princess Royal, Crown Princess, Empress Victoria and Empress Frederick
VL   Victoria Louise, Duchess of Brunswick
W   Emperor William II, as Prince, Crown Prince and Emperor

Chapter 1

1. Cecil, L., *Wilhelm II: Prince and Emperor*, p. 125, V to A, 27.1.1860.
2. Kohut, T., *Wilhelm II and the Germans*, p. 32.
3. Pakula, H., *An Uncommon Woman*, p. 168.
4. Poschinger, M., *Life of the Emperor Frederick*, p. 140.
5. Victoria, *Letters of the Empress Frederick*, p. 41, V to QV, 8.6.1863.
6. Corti, E., *English Empress*, p. 181.
7. Pakula, H., *An Uncommon Woman*, p. 287, F to V, 28.7.1872.
8. Ponsonby, A., *Henry Ponsonby*, p. 251, QV to Sir Henry Ponsonby, 18.11.1874.
9. Clark, C., *Iron Kingdom*, p. 557.
10. Kollander, *Frederick III*, p. 99, V to F, 6.1.1871.
11. Poschinger, M., *Life of the Emperor Frederick*, p. 362.
12. QV, *Darling Child*, p. 248, V to QV, 14.4.1877.
13. QV, *Letters 1862-85*, Vol. III, p. 169-70, Lady Emily Russell to QV, 27.12.1880.
14. Bennett, D., *Vicky, Princess Royal of England*, p. 204.

Chapter 2

1. Victoria, *Letters of the Empress Frederick*, p. 191, V to QV, 5.11.1881.
2. Müller, F., *Our Fritz*, p. 150.
3. Ludwig, *Kaiser Wilhelm II*, p .41.
4. MacDonogh, G., *Last Kaiser*, p. 89.
5. Müller, F., *Our Fritz*, p. 43, von Normann to Freytag, 20.1.1882.
6. *Ibid.*, p. 30.

7. Sinclair, A., *Other Victoria*, p. 190, V to QV, 30.10.1885.
8. Cecil, L., *Wilhelm II: Prince and Emperor*, p. 77.
9. Victoria, *Letters of the Empress Frederick*, p. 207, V to QV, 11.8.1886.
10. Müller, F., *Our Fritz*, pp. 25–6.
11. Corti, E., *English Empress*, p. 221, F to QV, 7.1.1885.
12. Müller, F., *Our Fritz*, p. 29.
13. Victoria, *Letters of the Empress Frederick*, p. 239, V to QV, 3.6.1887.
14. Poschinger, M., *Life of the Emperor Frederick*, pp. 436–7, F to Schellbach, 28.9.1887.
15. Victoria, *Letters of the Empress Frederick*, V to QV, 18.6.1888, p. 320.

Chapter 3

1. QV, *Letters 1886-1901*, Vol. I, p. 405, QV journal, 25.4.1888.
2. Victoria, *Letters of the Empress Frederick*, V to QV, 6.11.1888, p. 363.
3. Cecil, L., *Wilhelm II: Prince and Emperor*, p. 124.
4. Nowak, K., *Kaiser & Chancellor*, p. 29.
5. Whittle, T., *Last Kaiser*, p. 122.
6. Röhl, J., *Wilhelm II: The Kaiser's Personal Monarchy*, p. 8.
7. William II, *My Memoirs*, p. 3.
8. QV, *Letters 1886-1901*, Vol. 1, p. 417, QV to W, 15.6.1888.
9. Hough, R., *Louis and Victoria*, Princess Louis of Battenberg to QV, 16.6.1888, p. 143.
10. *Ibid.* V to QV, 4.7.1888 p. 144.
11. QV, *Letters 1886-1901*, Vol. I, p. 425, W to QV, 6.7.1888.
12. *Ibid.* Vol. I, p. 440–1, QV to Lord Salisbury, 15.10.1888.
13. Pakula, H., *An Uncommon Woman*, p. 528.
14. Taylor A., p. 247.
15. Corti, E., *The English Empress*, p. 331.
16. Pakula, H., *An Uncommon Woman*, p. 531, W to QV, 27.3.1890.
17. Nowak, K., *Kaiser & Chancellor*, pp. 217–8.
18. Palmer, A., *Kaiser*, p. 50.
19. William, Crown Prince, *Memoirs of the Crown Prince of Germany*, p. 15.
20. *Ibid.*, p. 14.
21. Victoria Louise, Duchess of Brunswick, *Kaiser's Daughter*, p. 4.
22. Howard, E., *Potsdam Princes*, pp. 30–40.
23. Victoria, *Letters of the Empress Frederick*, p. 351, V to QV, 11.10.1888.
24. Mallet, V., ed. *Life with Queen Victoria*, p. 52, diary, 21.4.1891.
25. Newton, T., *Lord Lansdowne*, p. 199.
26. Levine, I.., *Kaiser's letters to the Tsar*, pp. 24–5, W to N, 25.10.1895.
27. Bülow, Prince, *Memoirs 1897-1903*, p. 356.

Chapter 4

1. Röhl, J., *Wilhelm II: The Kaiser's Personal Monarchy*, p. 4, E to Princess Edward of Saxe-Weimar, 22.1.1901.
2. Lee, S., *King Edward VII*, II, p. 11.
3. Van der Kiste, J., *Crowns in a Changing World*, p. 10, W to E, 30.12.1901.
4. Brook-Shepherd, G., *Uncle of Europe*, p. 255, E to Marquis de Soveral, 1905, exact date unknown.
5. Jonas, K., *Life of Crown Prince William*, pp. 35–6.
6. Ludwig, E., *Kaiser Wilhelm II*, p. 230.
7. Brook-Shepherd, G., *Royal Sunset*, p. 103.
8. Bülow, Prince, *Memoirs 1903-1909*, pp. 190–1.
9. Jonas, K., *Life of Crown Prince William*, p. 38.

10. Andrew, C., *Listener*.
11. Lee, S., *King Edward VII*, II, p. 554, E to Knollys, 31.10.1907.
12. Palmer, A., *Kaiser*, p. 130.

Chapter 5

1. Palmer, A., *Kaiser*, p. 132.
2. Lloyd George, D., *War Memoirs*, I, p. 22.
3. Urbach, K., *Go-betweens for Hitler*, p. 52.
4. Cecil, II, p.135, W to Stuart-Wortley, 15.10.1908.
5. Magnus, P., *King Edward the Seventh*, p. 400, E to Hardinge, 30.10.1908.
6. Trevelyan, G., *Grey of Fallodon*, pp. 154–5.
7. *The Times*, 24.11.1908.
8. Lee, S., *King Edward VII*, II, p. 622, E to Knollys, 25.11.1908.
9. Clark, C., *Iron Kingdom*, p. 589.
10. Bülow, Prince, *Memoirs 1903-1909*, p. 375.
11. Daisy, Princess, *From my Private Diary*, p. 239.
12. Röhl, J., *Wilhelm II: Into the Abyss of War and Exile*, p. 747.
13. Massie, R., *Dreadnought*, p. 801.
14. Röhl, J., *New Interpretations*, p. 42, W to Lady Montagu, 1.5.1910.
15. Leslie, A., *Edwardians in Love*, p. 337.
16. William II, *My memoirs*, p. 124.
17. *Daily Chronicle*, 20.5.1910.
18. Rose, K., *King George V*, p. 165.
19. *Ibid*.
20. Battiscombe, G., *Queen Alexandra*, p. 274.
21. Nicolson, H., *King George the Fifth*, p. 182, W to G, 15.2.1911.
22. Davis, A., *Kaiser I Knew*, p. 143.
23. Victoria Louise, Duchess of Brunswick, *Kaiser's Daughter*, p. 48.
24. Röhl, J., Warren, M., & Hunt, D., *Purple Secret*, p. 152, Princess Charlotte to Baroness Heldburg, 25.7.1911.
25. Jonas, K., *Life of Crown Prince William*, p. 65.
26. *Ibid*., p. 68.

Chapter 6

1. Cecil, L., *Wilhelm II: Emperor and Exile*, p. 172, W to G, 10.6.1912.
2. Nicolson, H., *King George the Fifth*, pp. 206–7.
3. Röhl, J., *Wilhelm II: Into the Abyss of War and Exile*, p. 904.
4. Van der Kiste, J., *Crowns in a Changing World*, p. 86, Prince Henry to G, 14.12.1912.
5. Ponsonby, Sir F., *Recollections of Three Reigns*, p. 266.
6. Balfour, M, *Kaiser and his Times*, p. 339.
7. Ponsonby, Sir F., *Recollections of Three Reigns*, p. 97.
8. Rose, K., *King George V*, p. 166.
9. *Ibid*., p. 167.
10. Victoria Louise, Duchess of Brunswick, *Kaiser's Daughter*, p. 76.
11. Whittle, T., *Last Kaiser*, p. 256.
12. Jonas, K., *Life of Crown Prince William*, p. 82.
13. Victoria Louise, Duchess of Brunswick, *Kaiser's Daughter*, p. 80.
14. Palmer, A., *Kaiser*, p. 166.
15. Nicolson, H., *King George the Fifth*, pp. 245–6.
16. Victoria Louise, Duchess of Brunswick, *Kaiser's Daughter*, p. 82.
17. Cecil, L., *Wilhelm II: Emperor and Exile*, p. 204.
18. Blücher, E., *An English Wife in Berlin*, p. 14.

Chapter 7

1. Howard, E., *Potsdam Princes*, p. 39.
2. Vovk, J., *Imperial Requiem*, p. 262.
3. Rohl, J., *Wilhelm II: Into the Abyss of War and Exile*, p. 146, CPW to W, 6.10.1914.
4. Jonas, K., *Life of Crown Prince William*, pp. 96–7.
5. Victoria Louise, Duchess of Brunswick, *Kaiser's Daughter*, p. 84.
6. Gerard, J., *My First 83 Years in America*, p. 237.
7. Victoria Louise, Duchess of Brunswick, *Kaiser's Daughter*, p. 85.
8. MacDonogh, G., *Last Kaiser*, p. 371.
9. Müller, G., *Kaiser and his Court*, p. 42, diary 6.11.1914.
10. Aronson, T., *Crowns in Conflict*, p. 116.
11. Röhl, J., *Kaiser and his Court*, p. 207.
12. Ludwig, E., *Kaiser Wilhelm II*, p. 409.
13. Jonas, K., *Life of Crown Prince William*, p. 97, Tirpitz diary, 15.4.1915.
14. *Ibid.*, p. 96.
15. Röhl, *Wilhelm II: Into the Abyss of War and Exile*, p. 1130.
16. Balfour, M., *Kaiser and His Times*, p. 375.
17. Ludwig, E., *Kaiser Wilhelm II*, p. 415.

Chapter 8

1. Urbach, K., *Go-betweens for Hitler*, p. 100–1.
2. *Ibid.*, p. 131, Princess Löwenstein-Wertheim to her husband, 25.7.1918.
3. Petropoulos, J., *Royals and the Reich*, pp. 45–6.
4. Urbach, K., *Go-betweens for Hitler*, p. 104.
5. William II, *My Memoirs*, p. 283.
6. Cecil, L., *Wilhelm II: Emperor and Exile*, p. 288.
7. Huldermann, B., *Albert Ballin*, p. 285.
8. Victoria Louise, Duchess of Brunswick, *Kaiser's Daughter*, p. 141.
9. Balfour, M, *Kaiser and his Times*, p. 409.
10. Jonas, K., *Life of Crown Prince William*, p. 120.
11. Louis Ferdinand, Prince, *Rebel Prince*, p. 38.
12. Gore, J., *King George V*, p. 308, G's diary, 9.11.1918.
13. Cecil, L., *Wilhelm II: Emperor and Exile*, p. 294.
14. Victoria Louise, Duchess of Brunswick, *Kaiser's Daughter*, p. 139.

Chapter 9

1. Vovk, J. C., *Imperial Requiem*, p. 384.
2. Louis Ferdinand, Prince, *Rebel Prince*, p. 40.
3. Nicolson, H., *King George the Fifth*, p. 337, Stamfordham to G, 5.12.1918.
4. *Spectator*, 25.1.1919.
5. Victoria Louise, Duchess of Brunswick, *Kaiser's Daughter*, p. 145.
6. *Ibid.*, p. 145–6.
7. Rohl, J., *Wilhelm II: Into the Abyss of War and Exile*, p. 1195.
8. *The Times*, 5.12.1918.
9. *Ibid.*, 11.2.1919.
10. Rohl, J., *Wilhelm II: Into the Abyss of War and Exile*, p. 1221.
11. *The Times*, W to Fürstenburg, 2.1.1920, published 28.1.1920.
12. *Ibid.*
13. Urbach, K., *Go-betweens for Hitler*, pp. 133–4, W to Fürstenburg, 27.1.1920
14. Rohl, J., *Wilhelm II: Into the Abyss of War and Exile*, p. 1202.

15. *Ibid.*, p. 1203.
16. Victoria of Prussia, Princess, *My Memoirs*, p. 206.
17. Cecilie, Crown Princess, *Memoirs*, pp. 253–4.
18. William, Crown Prince, *Memoirs*, p. 209.
19. Rohl, J., *Wilhelm II: Into the Abyss of War and Exile,* p. 1203, Haehner diary, 6.12.1920.
20. Victoria Louise, Duchess of Brunswick, *Kaiser's Daughter*, p. 150.
21. Rohl, J., *Wilhelm II: Into the Abyss of War and Exile*, p. 1203.
22. Victoria Louise, Duchess of Brunswick, *Kaiser's Daughter*, p. 161.
23. Kurenberg, J., *Kaiser*, pp. 336–7.
24. Victoria Louise, Duchess of Brunswick, *Kaiser's Daughter*, p. 162.

Chapter 10

1. Urbach, K., *Go-betweens for Hitler*, p. 107.
2. Victoria Louise, Duchess of Brunswick, *Kaiser's Daughter*, pp. 167–8.
3. MacDonogh, G., *Last Kaiser,* p. 435.
4. Cecil, L., *Wilhelm II: Emperor and Exile,* pp. 323–4.
5. Victoria Louise, Duchess of Brunswick, *Kaiser's Daughter*, p. 149.
6. Waters, W., *Potsdam and Doorn*, p. 97.
7. Ponsonby, Sir F., *Recollections of Three Reigns*, p. 113.
8. Balfour, M., *Kaiser and His Times*, p. 416.
9. Van der Kiste, J., *Kaiser Wilhelm II*, p. 210.
10. Cecil, L., *Wilhelm II: Emperor and Exile*, p. 333.
11. MacDonogh, G., *Last Kaiser,* p. 444.
12. Cecil, L., *Wilhelm II: Emperor and Exile*, p. 330.
13. Victoria Louise, Duchess of Brunswick, *Kaiser's Daughter*, pp. 169–70.
14. *Evening Standard*, 17.12.1929.
15. Petropoulos, J., *Questions*.
16. Victoria Louise, Duchess of Brunswick, *Kaiser's Daughter*, pp. 175–8.
17. *Ibid.*, p. 180.
18. Urbach, K., *Go-betweens for Hitler*, p. 232.
19. MacDonogh, G., *Last Kaiser,* p. 447.
20. Louis Ferdinand, Prince, *Rebel Prince*, pp. 251–2.
21. *Ibid.*, p. 41.
22. Churchill, W., *Great Contemporaries*, p. 29.
23. Hamilton, Lord F., *Vanished Pomps of Yesterday*, p. 316.
24. MacDonogh, G., *Last Kaiser,* p. 447.
25. Röhl, J., *Wilhelm II: Into the Abyss of War and Exile*, p. 1249.
26. Victoria Louise, Duchess of Brunswick, *Kaiser's Daughter*, pp. 162–3.
27. *Ibid.*, p. 164.
28. *Ibid.*, p. 163.
29. Röhl, J., *Wilhelm II: Into the Abyss of War and Exile,* p. 1256, Ilsemann diary, 17.5.1935.

Chapter 11

1. *The Times*, 27.1.1934.
2. Clark, C., *Iron Kingdom*, p. 664.
3. Lockhart, R., *Listener*.
4. Röhl, J., *Kaiser and his Court*, p. 210, W to Bigelow, 15.8.1929.
5. Pope-Hennessy, J., *Queen Mary*, p. 592, W to Queen Mary, 1.10.1938.
6. *Ibid.*, p. 289, Queen Mary to King George VI, 4.10.1938.
7. Jonas, K., *Life of Crown Prince William*, p. 196, CPW to Chamberlain, 24.10.1939.

8. Röhl, J., *Wilhelm II: Into the Abyss of War and Exile,* p.1265.
9. Cecil, L., *Wilhelm II: Emperor and Exile,* p. 345.
10. Victoria Louise, Duchess of Brunswick, *Kaiser's Daughter,* p. 177.
11. Louis Ferdinand, Prince, *Rebel Prince,* p. 72.
12. *Ibid.,* p. 49.
13. *Ibid.,* p. 149.
14. Lockhart, R., *Comes the Reckoning,* p. 38.
15. Victoria Louise, Duchess of Brunswick, *Kaiser's Daughter,* p. 201.
16. *Ibid.,* p. 202.
17. Röhl, J., *Wilhelm II: Into the Abyss of War and Exile,* p. 1260, W to Bigelow, 14.9.1940.
18. Victoria Louise, Duchess of Brunswick, *Kaiser's Daughter,* p. 214.
19. Palmer, A., *Kaiser,* pp. 224–5.
20. Victoria Louise, Duchess of Brunswick, *Kaiser's Daughter,* p. 205.
21. Jonas, K., *Life of Crown Prince William,* p. 200, CPW to Hitler, 7.5.1940.
22. *Ibid.,* pp. 200–1, CPW to Hitler, 25.6.1940.
23. Röhl, *Kaiser and his Court,* p. 211, W to Margaret, Landgravine of Hesse-Cassel, 3 November 1940.
24. Petropoulos, J., *Royals and the Reich,* pp. 102–3.
25. Bradford, S., *King George VI,* p. 425.
26. Petropoulos, J., *Royals and the Reich,* p. 226.
27. Röhl, J., *Wilhelm II: Into the Abyss of War and Exile,* p. 1263.

Chapter 12

1. Victoria Louise, Duchess of Brunswick, *Kaiser's Daughter,* p. 208.
2. *The Times,* 5.6.1941.
3. Louis Ferdinand, Prince, *Rebel Prince,* p. 300.
4. Victoria Louise, Duchess of Brunswick, *Kaiser's Daughter,* p. 209.
5. *The Independent,* 18.11.2012.
6. Hassell, U. von, *Ulrich von Hassell Diaries 1938-1944,* p. 132.
7. Jonas, K., *Life of Crown Prince William,* p. 125, p. 206.
8. Louis Ferdinand, Prince, *Rebel Prince,* p. 312.
9. *The Times,* 28.9.1994.
10. Victoria Louise, Duchess of Brunswick, *Kaiser's Daughter,* p. 223.
11. Nelson, W., *Soldier Kings,* p. 455.
12. Louis Ferdinand, Prince, *Rebel Prince,* p. 347.
13. Petropoulos, J., *Royals and the Reich,* p. 320.
14. Victoria Louise, Duchess of Brunswick, *Kaiser's Daughter,* pp. 258–9.
15. Louis Ferdinand, Prince, *Rebel Prince,* p. 224.
16. Montgomery-Massingberd, H., *Telegraph Weekend Magazine.*
17. *The Times,* 28.9.1994.
18. Clark, C., *Iron Kingdom,* p. 673.

Bibliography

Books

Aronson, T., *Crowns in Conflict: The Triumph and the Tragedy of European Monarchy, 1910-1918* (London: John Murray, 1986); *The Kaisers* (London: Cassell, 1971)

Balfour, M, *The Kaiser and his Times* (London: Cresset, 1964)

Battiscombe, G., *Queen Alexandra* (London: Constable, 1969)

Bennett, D., *Vicky, Princess Royal of England and German Empress* (London: Collins Harvill, 1971)

Blücher, E., Princess, *An English Wife in Berlin: A Private Memoir of Events, Politics, and Daily Life in Germany throughout the War and the Social Revolution of 1918* (London: Constable, 1920)

Bradford, S., *King George VI* (London: Weidenfeld & Nicolson, 1989)

Brook-Shepherd, G., *Royal Sunset: The Dynasties of Europe and the Great War* (London: Weidenfeld & Nicolson, 1987); *Uncle of Europe: The Social and Diplomatic Life of Edward VII* (London: Collins, 1975)

Carr, W., *A History of Germany, 1815-1990*, 4th ed. (London: Arnold, 1991)

Carter, M., *The Three Emperors: Three Cousins, Three Empires and the Road to World War One* (London: Fig Tree, 2009)

Cecil, L., *Wilhelm II: Prince and Emperor, 1859-1900* (Chapel Hill: University of North Carolina, 1989); *Wilhelm II: Emperor and Exile, 1900-1941* (Chapel Hill, University of North Carolina, 1996); 'Wilhelm II and his Russian 'Colleagues'', in C. Fink, I. Hull and M. Knox, eds., *German Nationalism and the European Response* (Oklahoma: University of Oklahoma Press, 1985)

Cecilie, Crown Princess, *Memoirs (*London: Victor Gollancz, 1931)

Churchill, W., *Great Contemporaries* (London: Odhams, 1937, n.e. 1939)

Clark, C., *Iron Kingdom: The Rise and Downfall of Prussia, 1600-1947* (London: Allen Lane, 2006)

Corti, E. C. C., *The English Empress: A Study in the Relations between Queen Victoria and her Eldest Daughter, Empress Frederick of Germany* (London: Cassell, 1957)

Daisy, Princess of Pless, *From my Private Diary*, ed. D. Chapman-Huston (London: John Murray, 1931)

Davis, A. N., *The Kaiser I Knew: My Fourteen Years with the Kaiser* (London: Hodder & Stoughton, 1918)

Gerard, J. W., *My First 83 Years in America* (New York: Doubleday, 1953)

Gore, J., *King George V: A Personal Memoir* (London: John Murray, 1941)

Hamilton, Lord F., *The Vanished Pomps of Yesterday* (London: Hamish Hamilton, 1920)

Hough, R., *Louis and Victoria: The First Mountbattens* (London: Hutchinson, 1974)

Howard, E., *The Potsdam Princes* (London: Methuen, 1916)

Huldermann, B., *Albert Ballin* (London: Cassell, 1922)

Jonas, K. W., *The Life of Crown Prince William* (London: Routledge & Kegan Paul, 1961)

Kohut, T., *Wilhelm II and the Germans* (Oxford: Oxford University Press, 1991)

Kollander, P., *Frederick III: Germany's Liberal Emperor* (Westport, Connecticut: Greenwood, 1995)

Lee, Sir S., *King Edward VII*, 2 vols (London: Macmillan, 1925-7)

Leslie, A., *Edwardians in Love* (London: Hutchinson, 1972)

Levine, I. D., *The Kaiser's Letters to the Tsar* (London: Hodder & Stoughton, 1920)

Lloyd George, D., *War Memoirs*, 6 vols (London: Ivor Nicholson & Watson, 1933-6)

Lockhart, R. H. B., *Comes the Reckoning* (London: Putnam, 1947)

Longford, E., *Victoria R.I.*, (London: Weidenfeld & Nicolson, 1964)

Louis Ferdinand, Prince, *The Rebel Prince: Memoirs of Prince Louis Ferdinand of Prussia* (Chicago: Henry Regnery, 1952)

Ludwig, E., *Kaiser Wilhelm II* (London: Putnam, 1926)

MacDonogh, G., *The Last Kaiser: Wilhelm the Impetuous* (London: Weidenfeld & Nicolson, 2000)

Magnus, P., *King Edward the Seventh* (London: John Murray, 1964)

Mallet, V., ed. *Life with Queen Victoria: Marie Mallet's Letters from Court 1887-1901* (London: John Murray, 1968)

Massie, R. K., *Dreadnought: Britain, Germany, and the coming of the Great War* (London: Jonathan Cape, 1992)

Müller, F., *Our Fritz: Emperor Frederick III and the Political Culture of Imperial Germany* (Cambridge, Mass.: Harvard University Press, 2011)

Nelson, W. H., *The Soldier Kings: The House of Hohenzollern* (London: Dent, 1971)

Newton, T., *Lord Lansdowne* (London: Macmillan, 1929)

Nicholls, A. J., *Weimar and the Rise of Hitler*, 4th ed. (Basingstoke: Palgrave Macmillan, 2000)

Nicolson, H., *King George the Fifth, His Life and Reign* (London: Constable, 1952)

Nowak, K. F., *Kaiser & Chancellor: The Opening Years of the Reign of the Emperor William II* (London: Putnam, 1930)

Pakula, H., *An Uncommon Woman: The Empress Frederick* (London: Weidenfeld & Nicolson, 1996)

Palmer, A., *The Kaiser: Warlord of the Second Reich* (London: Weidenfeld & Nicolson, 1978)

Petropoulos, J., *Royals and the Reich: The Princes von Hessen in Nazi Germany* (New York: Oxford University Press, 2006)

Ponsonby, A., *Henry Ponsonby, Queen Victoria's Private Secretary: His Life from his Letters* (London: Macmillan, 1952)

Ponsonby, Sir F., *Recollections of Three Reigns* (London: Eyre & Spottiswoode, 1951)

Pope-Hennessy, J., *Queen Mary, 1867-1953* (London: Allen & Unwin, 1959)

Röhl, J., & Sombart, N. (eds), *Kaiser Wilhelm II: New Interpretations* (Cambridge: Cambridge University Press, 1982)

Röhl, J., *The Kaiser and his Court: Wilhelm II and the Government of Germany* (Cambridge: Cambridge University Press, 1996); *Wilhelm II: The Kaiser's*

Personal Monarchy, 1888-1900 (Cambridge: Cambridge University Press, 2004); *Wilhelm II: Into the Abyss of War and Exile, 1900-1941* (Cambridge: Cambridge University Press, 2014); *Young Wilhelm: The Kaiser's Early Life, 1859-1888* (Cambridge: Cambridge University Press, 1998)

Röhl, J., Warren, M., & Hunt, D., *Purple Secret: Genes, 'Madness', and the Royal Houses of Europe* (London: Bantam, 1998)

Rose, K., *King George V* (London: Weidenfeld & Nicolson, 1983)

Sinclair, A., *The Other Victoria: The Princess Royal and the Great Game of Europe* (London: Weidenfeld & Nicolson, 1981)

Steinberg, J., *Bismarck: A Life* (Oxford: Oxford University Press, 2011)

Taylor, A. J. P., *Bismarck: The Man and the Statesman* (London: Hamish Hamilton, 1955)

Trevelyan, G. M., *Grey of Fallodon: The Life and Letters of Sir Edward Grey, afterwards Viscount Grey of Fallodon* (London: Longmans, 1940)

Urbach, K., *Go-betweens for Hitler* (Oxford: Oxford University Press, 2015)

Van der Kiste, J, *Crowns in a Changing World: The British and European Monarchies, 1901-36* (Stroud: Sutton, 1993); *Dearest Vicky, Darling Fritz: Queen Victoria's Eldest Daughter and the German Emperor* (Stroud: Sutton, 2001); *Kaiser Wilhelm II: Germany's last Emperor* (Stroud: Sutton, 1999); *The Last German Empress: Empress Augusta Victoria, Consort of William II* (South Brent: Createspace/A & F, 2015); *The Prussian Princesses: Sisters of Kaiser Wilhelm II* (Stroud: Fonthill Media, 2014)

Victoria Louise, Duchess of Brunswick, *The Kaiser's Daughter: Memoirs of H.R.H. Viktoria Luise, Duchess of Brunswick and Lüneburg,* ed. Robert Vacha (London: W.H. Allen, 1977)

Victoria of Prussia, Princess, *My Memoirs* (London: Eveleigh, Nash & Grayson, 1929; Ticehurst: Royalty Digest, 1996)

Victoria, Consort of Frederick III, German Emperor, *The Empress Frederick writes to Sophie,* ed. A. Gould Lee, Faber, 1955; *Letters of the Empress Frederick,* ed. Sir F. Ponsonby, Macmillan, 1928

Victoria, Queen, *Advice to a Grand-daughter: Letters from Queen Victoria to Princess Victoria of Hesse,* ed. R. Hough (London: Heinemann, 1975); *The Letters of Queen Victoria: a Selection from Her Majesty's Correspondence between the years 1837 and 1861,* ed. A.C. Benson & Viscount Esher, 3 vols (London: John Murray, 1907); *The Letters of Queen Victoria, 2nd Series: a Selection from Her Majesty's Correspondence and Journal between the years 1862 and 1885,* ed. G. E. Buckle, 3 vols (London: John Murray, 1926-8); *The Letters of Queen Victoria, 3rd Series: a Selection from Her Majesty's Correspondence and Journal between the years 1886 and 1901,* ed. G.E. Buckle, 3 vols (London: John Murray, 1930-2); *Dearest Child: Letters between Queen Victoria and the Princess Royal, 1858-1861;* ed. Roger Fulford (London: Evans Bros, 1964); *Dearest Mama: Private Correspondence of Queen Victoria and the Crown Princess of Prussia, 1861-1864;* ed. Roger Fulford (London: Evans Bros, 1968); *Your Dear Letter: Private Correspondence of Queen Victoria and the Crown Princess of Prussia, 1865-1871,* ed. Roger Fulford (London: Evans Bros, 1971); *Darling Child: Private Correspondence of Queen Victoria and the Crown Princess of Prussia, 1871-1878;* ed. Roger Fulford (London: Evans Bros, 1976); *Beloved Mama: Private Correspondence of Queen Victoria and the German Crown Princess of Prussia, 1878-1885;* ed. Roger Fulford (London: Evans Bros, 1981) von Bülow, Prince B., *Memoirs 1897-1903* (London: Putnam, 1931)

von Hassell, U., *The Ulrich von Hassell Diaries 1938-1944: The Story of the Forces against Hitler Inside Germany* (London: Frontline, 2010)

von Kurenberg, J., *The Kaiser: A life of Wilhelm II, last Emperor of Germany* (London: Cassell, 1955)

von Müller, G.A., *The Kaiser and his Court: The Diaries, Note Books and Letters of Admiral Georg Alexander von Müller, Chief of the Naval Cabinet 1914-18*, ed. Walter Görlitz (London: Macdonald, 1961)

von Poschinger, M., *Life of the Emperor Frederick*, ed. Sidney Whitman (London: Harper, 1901)

Vovk, J. C., *Imperial Requiem: Four Royal Women and the Fall of the Age of Empires* (Bloomington: iUniverse, 2012)

Waters, W. H. H., *Potsdam and Doorn* (London: John Murray, 1935)

Whittle, T., *The Last Kaiser: A Biography of William II, German Emperor and King of Prussia* (London: Heinemann, 1977)

William II, Emperor, *My Early Life* (London: Methuen, 1926); *My Memoirs: 1878-1918* (London: Cassell, 1922)

William, Crown Prince, *The Memoirs of the Crown Prince of Germany* (London: Thornton Butterworth, 1922)

Journals, Newspapers, and Articles

Andrew, C., 'Secrets of the Kaiser' in *The Listener*, 7.6.1984

Boyes, R., 'Call to end exile of last Kaiser' in *The Times*, 24.11.1999

Lockhart, R.H.B., 'The Kaiser in exile' in *History Today,* January 1955

Montgomery-Massingberd, H., 'Kings without kingdoms' in *Telegraph Weekend Magazine*, 10.2.1990

Paterson, T., 'End of the line for Germany's last Emperor' in *The Independent,* 18.11.2012

Royalty Digest

Stone, N., '1914—Was Germany guilty?' in *The Listener*, 9.8.1984

The Spectator

The Times

Zeepvat, C., 'A silent good friend: Prince Eitel Friedrich of Prussia' in *Royalty Digest*, 36, June 1994

Internet, accessed January–May 2017

Questions for Jonathan Petropoulos (author of *Royals and the Reich*, q.v.). OUPblog, *Oxford University Press's Academic Insights for the Thinking World* blog.oup.com/2006/05/questions_for_j/#sthash.4Jr9MEaj.dpuf

The Mad Monarchist (articles on Hitler and monarchy) madmonarchist.blogspot.co.uk

Index